MEDIA UNBOUND

MEDIA UNBOUND

The Impact of Television Journalism on the Public

STEPHAN LESHER

HOUGHTON MIFFLIN COMPANY BOSTON
1982

Library of Congress Cataloging in Publication Data

Lesher, Stephan.
    Media unbound.

    Bibliography: p.
    Includes index.
    1. Television journalism — Social aspects — United
States. I. Title.
PN4888.T4L44   302.2'345   82–3063
ISBN 0–395–31827–0   AACR2

For Michael Halberstam
1932–1980

The intense atom glows
a moment, then is quenched
in a most cold repose.
— PERCY BYSSHE SHELLEY

Author's Note

*T*HE TITAN PROMETHEUS was chained to a rock and tortured by Zeus for using knowledge as a weapon to defeat evil, leading mankind from sinless ignorance to wisdom. He was offered his freedom, though, on condition that he disclose the secret of how Zeus' fall from power could be averted. Prometheus bought his pardon by revealing the secret. Chained and suffering, Prometheus represented to Shelley "courage, and majesty, and firm and patient opposition to omnipotent force...exempt from the taints of ambition, envy, revenge, and a desire for personal aggrandizement." Unbound, however, Prometheus, in the play by Aeschylus, was "unsaying his high language" and "reconciling...with the Oppressor of mankind."

Contents

MEDIA UNBOUND

The Best We Can Do

*N*EWS-GATHERING is a mistake-prone business. When its mistakes are magnified through television, our perception of reality is distorted, and sometimes our recollection of history is obfuscated. Occasionally, leaders of our institutions make decisions based on their journalistically induced misunderstanding of the recent past.

Media Unbound explores the intrinsically capricious nature of journalism, ironically, through a work of journalism. Writing a book, however, provides the luxury of time, the greatest single ally of journalistic accuracy. Moreover, I try to avoid the journalistic transgressions of which I am critical: self-importance, disguising one's own views, not giving wide enough range to conflicting ideas. If I sometimes fail—well, that's journalism.

Although I won't reveal the ending of the book, I will tell you now that, despite the increasingly profound and often negative impact of journalism on our lives, I disagree completely with any effort designed to constrain it by law or fiat. With that in mind, I try, in *Media Unbound,* to lay journalism bare in a way that allows us to see it for what it is: a quasi-intellectual exercise performed by reasonably intelligent men and women whose observations may or may not be as perceptive as the next person's, but whose loudness precludes almost anyone else from being heard.

The goal is to let the reader know journalism with an intimacy that comes from cohabitation; it may tarnish the luster of romance, but it gives the comfort and security of knowing what to expect.

Media Unbound examines journalism by showing how it is done and what it does to us when it is done wrong, which is distressingly often.

Because television news has the greatest impact on the greatest number of Americans compared to other media, this book pays more attention to it than to print journalism.

Because, within television news, *60 Minutes* reaches the most people regularly while exemplifying both the best and worst aspects of modern journalism, *Media Unbound* pays greatest attention to that program.

In the fall of 1980, I encountered Walter Cronkite on a street in downtown Washington, D.C., and we began chatting about this book, then at the reporting-and-research stage. "Maybe," he said, "we should just give it all up — trying, that is, to make journalism any better. Maybe we should just tell the people, 'Look, this is the best we can do,' and leave it at that."

To a large extent, *Media Unbound* does just that. It examines the limitations of journalism and, in so doing, tries to keep it at its proper rank — the court stenographer, not the judge or jury; the informer, not the decision-maker. The play within *Hamlet* may have caught the king's conscience, but it was, after all, a play with actors — a reflection of reality as understood by one imperfect man; the actors were long gone when Hamlet and the other principals were forced to resolve their conflicts. Journalists, too, reflect reality imperfectly and without bearing responsibility for resolving the conflicts they delineate. Too often, however, their misjudgments, magnified by their media, unduly influence the outcome of events and our understanding of them.

Media Unbound presents journalism closely, familiarly — misjudgments, misunderstanding, professional misprision, and all — in the hope that we may learn how to live together constructively, if not always pleasantly.

1

Beyond
Anybody's Power

ON THE EVENING of February 27, 1968, journalism was transmogrified from the public's Huck Finn into Banquo's ghost. Until then, journalism had been nearly everyone's favorite nephew—rascally, reckless, even intemperate, perhaps, but irrepressibly engaging and, despite the exasperated head-wagging and tongue-clucking it provoked sometimes, the beneficiary of unwavering loyalty and limitless, even affectionate, tolerance.

That night, however, fondness and patience began curdling into fear and aversion. There was an instinctive, dawning recognition that journalism—for three hundred years the people's gadfly, gossip, town crier, court jester, and sometime champion—had assimilated sinister power.

That night, with unmistakable clarity, television journalism demonstrated its astonishing force as the nation's self-appointed superego.

The vehicle was Walter Cronkite, an intelligent, moderately well-educated man whose on-air pleasantness had earned him permanent possession of the trophy for the person most frequently described in public encomiums as "avuncular."

An employee of a major corporation (CBS), unelected by anyone to anything, not privy to any comprehensive, analytical reports by America's military or intelligence resources, Walter Cronkite that evening decided unilaterally that United States policy in Vietnam was wrong, that the war must end in stalemate, and that the United States must negotiate with humility.

He told a national television audience that he had been "too often disappointed by the optimism of American leaders, both in Vietnam and Washington, to have faith any longer in the silver linings they find in the darkest clouds." Those optimists had been wrong before, he said. Why should they be believed now, when they claimed that military and political success had been achieved in the battles that had begun raging at the start of the 1968 Tet holidays? Cronkite was "certain that the bloody experience of Vietnam is to end in stalemate." The only "rational" solution, he concluded, would be "to negotiate, not as victors, but as an honorable people who lived up to their pledge to defend democracy, and did the best they could."

It is unlikely that punditry, no stranger to journalism, had ever before been exercised in front of such a vast, captive audience conditioned to viewing news reports as "objective," however loosely that term may have been applied.

Aware of a new phenomenon, President Lyndon Johnson, after watching Cronkite's televised declamation, told his press secretary, George Christian, that the centrist coalition constructed so painstakingly by the President to buttress America's Vietnam War policies now was jeopardized. The enormous reach and impact of the Cronkite report would deprive the government of the continued support of much of the population for aggressive prosecution of the war. He confided to Christian that "losing" Walter Cronkite meant losing the "center."

"It was the first time in American history," David Halberstam wrote later, "a war had been declared over by an anchorman." When, a few days later, Frank McGee told millions of viewers on NBC News that "the war is being lost," *New York Times* critic Jack Gould recognized that television had become "a new and unpredictable factor in influencing critical decisions."

The importance of the event did not hinge entirely on whether Cronkite and McGee were right or wrong in their analyses nor whether their reports represented one of those rare occasions in which the end justified the means. The overriding importance was that it demonstrated that America had become media-minded, believing and acting on journalistic information more than on any other source or institution. Journalism had stopped merely reporting on the nation's agenda; it had become *part* of the nation's agenda, with all the opportunity for good or evil that role entailed.

What Halberstam, Gould, and millions of others perceived, if only intuitively, was that the multitude's David, which occasionally had hurled stones at whatever Goliath might be vexing society, somehow had become a Goliath itself: generally benign, often beneficial — but potentially bellicose, bullying, smug, sullen, and self-righteous. Journalism as giant had lost its sense of humor and its sense of place.

In 1974, a survey by *U.S. News & World Report* showed that a cross-section of the nation's business and professional leaders ranked television ahead of the White House as the country's foremost power center. A few years later, Senator Adlai Stevenson remarked that the media are "the nation's only unaccountable institution, unrestrained by effective internal procedures or external checks." If journalism's mission was to transmit nationally what it determined to be important ideas and information, fulfilling its stated goal of meeting "the public's right to know," then television news had become the only journalistic game in town.

Its size alone was intimidating; it continued to grow with the passage of time and with the deepening sense of national dislocation. In periods of domestic or international ferment, television news attracted viewers as a horseshoe magnet attracts bunches of iron shavings. In late October 1979, the evening news programs of the three major television networks were drawing a combined audience of forty-five million people. Scarcely a month later, after American diplomats and Marines had been seized and were being held hostage by Iranian terrorists, the size of that audience surged by twelve million people, to a total of fifty-seven million Americans watching ABC, CBS, and NBC news every night. Whenever they sensed trouble, it seemed that people felt safer when, figuratively, they huddled as a nation around the tube.

By the end of the 1970s, three out of every four Americans learned most of their news from television. Every second American received *all* his or her news from television.

By 1980, whether the subject was Vietnam, black militancy, student rage, Watergate, Iran, Abscam, assassination attempts, or presidential primaries and elections, it could be argued that, to an extraordinary degree, until television reported it, it had not happened.

The *chutzpah* of a Walter Cronkite or a Frank McGee, without portfolio, telling millions of people that, to quote Oscar Hammerstein II's King of Siam, "what they do not know is so," is certainly unsettling; the awesome size of the medium through which they tell it is downright scary.

The real scare, however, results from the essence of journalism — all journalism — from that of Daniel Defoe, the acknowledged "father" of modern journalism, to the present. Journalism is an inherently imprecise, wholly subjective, seat-of-the-pants business, relying entirely on personal judgment and opinion in identifying, gathering, and presenting news. Yet because of the stupefying reach, immediacy, and impact of electronic journalism, reportage — however incomplete and misleading it may be — influences crucial decisions and, worse, becomes the foundation for what we remember as fact years later. That misconception then forms the basis on which we often make subsequent decisions.

The popular notion that American military forces are incapable of overcoming revolutionary insurgents abroad, for example, was instilled by the journalists covering Vietnam. Many of them were incorrect. Nonetheless, current national debates on the propriety and feasibility of using force to achieve diplomatic goals invariably start with the assumption by many that military intervention against foreign insurgents cannot succeed.

The political and ethical wisdom of any such action is, at the least, eminently arguable; the equation of political goals and ethical ideals with military capability, however, is a sophism fashioned by journalists, not by good historians.

Similarly, news media are responsible for the widespread belief that the series of political misadventures of the 1970s — "Watergate"—was as sordid as any in American history, threatening democratic institutions as they rarely had been threatened before. It was as if the Electoral College never had been manipulated to deny Samuel Tilden the presidency, or as if the impeachment of Andrew Johnson was merely a historic curiosity, or as if the Civil War and the Great Depression were no greater threat than Watergate in their onslaughts against the very foundation of the republican system. The media-induced perception of Watergate as a unique horror spawned a series of political "reforms" widely criticized by odd bedfellows like Eugene McCarthy, James Buckley, and David Broder as imposing more mischief on the political process than had Watergate itself.

Journalism is inclined to error, generally without memory, and almost always lacking in perspective. But its power to leave us with indelible impressions often overwhelms its functions to entertain and inform.

Sanford Socolow, former executive producer of *The CBS Evening News,* maintained that Vietnam coverage by television news included only a small proportion of vivid war scenes, but that these obliterated recollection of the "dull, turgid, 'responsible' stories we did, true or false, about land reform, or about the wonderful, bucolic programs to win the hearts and minds of the people. We bored the tears out of people, cumulatively speaking, for hours. You get one battle piece which lasts two minutes, and it erases the memory of everything you've done for two weeks...

"So it is almost—I'm not willing to say it, but I'm very close to saying—that it's almost beyond anybody's power to balance those things."

As an example, he cited television's coverage of a 1980 trial in Miami of white policemen accused of murdering a black man they had arrested for a traffic violation. The policemen were acquitted; the "live" television coverage of the jury returning the verdict and of the hysterical reaction of the victim's mother minutes later was cited by authorities as contributing to subsequent racial riots in Miami.

"I know what you're worried about," Socolow said during our conversation. "You're worried about us just showing the shrieking, hysterical mother in the absence of everything else in that trial.

"What I'm submitting to you is that the dilemma is even worse: that if, by any standards, you did a responsible story about that trial and the circumstances and the accusations and the denials and the verdict, and you have the hysterical mother in there as a minor portion of it in terms of time devoted to her, that's still all people'd remember about that piece. And you'd still be accused of going for tabloid journalism, the bumper-fender school of journalism, if you put [her] in at all."

(Socolow was only partly right in guessing what I was worried about. The thought of allowing still photographs or even artists' sketches of courtroom proceedings makes me uncomfortable; allowing live television coverage of criminal trials strikes me as outrageous. It adds nothing to the system of justice, no more than a film or photographs of an accused entering or leaving a courtroom shackled in handcuffs, with a coat draped over his head in a feeble attempt at anonymity. It amounts to prying to the point of prurience. I have yet to understand how the First Amendment is served by twisting the meaning of the right to a public trial, designed to protect an accused person from a star chamber proceeding, into some sort of raree designed for mass amusement. I am also troubled by the ubiquitous "mini-cam" outside a grieving mother's door, ready to record her immediate, almost certainly emotional, response. Not long afterward, that same woman, having had an opportunity to collect herself, appealed for calm among black Miamians — an action simply related to me, a viewer in Washington, D.C., by a newscaster, but apparently deemed unworthy of being shown on film.)

Socolow's suggestion that modern journalism, by its nature, can mislead us even when it is presented responsibly is alarming; the implication of what awful journalism can do to us is terrifying.

Put another way, his observation is that journalism defies responsibility, recalling Michel de Montaigne's description in 1572 of those prognosticators "who cite their authority in current events...With all they say, they necessarily tell both truth and falsehood. For who is there who, shooting all day, will not sometime hit the mark?...Besides, no one keeps a record of their mistakes, inasmuch as these are ordinary and numberless; and their correct divinations are made much of because they are rare, incredible, and prodigious."

James Dickenson, then a national political correspondent for *The Washington Star*, put it more succinctly, if less elegantly, 408 years later, when he said that journalists, interpreting the developments of the 1980 American presidential campaign, had been "wrong on just about every goddam thing."

In 1920, Walter Lippmann wrote that "the news of the day as it reaches the newspaper office is an incredible medley of facts, propaganda, rumor, suspicion, clues, hopes, and fears."

The tempo and volume of that "incredible medley" have been squared and cubed since then; yet the manner in which that cacophony of babble is sifted and sorted for retelling has not changed since the days of the pamphleteers. It is as if all the Third World delegates to the United Nations were condemning the United States simultaneously in their native tongues while a lone interpreter wrestled bravely with each oration.

"This is not a precise science," Dan Rather, with considerable understatement, said of his craft. "This, on its best days, is a very crude art."

Like graffiti on New York's subway cars, television journalism is not only a very crude art; it is also a very visible art. However well motivated its intentions, television journalism is like a combination of Gulliver in Lilliput with Godiva in Coventry: anything that big and naked certainly will get our attention, command our careful scrutiny, and arouse more than a little suspicion.

It is no surprise, therefore, that opprobrium is heaped on modern journalism with increasing frequency. Criticism of television news, though, usually is misdirected. The problem with modern journalism is not that television has made journalism any worse; television merely has made journalism's intrinsic weaknesses manifest.

Television news has taken the historic, unchanging, fundamental defects of journalism and jack-hammered them at the people of the United States at speeds guaranteed to maximize error and minimize thoughtfulness, and with a repetitious intensity certain to dull perceptions of reality and history.

It is not that reporters make any more mistakes than they used to; journalism always has been a disorderly, inexact olio of available information, opinion, and individual impression. It variously informs and misleads, educates and titillates, unearths abuses and is abusive. The news business is as helter-skelter and hit-or-miss as ever. The difference is that the boys and the girls on the proverbial bus really are riding a rocket ship. The means of reporting have undergone future shock, but the craft has remained unchanged since 1700;

Robin Hood and his Merry Men still roam Sherwood Forest in leotards and funny little hats—but they have been rearmed with jet-propelled bowstrings and atomic-tipped arrows, the kinds of weapons that, quite literally, can blow our minds.

In consequence, to paraphrase Fiorello La Guardia, when modern news media make a mistake, "it's a beaut!"

2

Mediazation

*I*T WAS 1968 when history and general perceptions of reality began undergoing "mediazation," the disturbing process by which journalism befogs memory and truth. It began with the news media's treatment of the North Vietnamese and Vietcong Tet offensive in late January of that year.

In the midst of the Tet holidays, with 50 percent of Saigon's troops on leave, Communist forces launched surprise attacks throughout South Vietnam, including assaults on Saigon's airport, on the Presidential Palace, and on the U.S. Embassy. Peter Braestrup, who covered Tet for *The Washington Post*, wrote, in a massive study of the nature and influence of news reporting during the Tet crisis, that "not since major U.S. forces first entered Vietnam in 1965 had Hanoi undertaken so ambitious a military effort—aimed largely at South Vietnamese installations amid calls for a popular uprising against the Thieu regime and its American allies."

Most news reports, like those of Cronkite, McGee, and Braestrup, described events in terms of unrelieved failure for South Vietnam and the United States. Consequently, with few exceptions, that is how people remember Tet.

That is not how they *ought* to remember Tet. Those

examining Tet from a historical perspective—observers as disparate in their views of American involvement in Vietnam as Henry Kissinger and Frances FitzGerald—agree, nonetheless, that Tet was a serious military and political defeat for the Communists.

Kissinger wrote that the Communists' "massive countrywide offensive...was massively defeated...We had decisively defeated the Tet offensive in 1968, but its shock to American public support for the war led to the bombing halt and multiplied pressures for our withdrawal...The Vietcong cadres had been decimated...[and] North Vietnamese regular army forces took up the slack. Almost all of the fighting was now done by *North* Vietnamese main force units—contrary to the mythology of 'people's war.'" FitzGerald, a vehement critic of American intervention in Vietnam, concurred that "the curious aspect of American public reaction to the Tet offensive was that it reflected neither the judgment of the American officials nor the true change in the military situation in South Vietnam," whose army "was not routed" and whose government "did not fall; and as a year would show, the Tet offensive had weakened the Front [Vietcong]."

Don Oberdorfer, in his book *Tet!*, published three years after the event, wrote that "it is clear that the attack forces...suffered a grievous military set-back...The Vietcong lost the best of a generation of resistance fighters...The war became increasingly a conventional battle and less an insurgency. Because the residents in the cities did not rise up against the foreigners and puppets at Tet—indeed, they gave little support to the attack force—the communist claim to a moral and political authority in South Vietnam suffered a serious blow." The South Vietnamese government, Oberdorfer wrote, "became more of a working institution than it had ever been before," nearly doubling its military strength through a general mobilization, a process requiring "more political will than the South Vietnamese had ever been able to muster."

London's Institute of Strategic Studies published in its 1969 *Strategic Survey* that the elite of North Vietnam's army had been destroyed, that the Vietcong's rural base in South Vietnam had begun to crumble, and that "villagers who had fled to the towns in earlier years were now returning in large numbers to their rural homes, under the increasingly effective protection of the central Government."

Although there is little question that the Communists won what Kissinger and others call a "psychological victory," it is doubtful that it resulted from the "shock" alone. The psychological victory was a result of the American public's understanding of, and reaction to, the message received from the news media. "That message, most simply put," Peter Braestrup wrote in his study, *Big Story,* "was: 'Disaster in Vietnam!' The generalized effect of the news media's contemporary output in February–March 1968 was a distortion of reality—through sins of omission and commission—on a scale that helped shape Tet's political repercussions in Washington and the Administration's response."

There is an abiding tendency to blame such distortions on the ideology—usually described as "liberal"—of most reporters. Whatever the ideology of most reporters may be, distortions result from the nature of journalism, not from the nature of journalists.

The fiercely competitive business of journalism demands words and pictures *now!* The pressure to be first with the news overwhelms all other considerations. The caveats available to reporters—"while it is not yet certain, it appears that...."; "though the situation remains unclear, knowledgeable sources say...."; "though officials continue to make optimistic statements, no one is placing any bets that...."—are crutches that support imprudent reporting.

Confusion, invariably, reigns during crises. At Tet, the action was dispersed, but reporters were not. Official spokesmen, whom journalists had learned to regard as adversaries, were themselves unsure of what was going on. Some issued misleading statements before they knew the truth—but deadline-pressured reporters lapped up available statements like thirst-crazed desert wanderers at a water hole.

The nuclear reactor accident at Three Mile Island was limited geographically, but its technical complexity made the action as difficult to follow as any on a battlefield. Reporters erupted on the scene, frightening the bejeezus out of businessmen, unaccustomed to pressure and publicity. Heeding foolish public relations advisers, they reacted by withholding information—which both angered reporters and made them suspicious. Journalists, required to file stories whether or not they understood what was happening, relied on their competitive juices to fashion their reports—almost always settling on the worst possible scenario. Zap! We were mediazated. We shall remember how the hydrogen bubble could have caused disaster at Three Mile Island—when, in fact, no such danger existed; reporters publicized the dire, incorrect predictions made in Washington and gave short shrift to the more sanguine (and accurate) technical reports issued by on-site experts. We shall recall the farm animals that died near Three Mile Island—but forget that they died of natural causes, not radiation.

When Professor Edward W. Said maintains in his criticism of American news coverage of Islam that reporters are "blindly serving [their] government," he reveals a thorough ignorance of journalism. Said contends, correctly, that American journalists seized on the most vengeful, bloodthirsty statements of Iranian mullahs, creating a false image of an entire, multifaceted religion. If the image of Islam was distorted, it was done so by reporters serving journalism— and journalism's insatiable lust for controversy and action— not by a government or policy.

Tet, Three Mile Island, the emerging political force of Islam—all are among the more significant developments of our time. The Tet offensive was indeed a shock; the accident at Three Mile Island was serious and the nuclear fuel core did, in fact, overheat; Iranian mullahs, without doubt, have given observers good cause to question the competency of their clergy-run government. Anyone relying on contemporary journalism, however, to understand the military and political ontogeny of Vietnam, the problems of and prospects for nuclear energy, or the outlook in the Middle East should certain nations be dominated by orthodox Muslims would have difficulty passing an examination in world history.

Journalists strive to be accurate, but journalism, too often, does them in. The reason is that it is journalistically "accurate" to report someone else's nonsensical assertions, whether or not that "someone" is identified.

A journalist's politics or ideals simply don't enter into his "interpretations." Rather, his "conclusions" are dictated by the desire to meet a deadline and the expectations of his editors. It is merely safer (and newsier, in terms of getting space or air time) to take the gravest view of circumstances. If you report that a nuclear plant may blow up or spew radiation everywhere, and it does not, a later story can always say the endangering problems were averted. Conversely, if you report that the plant won't blow up, and it does, you'll risk being hooted out of the business.

Besides, news outlets comprise a conglomeration of people and personalities and, depending on the characteristics of their audiences, acquire personalities of their own. *The New York Times* and *The New York Post;* the National Broadcasting Company and *The National Enquirer; Newsweek, Newsday, People,* and *Playboy* — all are in the journalism business. Journalism and journalists are polyphagous, devouring tidbits of information voraciously; the problem is that they feed on one another as well, which makes them the chief victims of history's mediazation. They spend their days reading and viewing one another's reports while the rest of the population is engaged in some form of commerce that limits its reading, watching, or listening to the news.

Harry Reasoner, for instance, who became prominent in television for his mildly acerbic wit, said his "general opinions about Vietnam would coincide very closely over the years

with Barry Goldwater's and Dwight Eisenhower's opinions."
He thought it "defensible," however, "if the decision to get
out of Vietnam was strongly influenced by the reaction of the
American people to seeing honest things on television."

What, I asked, if the American people had not seen honest
things on television? What if they had been misinformed on a
grand scale, as the books by FitzGerald and Oberdorfer
indicate?

"I am aware of this new theory that Tet was a disaster for
the Communists," Reasoner answered. "I went to Vietnam
first in 1953. I know Asia extremely well. I would not
[disagree] for a minute that the United States armed forces
responded very effectively in terrible circumstances in the
Tet offensive. But to say that this was somehow an American
cum South Vietnamese victory that the press concealed, I
think is arrant nonsense."

Reasoner said he had not read the books and that therefore
he would be "half-witted" to try to respond "chapter and
verse." Still, he added, "my answer to that is they're wrong.
They are grinding some very old axes...I know this: that in
terms of dealing with a South Vietnamese government able to
control its own territory and handle its own war, we were
beaten a long time before Tet. Tet merely demonstrated what
the enemy could do when it wanted to, and was driven back
by the United States armed forces. And this other thing is
wishful thinking. I think we would all like to think we had
done better than we had there. I am certainly not left wing,
and I am not a dupe, but this new theory that Tet was a
misreported victory for the allies is not one [that I hold]."

Granting that Reasoner is not easily duped, he nonetheless
suffers from a classic case of mediazation. While characteriz-
ing as some "new theory" the strikingly similar findings on
Tet by a diverse group of historians, Reasoner ascribes
unassailable truth to contemporary reportage of those events.
His colleague at *60 Minutes*, Morley Safer, was even less
inclined to consider the new theory—and reacted far less
equably—when author Robert Elegant, who had spent two

decades as a correspondent in Southeast Asia, wrote in the August 1981 issue of *Encounter* that "I believe it can be said...that South Vietnamese and American forces actually won the limited military struggle. They virtually crushed the Viet Cong in the South...It is interesting to wonder whether Angola, Afghanistan, and Iran would have occurred...*if* the 'Vietnam Syndrome' for which the press (my view) was largely responsible, had not afflicted the Carter Administration and paralyzed American will." Safer, according to columnist William F. Buckley, Jr., responded in an on-air commentary, in October 1981, by comparing Elegant's article "to the kind of thing Joseph Goebbels would have done." Buckley recalled that Safer added that the article was " 'appropriate for a Soviet department of agitation and propaganda'...and perhaps Elegant was after 'pieces of silver left from those dark days' [when *Encounter*]...once accepted CIA money." Buckley said CBS News refused Elegant's request for a response, a reaction Buckley found "at least as serious as any controversy over how to allocate the blame for the bloody fiasco in Vietnam. If such a reply is accepted as appropriate criticism, then civilized discourse, as the basis of democratic exchange, is dead."

In a single commentary, Safer had branded as a Nazi, a Communist, and a Judas someone whose view of history was different from his and from many of his colleagues' (although not different from many historians'). Most journalistic victims of mediazation, however, suffer less from an overdose of vitriol than from the all-too-human and widespread maladies of selective memories, rationalization, and sophistry. In January 1982, CBS presented information indicating that General William Westmoreland deliberately had underestimated enemy strength in Vietnam in the two years preceding the Tet offensive; civilian leaders, he and his generals reportedly feared, were not "sophisticated" enough to deal with bad news. Such despicable and dangerous action drew predictably outraged commentary; columnist Buckley wondered how American policy and strategy might have been altered had the nation· not been fed what he described as "informational garbage." A number of reports, however, like one in *The Washington Post*, described the CBS program as "timely" because "revisionists" had been maintaining that the military outcome in Vietnam might have been different if Tet had not been misreported. With the sort of illogic that might have started Aristotle turning in his grave, some journalists inferred that, because enemy strength *before* the Tet offensive was greater than the American people knew, and because the fighting was bloodier and more intense than the people and the press had anticipated, the military and political *outcome* of the Tet battles was *not*, therefore, portrayed incorrectly by the news media.

Despite the nature of reporting—its haste in sifting the meaning and import of events, the inevitably conflicting information and viewpoints, the necessarily limited access of any observer to events occurring in several places at once— journalism, through television, is pounded into our brains with a completeness that makes dispassionate history impotent as a contestant for our attention, much less for our recollection.

Amplifying journalistic farrago to decibel levels beyond the wildest, drugged fantasies of even the most frenzied acid-rock freak is, alone, a guarantee of widespread, irreversible absorption of misinformation. In addition to its blare and omnipresence, however, there are related media phenomena that compound the likelihood of misreporting: a legal womb in which journalists find increasing comfort and protection, and growing reportorial self-indulgence in interpretive reporting, or editorializing, or "I" trouble—the overweening need to tell us "what it all means." Bigness and virtual invulnerability to libel suits have created a generation of reporters for whom speed and conflict, rather than measured accuracy and balance, are the stuff of prestige, promotion, and pay.

Journalistic involvement in, or even provocation of, turmoil is not new. It was in 1898 that publisher William Randolph

Hearst cabled this response to the on-scene report from the artist Frederic Remington that there was no war in Cuba: "You furnish the pictures and I'll furnish the war." Much more recently, coverage of the American hostages in Iran produced the controversial (and, some columnists like Ellen Goodman and James Reston suggested, provocative) daily captivity reminders or "countdowns" on CBS and ABC.

For the most part, though, journalism is content simply to point its cameras or pencils at controversy and, without fear or favor, emphasize whichever side of the dispute makes the direst predictions of the outcome. As Jerry Manders, a public relations and advertising executive, wrote in a tract advocating that television be outlawed, "The machine doesn't care about its fantasies. A new one will do. Bringing Nixon down was just as good for ratings as supporting him. Better. More action. . . If people believed the images of historical events or news events were equal to the events or were even close approximations of them, then historical reality was in big trouble."

3

A Sensational Story

A NOTORIOUS EXAMPLE of the pitfalls inherent in encouraging reportorial style over substance was the *Washington Post*–Pulitzer Prize–"Little Jimmy" fiasco of April 1981. *Post* reporter Janet Cooke, twenty-six, had been awarded a Pulitzer Prize for her story the previous fall about Little Jimmy, an eight-year-old boy whose mother watched without objection while her lover, a drug-pusher, injected heroin into the boy's veins as reporter Cooke looked on. Cooke kept the identities of the principals secret from her editors as well as from her readers.

The day after the story appeared, a therapist at Howard University, in Washington, D.C., who had been interviewed for the story, told a *Post* editor she thought Cooke had manufactured Little Jimmy. The therapist, who specialized in treating young drug-users, was afraid her patients might think they were being compromised; if their identities were being disclosed indiscriminately, they might stop seeking medical help. She said the *Post* editor to whom she spoke, Patrick Tyler, accused her of anger and jealousy because her drug-abuse program had not received more attention in the article.

Shortly after the Cooke article appeared, Washington

police launched a citywide search for Jimmy, but were unable to find the boy. Washington's mayor, Marion Barry, while conceding there was a serious drug problem in the city, said publicly that he doubted the existence of Little Jimmy.

The publicity attending a Pulitzer Prize–winner soon exposed serious misrepresentations Cooke had made to her employers about her academic background. Suspicious, her editors wrung from her a confession that she had fabricated her story. Little Jimmy, she admitted, was a "composite" of some of the young addicts described to her by therapists and others she had interviewed. She had never met him, nor anyone like him, nor, indeed, had she seen anyone "shoot up."

The subsequent agonized soul-searching throughout the news industry concentrated on the symptoms rather than the disease: How could newsroom "systems" be instituted to minimize the chance that embroidered news stories could slip through a phalanx of editors? Should reporters confide the identities of confidential sources to a superior sworn to secrecy? Should news organizations exercise greater care in checking the credentials of applicants?

Receiving less attention were more fundamental questions about modern journalism: Had its adversarial stance in relation to constituted authority created a self-delusion that journalism was a law unto itself? Had the popularity and profits of reportorial confrontation and controversy led inevitably to the giving of the greatest rewards to sensationalism? Would a thoughtful, thorough, but less dramatic analysis of Washington's drug culture have won a Pulitzer Prize?

"It's the toughness of journalism," Joseph Mastrangelo, a veteran *Post* reporter, said of his young colleague's perfidy. "These kids have got to come up with a sensational story to get noticed."

During the initial stages of Cooke's reporting, when she discussed her findings with her city editor, Milton Coleman, "she talked about hundreds of people being hooked," Coleman recalled. "And at one point she mentioned an eight-year-old addict. I stopped her and said, 'That's the story. Go after it. It's a front-page story.'"

Cooke could not locate the eight-year-old the therapist had mentioned to her, nor anyone else fitting the description. It is a reasonable assumption that the attraction of "making" the front page outweighed her fear of being caught in a monstrous lie.

Ironically, the *Post's* Bob Woodward was the editor principally responsible for authorizing Cooke's reliance on anonymous sources to propound her myth—the same Bob Woodward who had climbed to fame and fortune on the strength of anonymous sources in his reporting of the Watergate scandal, in two books about the fall of Richard Nixon, and in his subsequent book, *The Brethren: Inside the Supreme Court.* (The dewy-eyed romance between Woodward and his journalistic brethren began to pall with the publication of the last book. Writer-lawyer Renata Adler, in reviewing the book, concluded "that certain techniques, well suited to investigation of breaking stories of a criminal nature, are entirely unsuited to extended, serious analysis in other contexts...Investigative reporting, perhaps, might think again.")

During his reporting of the Watergate crimes, Woodward had refused to identify Deep Throat, his most important anonymous source, to his editors. In an incredible abdication of responsibility, the *Post's* publisher, Katharine Graham, went further and told Woodward she did not even want to know the identity of Deep Throat.

Interestingly, at that time, Woodward was about the same age and at the same level of inexperience as Cooke when she created her story of whole cloth.

For years, many respected Washington journalists have speculated that Deep Throat was, like Little Jimmy, a composite. One disbeliever, political writer and commentator Richard Reeves, said to me once that if Deep Throat came forward, "he'd be worth ten million dollars on the hoof" from publishers and film producers. Yet, perhaps because the Watergate story proved out, the extensive, often exclusive use of unidentified sources in making serious allegations against high-ranking government officials was deemed justified.

Whatever the validity of Deep Throat, and whatever the contributions of Woodward, Carl Bernstein, and other reporters through their exhaustive searches of records and numerous, thorough interviews, journalism's role in "uncovering" Watergate has been exaggerated considerably. Congress, with no help from media, discovered the taping system in President Nixon's White House. The courts forced delivery of those tapes to investigative and prosecutorial authorities. Without the tapes and their incontrovertible proof of "cover-up," a presidential resignation would have been unlikely.

Nor can it be argued that media were working consciously in the nation's best interest. Reporters and their print or electronic outlets valued the "beat" above all; they worked in a caldron of competition. In that context, young, ambitious, untested reporters might well create an all-knowing source, as has been speculated about Deep Throat, to buttress what they know or feel to be true but cannot otherwise document sufficiently for doubting editors.

The *Post*'s executive editor, Benjamin C. Bradlee, when criticized for not notifying authorities about Jimmy rather than giving higher priority to publishing the story, responded, "I don't think of the journalist as cop"—implying that notifying the police in connection with the commission of a crime is unjournalistically coplike, though *acting* like a cop (as in undercover, investigative reporting) is not.

A significant segment of major media considers itself, obviously, to be somehow extralegal, if not actually above the law—at least, in an institutional sense. Mike Royko, a columnist for *The Chicago Sun-Times* captured this growing conceit when he said, "There's something more important than a story here. This eight-year-old kid is being murdered.

The editors should have said, 'Forget the story, find the kid.' Who do they think they are? God? People in any other profession would have gone right to the police."

When the occasion suits their purposes, moreover, investigative reporters are not above enlisting the aid of authorities in sometimes unwholesome ways.

Gerald Rafshoon, President Carter's media adviser, was investigated by the Department of Justice and the Federal Election Commission to determine any wrongdoing on his part in connection with financing Carter's 1976 political advertising campaign. Though he was cleared of any violations, Rafshoon told me the exercise had cost him $300,000 in legal and accounting fees. His attorney, William Stack of Atlanta, told me the investigation was undertaken after two journalists, unable to substantiate their own suspicions of Rafshoon, presented the results of their reporting to federal authorities.

Ethics-in-government laws passed in the wake of the Watergate disclosures compelled government agencies to investigate the allegations. Subsequent news stories, listing the unproved (and, as it turned out, unfounded) charges against Rafshoon, thus were "justified" because Rafshoon was being investigated by government agencies. Hence, the reporters caused the investigation that, in turn, provided them with the news peg on which to hang the charges in print.

Journalism has undergone a wholesale relaxation, if not disappearance, of erstwhile news-reporting requirements to identify accusers when airing their accusations, and of not erring on the side of caution when presenting material damaging to groups or individuals. Rashness has replaced caution, and a wave of journalistic McCarthyism — guilt by anonymous innuendo — has replaced workmanlike, even-handed reporting.

In one bizarre example, two reporters for *The Alton* (Illinois) *Telegraph* sent a "confidential memorandum" in 1969 to federal investigators. They alleged that there were connections among an Alton contractor, a local savings-and-loan association, "hoods," and a "crime boss" and that the Mafia was pumping money into the financial institution, which then funneled large loans to the contractor. Whatever the motive of the reporters in sending the memorandum, had it set off an investigation, the allegations could have been published as the news that federal officials were probing the "charges."

Federal authorities, however, decided against opening a criminal investigation. One of them, though, forwarded details of the reporters' memorandum to federal banking officials, prompting an examination of the savings-and-loan association. The institution cut off credit to the contractor, James C. Green, whose multimillion-dollar development business collapsed for want of capital infusions. Six years later, Green learned why his credit had been stopped.* He filed suit in 1976, and in 1980 was awarded an astounding $9.2 million, an amount extraordinary both because of its size and because the allegations never were published. (By mid-1981, the size of the judgment was being appealed and negotiated simultaneously. Whatever the outcome, it is important to note that had Green been a public official or designated by the courts as a public figure, he would have been required to prove that the reporters had acted with malice or reckless disregard of the facts, making it extremely unlikely that he could have won his suit.)

Whether or not material is published, a rapidly spreading fancy in journalism is that the act of investigative reporting is a legally protected, morally justified end in itself, a notion that troubles even such champions of the First Amendment as Supreme Court Justice William J. Brennan. In its role of speaking out freely, Justice Brennan contends, the press "requires and is accorded the absolute protection of the First

---

*Ironically, one of the *Telegraph* reporters who had written the "confidential" memorandum gave a copy of it to an officer of the savings-and-loan association in 1976; it was passed along to Green by that officer.

Amendment." But in its role of gathering and disseminating the news, Justice Brennan maintains, "the press's interests may conflict with other societal interests and adjustment of the conflict on occasion favors the competing claim." Brennan adds, "It matters a great deal whether the press is abridged because restrictions are imposed on what it may say, or whether the press is abridged because its ability to gather the news. . . is impaired. . . The strong, absolutist rhetoric" to the contrary, he says, "is only obfuscatory."

Yet an eminent attorney like Floyd Abrams, frequently retained by major media to argue First Amendment cases in their behalf, has contended that for a journalist to be protected legally when he conceals his news sources is no different from a doctor asserting the confidential status of his communications with patients. "In fact," he has asked, "as between doctors and journalists, who needs the protection more?"

Abrams' argument turns on its head the justification for extending the right of privileged communications to doctors, lawyers, and some others: it is to protect the patient and client, each of whom wishes to confide personal information necessary for receiving medical or legal help; the information, each trusts, will go no further. In the case of a reporter's confidential source, it is the overt intention that the information be trumpeted far and wide—with only its source to be kept secret—creating, as it has so often, a perfect opportunity to grind an ax while professing righteous concern.

Reporters have become profligate in the use of protected sources. Anonymous finger-pointers promote laziness and sloppiness in news-gathering. Quotes can be made a bit sharper or made up entirely—who'll know the difference? Allegations need not be checked as thoroughly—what public figure can sue? Meanwhile, the more journalistic heat that "confidential sources" generate, the less a reporter need grapple with the substance of an issue. The shadows that are created darken our memories.

The value of excessive journalistic vilification, and the

ultimate purposes and contributions of those who, like the character in *Pilgrim's Progress*, wield the muckrake, have been questioned for some time. President Theodore Roosevelt, in a 1906 speech, lashed out at Lincoln Steffens, Upton Sinclair, and other journalists he had come to regard as "the lunatic fringe":

> There are times and places where...there is filth on the floor and it must be scraped up with the muckrake...But the man who never does anything else, who never thinks or speaks or writes save of his feats with the muckrake, speedily becomes, not a help to society, not an incitement to good, but one of the most potent forces of evil.

Save for his use of political hyperbole, Roosevelt wasn't alone in his assessment of the muckrakers' worth. The young Walter Lippmann, an acolyte of Steffens', wrote in 1913 that Steffens was "too whimsical for a permanent diet" and that a series of articles supposedly exposing the banking monopoly never "got down to grips with anything." Steffens' biographer Justin Kaplan wrote that "Lippmann concluded...the work of the muckrakers had been a waste."

At the root of its failure and, in its contemporary embodiment, that of investigative reporting, is the substitution of cynicism and pretension for healthy skepticism and a delight in inquiry—not to mention the prodigious egos required of those capable of convincing themselves that they alone recognize truth. The muckraking spirit was captured in a 1918 story by Willa Cather, describing her friend, magazine editor S. S. McClure, and his staff:

> He found he could take an average reporter from the daily press, give him a "line" to follow, a trust to fight, a vice to expose—this was all in that good time when people were eager to read about their own wickedness—and in two years the reporter would be recognized as an authority...The strangest thing was the owners of these grave countenances, staring at their own faces on newspapers and billboards, fell to venerating themselves.

A reportorial air of frigid cynicism often guarantees dramatic copy and success in journalism—but not necessarily *good* journalism. Columnist Joseph Kraft writes that, for reporters, "Watergate and Vietnam make it easy to disbelieve. But unrelenting doubt, systematic imputation of bad faith and evil motives breed a climate of universal distrust and absolute cynicism. In the end, those who disbelieve everything are themselves disbelieved."

Dr. Michael Halberstam, putting it another way, said once, "If I need an adversary, I'll hire a lawyer." Halberstam blamed the adversarial standard in journalism for many of its failures; yet in the January–February 1980 issue of *The Washington Journalism Review*, he wrote that "foolish, biased, and inaccurate" reporting—which, he maintained, dominated media coverage of his own field, medicine— resulted primarily from "systematic, built-in flaws in journalism that are reflected in its coverage of other fields."

Halberstam, himself a journalist and author of note, accused the media of "minnow journalism" rather than the "herd journalism" described by author Tim Crouse as the dominant characteristic of political reporters. "A herd of cattle takes a bit of work to get headed in one direction," Halberstam wrote, "but a school of minnows changes direction 180 degrees instantly, and for no apparent purpose."

Except for a report by a CBS correspondent, Halberstam wrote, "no medical reporter seriously questioned the alleged shortage of 50,000 doctors in 1973 or that it had turned into a vast surplus by 1977." In the three years before the Nobel Prize was awarded to the developers of computerized (CT) scanning, Halberstam counted about twenty-five hundred separate stories under the heading "Medicine and Health" in *The New York Times* Index; five, he said, were about CT scanning, and all of those stories focused on its cost, not on its medical or scientific value.

Halberstam added that newspaper stories in 1974 reported allegations of 30,000 to 140,000 deaths a year from drug reactions. When "a careful study in 1976 revised that figure to 9000, of which only a quarter were estimated to be preventable, the story was ignored." The same thing happened, he said, when "reams of publicity" were devoted to a study estimating that as many as a third of all operations performed in the United States were unnecessary.

> When a study by the New York Board of Health (no great advocate of the private practice of surgery) showed only 8 percent to be definitely questionable, the story ended up on page twenty-six of The [*Washington*] *Post*...
>
> The overriding sin...is the persistence of advocacy reporting [Halberstam wrote in his article]. Too many reporters have their stories in advance and gather facts to support it...Too many reporters start an assignment knowing everything and, not surprisingly, leave without having learned one damn thing. Advocacy disguised as straight reporting is an abomination. It is the ultimate insult to tell readers that we are too dumb to make up our own minds, and that we require a reporter to do it for us.

Advocacy, confrontation, "exposing" wrongdoing, all contribute to exciting, dramatic reading and viewing. Good guys and bad guys are delineated as sharply in modern journalism, especially in programs like *60 Minutes,* as in the old Grade B Western movies.

In February 1976, Mike Wallace narrated a *60 Minutes* segment on safety hazards in nuclear plants that *New York Times* television critic John J. O'Connor criticized for its "almost blatantly apparent" bias against nuclear power.

Wallace, asked four years later whether he recalled O'Connor's rebuke, remembered it well: "'Bordering on entrapment,' he [O'Connor] said. 'The antinuclear power bias of the piece was almost blatantly apparent...' Read the piece. It is absolutely prophetic," Wallace told me, referring to the subsequent accident at Three Mile Island. Without question, the segment was aimed at potential dangers—especially fire hazards—that might lead to a melt-down. The program generated its own considerable heat and seemed prescient when viewed from the perspective of the alarms sounded at Three Mile Island. Whether it shed much light is another matter.

The idea for the story originated with the Union of Concerned Scientists, an organization critical of nuclear development. A representative of the group introduced Wallace to Robert Pollard, a project manager of the Nuclear Regulatory Commission. Pollard told Wallace that he was concerned about licensing for operation a nuclear plant near New York City, and had "tried to say so inside the agency and was shushed." Pollard was earning about $30,000 a year, Wallace recalls, supported a family, but had decided, nonetheless, to "resign on principle." The Union of Concerned Scientists, "a perfectly reputable organization," in Wallace's view, "obviously...wanted [Pollard] to resign with a splash to call attention to the fact that...Con Ed [was] doing something that, in their estimation...was potentially dangerous to New York City." Pollard's resignation would dramatize the Nuclear Regulatory Commission's practice of licensing nuclear power plants despite what Pollard believed was inadequate attention to safety.

In the televised interview, Pollard said that "it will be just a matter of luck" if Consolidated Edison's nuclear plant, Indian Point Number 3, "doesn't some time during its life have a major accident."* Pollard was quoted as issuing one specific criticism to support his allegation that "the plant does not meet today's regulations." He said that "the separation ...between the backup safety systems at Indian Point is worse, probably, than Brown's Ferry."

Pollard's reference was to a fire at a nuclear power plant at Brown's Ferry, Alabama, in March 1975, in which cables supplying power to pump cooling water into the reactor were

*Before its completion, Indian Point Number 3 was sold to the Power Authority of the State of New York to meet what a Con Ed spokesman described as "a cash-flow problem."

destroyed, along with backup cables. The problem was solved when engineers devised a means to use auxiliary water pumps powered by undamaged cables. There was no regulation about what constituted proper separation between main and backup power cables; still, Pollard's general complaint was that problems of that kind should be anticipated and solved before nuclear plants are licensed.

60 Minutes arranged a tour of a plant, similar to Indian Point Number 3, accompanied by a Con Ed official, John Conway. In the middle of the tour, Wallace, on camera, told Conway about Pollard's complaint. "You obviously have me at a disadvantage," Conway complained on camera, "because I haven't read what this man has said, nor had I heard he made these statements." Conway maintained that a fire of the sort that occurred at Brown's Ferry could not happen at Indian Point, because the cable was insulated properly and an automatic fire-fighting water system had been installed. But Wallace countered that that wasn't the point. "If you had a fire in this cable tunnel, aren't these redundant systems, the backup systems, too close to the—isn't it all too confined? Couldn't there be the possibility of a disaster with, with the backup systems not working properly?"

Conway tried explaining again about fire-resistant coatings on the cables and the water system to extinguish a fire before it developed. "So now you ask me a question—if we had something, which I don't believe can happen here—[but] if a fire were to occur here...and if I had three different tunnels, separated, it would be better."

Wallace struck. "Why don't we have three different tunnels?"

"Because we don't think it's necessary," Conway said. "Obviously, when we designed it, we didn't think it was necessary."

"Well," Wallace said, "it's conceivable you could have a catastrophic event. That's what all these safety precautions are all about. Isn't that a fact, Mr. Conway?"

"All I can tell you is, we've had over twenty years of operating nuclear power plants...without any member of the public even being injured, never mind killed."

Wallace conceded that was true, and then mentioned a 1972 fire set by arsonists at another Consolidated Edison plant that "destroyed the power cables for several backup safety systems. Fortunately," he added ominously, "the plant was not yet in operation."

In describing that interview to me four years after it occurred, Wallace said Pollard had told him to "'take a look at the backup systems in the cables at Indian Point Number Three because they're too damn close together and a fire in one could jump over to the other,' and Con Ed was saying, 'First of all, there won't be a fire and, secondly, they couldn't jump—and besides [Wallace smacked the table for emphasis], we don't, we simply do not have—our safety is so intense here, nobody smokes, nobody...' And I look up, I swear, and right there tucked into the cables was a pack of Marlboro cigarettes. Well, when I showed it to, I think his name was Conway, to the fella who was giving us the tour..." Wallace and I laughed at our mental picture of poor Conway. Wallace then whispered, "He shit!"

Actually, on the program, Conway said nothing about smoking or the "intensity" with which safety is enforced. Wallace simply said, "We saw something that gave us pause; wedged between two cable bins in a no-smoking area was a pack of cigarettes."

Wallace's second attack was aimed at William Anders, a former astronaut who was then chairman of the Nuclear Regulatory Commission. "We set up an interview with Anders for the day on which Pollard was planning his resignation...First of all," Wallace said, "he didn't know Pollard by name, but that's perfectly understandable...Anders did not know Pollard was going to resign. He sure did not know he was going to resign in public. And we did, and we already had Pollard on film."

Anders asserted that nuclear plants cannot begin construction or operation, "nor will we allow them to continue to operate, unless we are satisfied at all times—we and our extensive staff...that these plants are safe."

WALLACE: Have you ever heard of a fellow by the name of Bob Pollard, Mr. Anders?

ANDERS: The name does not jump to my memory.

WALLACE: Bob Pollard is one of your project managers and he resigned today. Reason he resigned was he is not sure about the safety of your program.

ANDERS: Bob Pollard has never tried to contact me or any members of the Commission. I never even heard of Bob Pollard before.

Anders was upset that Wallace knew about an employee's complaint before he himself knew. He telephoned the director of the Office of Nuclear Regulation while the cameras continued to roll. The director knew Pollard, who, he conceded, had "given very specific and acute attention to a number of the fine points of rules and regulations which appear to give him some internal problems." He had no idea, however, that Pollard had been considering resigning.

Anders complained that *60 Minutes* was "being used...I think that it's very unfortunate...that this young man didn't express his views to his senior supervisors and to the Commission before he made his splash." Pollard argued that he "did try. I didn't try necessarily with Mr. Anders, but I tried with my supervisor." Wallace hadn't interviewed the supervisor. Pollard subsequently became a nuclear safety engineer in the Washington office of the Union of Concerned Scientists.

"Very dramatic," Wallace told me. "That's the technique. All [Anders] had to do was stop. We would've stopped. Now, they coulda said, they might say, 'Yes, but you'd use that business of where we said, "Stop!"' Believe me, we wouldn't have, we wouldn't have..."

The accident at Three Mile Island had nothing to do with fire hazards, so in that sense the *60 Minutes* segment was not, as Wallace boasts, "virtually a shooting script for Three Mile."

Further, in connection with Three Mile Island, several NRC employees had expressed deep concern about the cooling system, the very thing that did fail and trigger the accident there. One employee, James Creswell, mentioned his concern to a member of the Nuclear Regulatory Commission, who then demanded some answers from the plant's designers. Unfortunately, the commissioner's memorandum of inquiry was issued just as the Three Mile Island cooling system jammed. Still, the commissioner had listened and had acted.

Regardless of whether it represents an issue fully and fairly, *60 Minutes* reaches as many as forty million people each week. "*Everyone* watches your show," Betty Ford wrote ruefully to *60 Minutes*' executive producer, Don Hewitt. She was referring to the reaction that followed her comment on the program that she wouldn't be surprised if she learned that her daughter was having an affair.

In February 1975, Wallace and a *60 Minutes* crew were allowed to enter Syria and film inside Damascus' Jewish Quarter. The resulting program created a storm of controversy among American Jews. Wallace had reported that "life for Syria's Jews is better than it was in years past." The American Jewish Congress contended that Wallace's reporting was "inaccurate and distorted." CBS spokesmen said the network was "deluged" with mail objecting to Wallace's "bias." Some even accused Wallace, a Jew, of anti-Semitism.

In May 1980, Dan Rather tried to demonstrate that when Henry Kissinger was Secretary of State, he encouraged the Shah of Iran to lead an effort in OPEC to raise oil prices (or failed to discourage him from holding the line) so that the Shah would have more petrodollars with which to buy American armaments. These would ensure the Shah's role as the policeman of the Persian Gulf. It seemed, on the surface, a somewhat labyrinthine method of arming the Shah. The resulting *60 Minutes* program did nothing to unravel the convoluted mess.

The program left no doubt, however, that persons knowledgeable about America's role in the Persian Gulf believed in what *60 Minutes* called "The Kissinger-Shah Connection." George Ball, former Undersecretary of State, was asked by Rather on the broadcast, "Have you ever seen the evidence that Dr. Kissinger did try to use his influence with...the Shah to keep prices down?" Ball answered, "No."

But Ball said in a later interview, with *The Los Angeles Times*, that he had never looked for any such evidence: "It wasn't of any importance to me." Ball, a frequent critic of Kissinger, maintained in the post–*60 Minutes* interview that he does not subscribe to Rather's theory— "and I wasn't asked about it."

William Simon, former Secretary of the Treasury, did respond to Rather's on-air statement of the theory with the observation that "well, there could very well be some truth in that."

"But if that's true, we paid one hell of a price for arming the Shah," Rather said.

"Yeah..." Simon agreed, "and I suggested it was an unnecessary price to pay, if that were true."

Within the context of the program — that Kissinger helped inflate oil prices to finance the Shah's expensive purchase of sophisticated weaponry— Simon's and Ball's statements appeared supportive. Simon complained later that his attitude seemed "fuzzy," because, in an hour's interview, *60 Minutes* included only a few of his remarks.

That Ball was critical of the segment indicates that it probably was flawed. On the program, Kissinger was quoted as describing Ball as "a partisan political opponent...jealous of me...and long engaged in a personal campaign to destroy me." Remarks like that would seem unlikely to win unsolicited support from George Ball.

What infuriated *60 Minutes* and Rather was Kissinger's on-again, off-again attitude toward appearing on the program to respond to the allegations. CBS even delayed broadcasting the segment for a week on the strength of Kissinger's promise to appear if he had another week to prepare. He said he decided not to appear "when I concluded that I was being put on a show as a defendant by a man who had developed an erroneous thesis and had a vested interest in defending it."

Rather said in a *Los Angeles Times* interview, "I am absolutely convinced of the ultimate accuracy of the story. We bent over doubly backward, we went into circus contortion fits to be fair to him. . . We found a lot of what was alleged was untrue. A lot else required you to think the worst possible interpretation was true." On the air, however, Rather summarized the presentation by concluding, "Whatever the truth of these allegations, they are as of this date unproven."

A few days before the segment was aired, I sat in Dan Rather's office for an hour and a half while he listened to Henry Kissinger. Rather spoke barely a word.

"Henry's version of that conversation is exactly the opposite," Don Hewitt said when I told him of my observation. When Kissinger talked to him, Hewitt said, the former Secretary of State claimed that Rather had done all the talking and explaining. According to Hewitt, Kissinger "told Dan that he didn't hold Dan responsible; it was Hewitt who was out to get him. And he told me, 'Ah, no, no, no, no, no.' He said, 'I never said that. I said I know you're not responsible. I *know* it's Dan. Dan Rather's too big in this company for you to tell him what to do—so it's got to be him.'"

Clearly, so-called advocacy and confrontational journalism is provocative, provoking even a professional diplomat like Henry Kissinger to engage in a new form of shuttle diplomacy among CBS executives and reporters. Provocation is not synonymous with enlightenment, however. The *60 Minutes* segment entitled "The Kissinger-Shah Connection" was described as "a lynching" by William F. Buckley, Jr.; Fred W. Friendly considered it, less delicately, "a piece of shit."

Nonetheless, reporters often maintain that their freedom to gather and report the news should be absolute and unlimited. Yet the press always has considered its freedom somewhat more important than anyone else's. "Except when their own freedom was discernibly at stake," John Lofton wrote in a carefully researched book on the press and the First Amendment, "established general-circulation newspapers have tended to go along with efforts to suppress deviations from the prevailing political and social orthodoxies of their time and place rather than to support the right to dissent." Lofton, an editorial writer for *The St. Louis Post-Dispatch*, documented how leading newspapers supported the Alien and Sedition Acts in the nation's first quarter-century, how, before the Civil War, they failed to support the right of antislavery publications to use the mails, and how, for the most part, they were silent through the free-speech struggles of radicals and labor activists in the early 1900s. That freedom of the American press today is accepted almost unquestioningly and championed almost unanimously is a tribute to the cumulative influence of those who own and operate it.

The assertion of special privilege and prerogatives in pursuit of news lately has been couched in terms of protecting the "people," not the journalists or their editors or the publishers. The demand for special treatment would make it appear that journalists are toiling ceaselessly and single-mindedly in the public interest—salaries and profits be damned.

On the contrary, said CBS's Sanford Socolow. "If a newsman, whatever the medium he or she is in, stops for a split second to concern himself with the effect of what he's reporting, then he ought to get out of the business. Because that's going to paralyze his reporting in one way or another. Then, he's not a reporter any more. Theoretically, I would submit to you, you report as objectively and as factually and as quickly as you can—and devil the consequences. Let them flow."

In practice, if not in theory, the consequences can mislead many, impugn some, and devastate others.

4

A Mad Dog

WITHIN A FEW WEEKS of the Janet Cooke episode at *The Washington Post,* Michael Daly of *The New York Daily News* was forced to resign when he conceded that he had made up part of an account about a British soldier shooting a youth in Belfast. London journalists had uncovered the hoax, and there was considerable outrage in England. It was the sort of thing, British editorialists complained, that wrongly polarized world opinion. "The question of reconstruction and using a pseudonym [for someone quoted] — I've done a lot of it," Daly explained in his own defense. In terms of accounting for why talented journalists risk their careers by fabricating material, Daly added, "No one has ever said anything."

In another caprice of fate, the reporter who was awarded the Pulitzer Prize for feature writing, after Janet Cooke was disqualified, was herself accused of "journalistic malpractice" in her prize-winning account of the murder of former Representative Allard Lowenstein. The reporter, Teresa Carpenter of *The Village Voice,* wrote of the murderer, Dennis Sweeney, as if she had interviewed him personally, when, in fact, she had never met him.

One passage that drew complaints from friends of the deceased suggested there had been a homosexual relationship between Lowenstein and Sweeney. "Now," Carpenter wrote, "from his cell at Rikers Island, Sweeney denies that they ever had a relationship. Once, while he and Lowenstein were traveling through Mississippi together, they checked into a motel. According to Sweeney, Lowenstein made a pass and Sweeney rebuffed it. Sweeney is not angry with Lowenstein, he claims, nor does he feel any shame."

Carpenter defended the passage by pointing out that none of the statements was in quotation marks. Besides, she said in an interview at the time, "in my research, I was satisfied that what the story says was true. The reader has got to trust me when he or she is reading the piece. I do not feel compelled to attribute each and every piece of information to its source. I don't mean to sound arrogant, but I do mean to sound confident."

I have met neither Carpenter nor her editor, David Schneiderman, who said that he retained complete confidence in the accuracy of the article. I know nothing about either—and I really don't think any reader should be required to learn anything about the reporter as a prerequisite to reading her articles. Even if we should, could we know her well enough to rely on her personal conclusions concerning a delicate matter like alleged homosexuality (assuming that it was important that we know anything about those allegations in the first place)? Did *she* know Lowenstein and Sweeney well enough to reach her conclusions? Why couldn't Carpenter have written simply that some people to whom she spoke mentioned this aspect of their relationship, which, if true, could have angered Sweeney—although he told friends it had not? Why was it necessary to suggest she had wrung this crucial information directly from Sweeney?

Carpenter's statement is indeed arrogant; it is not so much confident as it is cocky. It is not a question of trust; it is a question of duplicity. She wrote that she got this information, for what it is worth, from the horse's mouth; there is no other way to interpret her remarks. The absence of quotation marks hardly makes a difference. There can be only two reasons for writing it her way. The first is that had she conceded that this somewhat salacious information had come to her second- or third-hand, readers would have been less likely to believe it. The second is that telling it her way, rather than the way it happened, had greater literary impact. As seen in the case of Janet Cooke, pizazz is more likely to be rewarded in journalism than thoroughness. (Imaginative, brightly written journalism can be thoughtful and thorough, too; it's just that with the emphasis placed on speed and "sex appeal," reporters who crave attention—and most do—know that editors pay more of it to those who find and exploit some gimmick.)

Whether it is arrogance, naïveté, or merely naked lust for success, the sense of "mission" infecting many reporters and editors has weakened journalistic moderation. Relentless pursuit of an alleged wrongdoer is almost always noticed and admired by colleagues and superiors, but moderation in reaching judgments, as in other walks of life, often is mistaken for weakness or wrong-headedness.

Few tragic examples of unceasing—and, by the newspaper's own admission, unwarranted—journalistic attacks can match the campaign by *The Green Bay Press-Gazette* in 1979 and 1980 against a county juvenile court judge named James W. Byers. Over a six-month period, the crusading newspaper published a hundred articles and editorials alleging irregularities by the judge in the performance of his duties. Procedures in the juvenile court were being investigated by a special prosecutor. The newspaper used the investigation as the basis for carrying out what its relatively new editor, Robert Gallagher, had said, in another context, was its "vital responsibility to aggressively pursue the real story of the way government operates."

On September 25, 1979, the paper ran an article by an

investigative reporter, Dennis Chaptman, quoting a county social worker to the effect that the failure of Judge Byers and others to move quickly in scheduling a custody hearing had risked "permanent brain damage...for a four-month-old infant in 1977." Chaptman had not examined the records in the case. Not only was there no brain damage, but the story failed to support the social worker's charge of undue delays. When the child's father said later that delays were caused by social workers trying to gain time to build their case, the story ran on the second page. Still, subsequent stories rarely failed to include charges of "health risks" leveled against Byers. Finally, however, on January 15, 1980, the newspaper was forced to run a front-page retraction of potentially libelous language used in a dozen articles and editorials; it also published eight columns of a "claim of true facts" prepared by attorneys. "That," reporter Chaptman, then twenty-six, said, "was one of the blackest days of my life. I got as drunk as I'd been in a long time."

Two weeks later, the special prosecutor reported that juvenile court officials "have not at all times followed the procedures set forth in the Wisconsin statutes," but that no one had "committed any crime which would warrant or justify criminal prosecution." The headline in the *Press-Gazette:* NO INDICTMENTS...DESPITE VIOLATIONS.

The newspaper story also omitted an important sentence from the special prosecutor's report: "I find that it does not appear probable that a crime was committed." The newspaper then resumed publishing stories attacking Byers' term, which he since had completed, as juvenile court judge.

One night in February 1980, the judge's wife, Nancy, left a note for her husband: "I can't stand the attacks of the *Press-Gazette.* I love you. I'm leaving."

Several hours later, police found her lying face down in the snow, unconscious but alive. At the hospital, Judge Byers, who previously had refused to fight the newspaper's allegations openly ("I can't fight back," he was quoted as telling a family member. "There's nothing you can do against a newspaper"), told one of his sons that next day he finally would go the *Press-Gazette.* "It's hurting your mother."

A few hours later, Judge Byers, fifty-three, died of a heart attack.

The reaction of John Brogan, a friend of Byers', is worth remembering:

"It started with the investigation of Watergate...but now you've overdone it. You think everybody in a public job is a kink, a sleaze, a scumbag...Thirty years ago, thirty miles south of here, came Joe McCarthy. Now we have editorial Joe McCarthys. Yes, you are the Fourth Estate. But what guarantees me that you won't turn into a mad dog, snarling and biting people without restraint of any kind? I feel threatened. I genuinely feel threatened."

Two other reactions also are worth remembering.

Reporter Chaptman says that "when I do these stories, I try to make them disappear. I don't let them intrude. You have to detach yourself from a story. After ten hours of working on it, you want to go home and eat your dinner and get done with it."

Editor Gallagher says he does not "feel any sense of responsibility. It is extremely difficult, if not dangerous, to allow personal considerations to affect news judgment. The issues we report are of vital interest to the public and, in effect, supersede any personal situations."

Underlying the penchant for cowboy journalism is the 1964 U.S. Supreme Court decision in *The New York Times* v. *Sullivan,* which, with subsequent, related decisions, has made exceedingly remote the likelihood of a public official or a public figure mounting a successful libel suit. No longer is it enough that a news organization utter lies about a public figure; now a plaintiff must show that the libel was uttered "with knowledge that it was false or with reckless disregard of whether it was false or not."

Proving that a reporter and his news organization deliber-ately and maliciously lied is an imposing task. The Catch-22, though, is that people frequently become public figures precisely because the news outlets that libeled them paid them so much attention in the first place. In the series of murders of young people in Atlanta, the media descended on the residence of Wayne Williams, who had been held by the FBI for twelve hours, questioned, and then released without being charged in any crime. Surrounded by reporters and camera crews, Williams agreed to conduct a news conference "to clear the air." "From that point," a later *New York Times* account said, "the public was deluged with news accounts of [his] activities and the events surrounding his questioning by the police." When Williams sought to limit the publicity, lawyers for seventeen news organizations argued that he was a public figure and therefore open to unlimited media exposure. U.S. District Court Judge Orinda D. Evans asked, "Can the press create a public figure, then rely on that as a defense in publicizing him?" Later, when he was charged and tried for two murders, Williams suggested, through his lawyers, that publicity may have pressured authorities into leveling their allegations prematurely.

The Supreme Court decision of 1979 in *Herbert* v. *Lando,* holding that a public figure suing for libel may inquire into the thoughts and editorial processes of journalists, did little to pierce the legal armor surrounding news organizations — armor that, in effect, gives reporters freedom from responsibility.

A major figure in journalism who understands the extent of that freedom is Don Hewitt of *60 Minutes,* the world's most far-reaching news program.

"I'm so fucking sick and tired hearing about the First Amendment," Hewitt said — as he says almost everything — animatedly. "I don't live in a fantasy land about it. I think part of the problem that journalists run into today is...that they've given the country the impression that they don't believe there are any other amendments in the Constitution but the First Amendment.

"I mean, I always used to kid and say, 'You know why those

Founding Fathers went to Philadelphia in 1776? They went there for one reason only: they went there to protect Dan Schorr. That's all they had on their minds.'

"I mean, to me [there is a] preoccupation with ourselves. I don't think reporters as a group are any better or worse than, you know, meatcutters or piano tuners or schoolteachers ... And I'm sick and tired of the reporter who tries to give the rest of the world the impression that he wasn't hired for that job: he was ordained. 'Journalism is the priesthood.' It isn't. It's a job. You know, as [Senator] Bob Dole said about the vice presidency, 'There's no heavy lifting and it's indoors in the winter.' You know, it's pretty good.

"I'm not really convinced that the courts are out to get the press. I've never caught cold from one of those chilling-effect court decisions. And I can honestly say that I don't ever remember doing anything differently because of Spiro Agnew or Warren Burger. I don't remember the atmosphere around here ever changing."

As to the *Herbert* decision, which resulted from a libel suit against *60 Minutes*, Hewitt said, "Wait a minute. How're they gonna prove malice if they don't ask what's on your mind? I don't mind telling anybody what was on my mind. But then... the hysteria starts: 'Then the next thing [they] wanta know is, "Who did you vote for when you went into that polling booth?"' I don't believe that. I believe if a guy is libeled, he has a right to find out [if the reporter had] a malicious intent." To find that out, Hewitt said, "I gotta ask him.

"Conversely, I don't believe anybody with malicious intent is gonna admit to it, so I think the whole thing is kind of silly. But it doesn't worry me. And all of a sudden [it] became, 'That is one of those chilling-effect court decisions.'

"'What was on your mind, Mr. Hewitt, when you did that meatpacking story?' 'Good story. Better be looked into.' A lady at [the Department of] Commerce was the one that turned us on to it. I said, 'That's a good story. Let's do it.'

That's what was on my mind. I don't mind tellin' you what was on my mind.

"Now, if there is a guy who said—not me, but somebody—'Oh, I didn't like that. I had some problems with that supermarket chain. I was out to get that guy.' Is anybody gonna say that? But that's one of those 'chilling-effect court decisions' that I don't think has chilled anybody—and it hasn't chilled me."

(Interestingly, it was *60 Minutes* producer Barry Lando's off-camera statement, following Mike Wallace's interview with Anthony Herbert, that he would "get" Herbert, that was a factor leading to the *Herbert* v. *Lando* decision by the Supreme Court.)

Daniel Schorr, on the other hand, believes that a journalist is "chilled" by the mere requirement to answer questions, even on subjects about which he may lecture publicly. Schorr, who risked imprisonment in 1976 by refusing to tell a congressional committee the source of classified materials disclosed in his news reports, believes that "the downfall of the First Amendment is going to come more from civil suits than from anything else. The libel suit is really an entering wedge. All you have to do now is just file a libel suit, even though you're not ever expecting to win or even pursue it very far, just to get that discovery process and get people to sit down and have to answer all those questions you want to ask them. I think that's a terrible weapon against the press."

To those who have sued for libel, however, it is less a weapon than a financial and emotional burden.

A 1980 publication of the Reporters Committee for Freedom of the Press (with a cover montage depicting a reporter handcuffed by the courts) recounted how, beginning in 1969, newspapers in Palm Beach, Florida, published "several hundred news articles, editorials, and cartoons" accusing the school superintendent "generally of incompetence, indecisiveness, and nepotism." In 1970, the superintendent, Lloyd F. Early, sued. In 1974, a county court jury awarded

Early $1 million on finding the statements made by the
newspapers were false and malicious. In 1976, a Florida
appeals court reversed the decision.

The court ruled, "While most of the articles and cartoons
can fairly be described as slanted, mean, vicious, and
substantially below the level of objectivity that one would
expect of responsible journalism, there is no evidence called
to our attention which clearly and convincingly demonstrates
that a single one of the articles was a false statement of fact
made with actual malice."

Early suggested that the courts had, in effect, "granted an
absolute protection to libelous news commentary, no matter
how vilifying or false," because the commentary "can argu-
ably fit within the category of editorial opinion rather than
reportorial fact." In October 1978, the U.S. Supreme Court,
supporting the malice doctrine, declined to review the case.

It took Early eight years to find out that "slanted, mean,
vicious" journalism is legally acceptable, provided that malice
cannot be proved.

It was also acceptable to publish allegations about the
police chief in Baton Rouge, Louisiana, having accepted
bribes twenty years earlier to protect owners of a whore-
house. The courts ruled that the newspapers had acted
reasonably by relying on unsupported statements—from
gamblers and barmaids. An Ohio state senator narrowly lost
his re-election campaign in 1974 after a labor publication
erroneously reported that the legislator had supported anti-
union legislation a decade earlier. His suit for libel failed
because he could not establish by "clear and convincing
proof" that the error resulted from "actual malice."

Even notable libel victories, like the large jury award to
actress Carol Burnett for a libel committed against her by *The
National Enquirer,* often require tenacity and money in
amounts available to a relative few. Burnett compared the
lengthy process of litigation to being pregnant for five years.
The appeals process, which began with a ruling that cut

the financial award in half, was expected to add perhaps another two years to the case before final disposition.

The Herbert case may be among the longest, as well as most celebrated, libel cases in recent years. In late 1973, Herbert, a retired Army lieutenant colonel, brought a multimillion-dollar libel suit against *60 Minutes*, CBS, *The Atlantic Monthly*, and others. By mid-1981, seven and a half years later, the case still had not come to trial. Herbert had exhausted all his savings and holdings, he said, and his attorneys, despite winning their prestigious Supreme Court victory, were growing impatient with their nonpaying client. "You can't eat prestige," Jonathan Lubell, Herbert's lead lawyer, complained gently.

Winning a libel suit is not an everyday occurrence. Winning one that carries a lucrative judgment in which the lawyers will share is rarer still. The investment by attorneys of enormous amounts of professional time and talent in libel cases is risky, and when clients have difficulty even paying expenses (the printing costs alone in connection with a Supreme Court appeal can be several thousand dollars), it is costly and counterproductive. The pressure begins to mount to urge a client to consider a settlement, even in a case the lawyers think they can win. Such settlements often preclude any acknowledgment of wrongdoing and prohibit public statements by the affected parties. The opportunity to clear a name besmirched by the media is therefore limited.

Correcting its mistakes is not one of journalism's strengths. A number of *Washington Post* reporters and editors had openly expressed doubts about Janet Cooke's story, and still it was nominated for a Pulitzer Prize. During the 1976 presidential campaign, I had reported incorrectly in *Newsweek* that Carter's representatives to the committee organizing the debates between the nominees had blackballed David Broder, the highly regarded political writer for *The Washington Post*, from the panel of journalists that was to question the candidates. Carter's press aide, Jody Powell, was understandably angry when he read the report. When I rechecked the source of the information, I was told that Powell had been highly critical of Broder during a meeting of the committee, but had not, in fact, "vetoed" Broder's appearance on the reporters' panel. But when I sought a correction in the next issue of *Newsweek,* an editor in New York refused my request. "If we had reported what Powell *really* said," the editor submitted, "it would have looked even worse."

No correction was made. However, I telephoned Broder to tell him I had been wrong. "Are you sure?" Broder asked. By then, the item had stirred up considerable gossip. I assured him that the source, who had no great love for Carter or Powell, was certain that he (or I) had gotten it wrong. I then informed Powell of the mistake and reassured him that Broder had been similarly notified.

Once, when I had failed to check thoroughly enough before publishing a tip I had received, I telephoned the source to tell him I had been wrong; the error had resulted from my carelessness, not from his information. The source, a veteran Washington lawyer with numerous media contacts, said, "You know, that's the first time in twenty-five years a reporter has ever said to me, 'Hey, I blew it.'"

In October 1981, *The Washington Post* underwent logical contortions for two and a half weeks before admitting an error. The newspaper's gossip column had reported, in breezy, chatty prose, that President Carter had bugged Blair House, the mansion across the street from the White House in which foreign heads of state are quartered during official visits to the American capital. President-elect and Mrs. Reagan were guests at Blair House just before Reagan's inauguration. It was through the bug, the gossip column reported, that the Carters had learned that Nancy Reagan wanted them to vacate the White House before the inaugural so that she could begin redecorating immediately—a report Mrs. Reagan denied at the time.

An infuriated Carter threatened to sue; the implications of the item, he stormed, reached to the heart of America's foreign policy, because foreign dignitaries would think they had been spied on by their American hosts—an absolute falsehood, Carter insisted.

Post executive editor Ben Bradlee adamantly stood by the story; he said he had talked to the writer's source, who insisted that a Carter family member had been *his* source. Carter spokesman Jody Powell was unconvinced; if *The Post* believed a story of that magnitude to be true, he wondered, why hadn't it been printed more prominently? Why was it published as a mere item in a gossip column?

The point seemingly struck home. A few days later, *The Post* ran an astonishing editorial, maintaining that the newspaper had reported only that a rumor about Blair House having been bugged was circulating in Washington; that did not mean the rumor was true. On the contrary, the editorial noted, "we find that rumor utterly impossible to believe." Having taken the incredibly untenable position of publishing a rumor it did not believe to be true, the newspaper's editors found themselves in even deeper hot water than before —ethically and legally.

A week later, for reasons unexplained, *The Post* no longer trusted its source. In a letter to Carter, *Post* publisher Donald Graham wrote, "We now believe the story he told us to have been wrong and that there was no 'bugging' of Blair House during your administration. Nor do we now believe that members of your family said Blair House was 'bugged.'"

"Why," *Philadelphia Bulletin* editor Craig Ammerman asked rhetorically, "didn't they simply run a correction?"

What had happened, according to reporter Phil Gailey, writing in *The New York Times,* revealed a greater irony about journalistic procedures and ethics. The twisted trail of the rumor began during an interview with Nancy Reagan by free-lance writer Dotson Rader in September 1981. Rader told Mrs. Reagan that he had been told by Rosalynn Carter and Jean Carter Stapleton that they had heard a tape of Mrs. Reagan saying she wished the Carters would leave the White House immediately. Mrs. Reagan told a friend, Nancy

Reynolds, who told Diana McLellan, *The Post's* gossip
columnist. McLellan telephoned Rader, who maintains he
warned McLellan not to print the item. (She denies that
anyone warned her off the story.) When Carter threatened to
sue, Bradlee said he spoke to Rader personally to corroborate
McLellan's story. Bradlee visited Rader at his home in
Princeton, New Jersey, taking with him affidavits that, Rader
said, Bradlee wanted him to sign. They disclosed his
"sources" as Mrs. Carter and Mrs. Stapleton. Unless he
signed, Rader said, Bradlee threatened that *The Post* would
subpoena him if there was a libel suit. Rader, vowing to go to
jail first, thought it strange that the newspaper that had relied
on Deep Throat, the most celebrated undisclosed source in
modern journalism, to achieve national acclaim would force a
writer to reveal his sources. In Rader's recollection of what he
initially told *The Post,* however, it is clear that he was less
than firm about maintaining that he actually had heard the
story from the Carter family. At any rate, Rader himself never
reported the tale in print, which suggests that its foundation
was indeed flimsy.

Sometimes there is even a tendency to duplicate the
mistakes of others rather than to challenge them and risk
"breaking from the pack." In the summer of 1975, for
example, there was a spate of stories suggesting that when he
was a member of Congress, New York's Governor Hugh
Carey had used influence inappropriately to win special favors
for his brother Ed, the head of a large, independent oil-
refining company located in the Bahamas. With a special
permit, due for renewal in a few weeks, the Bahamas-based
company was allowed to import oil from an American
producer at a time when high-grade foreign oil was limited in
supply and, when available, overpriced. The arrangement
enabled Ed Carey's company to compete with domestic
refiners during the oil-import crisis. Within two days of being
assigned the story, I had identified the source of the
allegations and learned he had a vested interest in seeing that
Ed Carey's special permit was not renewed; the man secretly

worked for Carey's chief competitor. Confronted by this information, he backed off the story. Now that he had a chance to check his facts, he told me, he could not prove that Representative Hugh Carey had used undue pressure. It appeared that his earlier allegations to newspapers had been exaggerated, he said.

My editors, however, were reluctant to publish my version of the story. Major newspapers, after all, were saying Hugh Carey had acted improperly. I won out in the end, but was not vindicated until the following week, when a *New York Times* reporter independently confirmed my story. (In the heat of the publicity, the federal agency with authority over Ed Carey's permit refused to extend it—just as his competitor had, in all likelihood, figured. Once the media had moved on to other stories, though, the permit was extended, with a minimum of public attention, on the grounds that there had been no wrongdoing.)

To err, without malice, is human. But when journalistic error is difficult to set right, when reporters and editors are reluctant to admit mistakes, and when stories that emphasize drama, conflict, and misbehavior (often relying on anonymous sources for corroboration) are encouraged and rewarded, an abundant supply of misinformation is bound to result.

When misinformation is magnified through television news, the resulting misconceptions can be irreversible. It is easier to poison a city's water supply than to purify it.

5

The Reporter
Gets in the Way

*N*OVEMBER 1969 was a tough month for journalism. That was the month Vice President Spiro Agnew accused newsmen, especially network reporters, of reflecting the views of a closed, like-minded, provincial, Eastern "establishment."

Immediately, journalistic luminaries like Norman Isaacs, then president of the American Society of Newspaper Editors, columnist James Reston of *The New York Times*, and, a bit later, Gloria Steinem in *New York* magazine suggested that support of Agnew's view connoted a smidgin of racism and anti-Semitism. Yet some independent polls disputed that notion; one published in *Newsweek* demonstrated that more than half the people with college training considered television news slanted and that distrust of television news increased with the amount of education people received. (A year later, a Gallup Poll reported that two of every three college graduates agreed with Agnew.)

Because of the public reaction to the Agnew speech, journalists were eager to convince their readers and viewers that newsmen adhered to rules governing objectivity and fairness—rules transcending personal views and backgrounds. Journalistic integrity, many believed, was on the line.

60 Minutes, into its second year of telecasts at the time, interviewed Walter Cronkite on the subject of journalistic integrity. *The CBS Evening News,* on which Cronkite was the anchorman, recently had gained a slim ratings lead over NBC's venerable *Huntley-Brinkley Report.* Further, Cronkite's reporting on space shots and political conventions had established him as an extraordinary news force.

Cronkite made a stab at explaining objectivity in journalism: "What is objective reporting?...Well, we have our prejudices, we all have our biases, we have a structural problem in writing a news story and presenting it on television as to time and length, position in the paper, position on the news broadcast. These things are all going to be affected by our own beliefs; of course they are. But we are professional journalists. This is the difference. We are trying to reach an objective state; we are trying to be objective. We have been taught from the day we went to school—when we began to know we wanted to be journalists—integrity, truth, honesty, and a definite attempt to be objective. We try to present the news as objectively as possible, whether we like or don't like it. Now, that is objectivity."

It would seem, then, that besides taking courses in Integrity 101 or the History and Principles of Honesty, objective journalists are those who try to be objective. Even if trying meant succeeding, though, we were no closer to learning what professional journalists were about. Cronkite hadn't defined objectivity.

In any event, journalists were more likely to describe their efforts as attempts at "fairness"; "objectivity" was a mythic Shangri-la dreamed of but never reached.

Fair enough. But when Fred Friendly, who had been president of CBS News and later became a professor of journalism at Columbia University, was asked in November 1969 to explain fair play in news, he replied: "Anybody that has to be told will never know. . . I think fairness is something you know in your gut you're doing." Harking back to one of his great news triumphs, the *See It Now* program he produced with Edward R. Murrow as the reporter, Friendly said journalists "try to be fair by doing interpretive journalism when it is required, not letting a Senator McCarthy. . . say there are 205 Communists in the State Department, and letting an outrageous, unsubstantiated charge like that go unidentified for what it is."

In describing why and how journalists should exercise skepticism, Friendly failed to define "fairness."

The problem these two eminent wordsmiths encountered in trying to define two seemingly simple English words was that they understood all too well the impossibility of imposing standards of fairness or objectivity in journalism. News-editing relies, essentially, on instinct. It does not lend itself to originality, intellectuality, or courage.

Since the founding of the Republic, a great deal has changed in the way journalism is disseminated; nothing has changed in the way journalism is performed. When American reporters were expelled from Iran in January 1980, Walter Cronkite moderated a CBS News discussion of the implications of that action. Cronkite's comments that night were understandable in terms of American frustration with Iran, but they hardly constituted disinterested reportage. As much the irrepressible chauvinist as Thomas Paine a couple of hundred years earlier, Cronkite couldn't disguise his disdain for Iran:

> Now, they've got a presidential campaign going on in Iran. A thing that was a little hard for us to accept and to swallow was several hundred people, or something like that, running for the presidency in a wide-open race. Ghotbzadeh — if that's his name, or [if] that's the way it's pronounced, at any rate; none of us seem to agree because I gather he won't tell us. We ask him, "How do you pronounce [your] name?" He said, "That's good enough." And that's maybe the way it's pronounced: "Thatsgoodenough." But Thatsgoodenough is himself running

for president of Iran. Other members of the Revolutionary Council [are] running. Is there are possibility...I'm serious about this—that this is an election ploy in Iran? That maybe it's good to go out to the countryside and be able to say, "We've thrown...the American reporters out of Iran?" Is it possible?

Cronkite has not always been unflappable as an anchorman. He wept when Kennedy was killed, and he was openly ecstatic in reporting the successes of the American space program. But rarely has Cronkite displayed more emotion than on the occasions when his own business was threatened. When Dan Rather was roughed up and ejected from the floor of the 1968 Democratic National Convention, Cronkite, on the air, blamed Mayor Daley and his "thugs." And during the CBS News program commenting on the media's ejection from Iran, Cronkite made no effort to disguise his anger:

> Americans may not be the last group of newsmen to be expelled from Iran...The Revolutionary Council also warned today that reporters from other countries may be thrown out, too, if they—quote—"distort news of the Iranian revolution." If they tell of continuing anti-American protests outside our embassy, they're probably on safe ground. But if they report uprisings by Iran's ethnic minorities, watch it, buddy, that may be bias! If they send out word of more grievances against the Shah, well, right on! But if the word, instead, is of followers of rival ayatollahs killing each other, that's a good bet to be construed as antirevolutionary distortion.

A time-worn journalistic shibboleth is that a reporter is not a stenographer. Their job, journalists say, is not to parrot events, but to interpret them.

In truth, reporters parrot events most of the time, giving us the traditional "who, what, when, where, why, and how." Because the reporter and editor still must decide which portions of an event to feature, which quotes to use, and, as Cronkite pointed out, where to place them in the newspaper or on the newscast, the exercise remains essentially subjective. Because an effort usually is made to minimize personal judgment, however, basic reporting of this kind has been the meat and potatoes of our daily news diet—mostly informative, rarely misleading.

The trouble comes because, on complicated or developing events, news media in recent years have assumed a mantle of responsibility to explain those events to the unwashed. What did the vote against President Johnson mean in the 1968 New Hampshire primary? Did we win or lose during Tet? What caused the riots at the Democratic National Convention in Chicago in 1968? To what extent has Watergate eroded our political system?

These analyses are not offered in the spirit of a Jeanne Dixon or your county-fair palm reader; they are made in dead earnest, and, as Montaigne told us, few can remember whether they were right or wrong. Columnist Meg Greenfield wrote that politicians, press, and public "have no collective memory, none. If it happened more than six hours ago, it is gone."

What happens in complicated situations is that reporters tend to play stenographer precisely when they should exercise independence, and they tend to expound their own ideas when they should be quoting someone much more knowledgeable to help us better comprehend the event.

The truth about the press versus Joe McCarthy is that the senator's outrageous charges were trumpeted loudly, widely, and rarely critically by the press. Had it been otherwise, McCarthy could not have become a sinister national power. Despite the belated, if highly touted, challenge to McCarthy by *See It Now*, the senator's downfall resulted primarily from the public's opportunity to view him not through the eyes of journalists, but for itself—as in the televised Army-McCarthy hearings. When the camera revealed a bellicose, crude Joe McCarthy contrasted to a distinguished, if inconstant, Secretary of the Army, Robert Stevens, and the gentle but piercingly shrewd civilian counsel, Joseph Welch, citizens started providing the underpinning that previously silent politicians required before daring to give voice to their anti-McCarthyism.

A more recent example of parroting at the wrong time came during the frantic television scramble over the shooting of President Reagan in March 1981. In late afternoon, with much of the nation waiting nervously to learn if its none-too-young President would survive his ordeal and be able to resume his duties, NBC's Chris Wallace rushed on the air with a breathless summary of a report from a radio journalist who had managed to sneak to the hospital's third floor. Wallace told us the radio reporter had said he learned from a physician (who did not wish to be named) that President Reagan was undergoing open-heart surgery. Serving as the anchorman, Marvin Kalb wisely and modestly admitted that he didn't know anything about open-heart surgery, but it certainly sounded serious. Wallace stared at his notes for what seemed like minutes, apparently realizing for the first time the gravity of his words and wishing the notes would magically change. They did not, and after confessing that he didn't really know either what open-heart surgery was, he launched into a silly oration about the public's right to know everything everybody was saying, whether it was right or wrong. Sure enough, it wasn't long before NBC's medical expert, Dr. Frank Field, was interviewing a New York thoracic surgeon, who informed viewers that if Reagan was undergoing open-heart surgery, the situation had to be viewed as grave.

As we all now know, Wallace had misunderstood the radio journalist. As *Newsweek* pointed out rather smugly, Wallace hadn't gotten it right; what the radio reporter (who said he got it from a doctor, remember) *really* said was that Reagan was undergoing *open-chest* surgery, not open-heart surgery. That should have been the tip-off to Wallace, *Newsweek*, and everyone else that the radio reporter and his source hadn't the vaguest notion of what they were talking about. Referring to the removal of a bullet from someone's thoracic region as "open-chest surgery" is like describing the removal of a tooth as open-mouth dentistry.

What most reporters never seem to learn is the wisdom of the aphorism "When in doubt, leave it out." If reporters possess the skill and have the time to develop information that challenges the assertions of a Joe McCarthy or the questionable report of a radio newsman who obviously cared more for his moment in the sun than for accuracy, they should, by all means, do so. Most opt for running off half-cocked with half-baked assertions because it's easy for them and for their editors; besides, every reporter worries that the "competition" may use what he or she overlooks—and that the editor will then wonder why the reporter wasn't with the pack.

If a reporter and editor cannot find cogent, third-party material to contradict questionable assertions, they best serve readers and viewers when they simply repeat what others say, omitting that which is suspect. Unfortunately, the desire to appear knowledgeable is an overpowering one in journalism. Questionable assertions often are featured, not omitted. Media thrive on exchanges of bombast, rarely spoiling the fun by finding the facts that would indicate there is no story at all.

When President Carter's naïvely brutish brother, Billy, was being grilled by a congressional committee about the propriety of his role in American-Libyan affairs, an assertion was made that Billy Carter was being investigated in connection with drug-smuggling. Carter was struck dumb; his alleged associates were sought and interviewed by journalists. Before the day was out, it was clear that Carter was under no cloud. Still, the episode—which had no connection to the ostensible purpose of the hearing, and which was demonstrated to be untrue—was aired prominently on the evening news programs of all three networks.

If reporters were rewarded for providing us with intelligent, lean accounts of happenings, leaving it to columnists to exhort and provoke, and if editors were content to provide us with more diversion and less salvation, our minds would be less scrambled by the daily news drumfire of imminent disasters, denunciations and denials, allegations and verbal counterthrusts — most of which, fortunately, fade from public view *sans dénouement,* which suggests that they were more the product of journalistic hype than of the irresistible forces of history. If journalism would concentrate on its two primary functions — to inform and, yes, to entertain — rather than trying to direct and save us, its output would be more salutary and more engaging. Many, if not most, of today's journalists wallow in their imagined intellectuality, wrestling with "meaning," intent on attacking, superficially and humorlessly, matters best left to history, fiction, and philosophy. It's not that reporters think too much; it's that they say too much, too soon, too glibly.

In reaction, few have gone as far as Walter Cronkite, who urged, in an interview, "thinking the unthinkable. It may just be that total freedom of speech and press are not possible when technology has so compressed time and distance."

Nonetheless, he made a point that Roger Mudd, who abjures any such "unthinkable" thought about restricting freedom of the press or of speech, put differently but tellingly.

"My problem with most television reporting," he said, "is that the reporter gets in the way of everything. And there's a great pressure on a television reporter to stand up and 'say what it all means' or give the answer before the thing has been written. And there's always a producer [saying], 'Yeah, but what's the bottom line? Is he gonna win or not? Who's gonna get the nomination?'

"There's that weight on you all the time not to let things unfold as they would, but to force things, to speed up the action, hastening the conclusions. Then you get involved in the story yourself. You wind up arranging the confrontation, which has not been allowed to unfold naturally, but has been stimulated and provoked so that the confrontation occurs on camera, and I think that's toying around with reality."

Mudd was troubled by "little bits and pieces" — small but

significant ways in which television journalists "are allowing ourselves to dibble around with reality." For example, he explained that when a news anchorman turns to a wall to conduct a two-way conversation with a large picture of a correspondent at another location, "he's not on that wall. That's a blank wall. That's a trick. The picture of, say, Ike Pappas [of CBS News] talking to me from the Pentagon, and I'm in the studio in New York—I can't see Ike Pappas on that wall. That's a green wall and his picture is projected [on the home screen] electronically. But I am asked to turn and look at the wall as if he were there, and to talk to that dumb, blank wall...I don't see anything. I see a blank, green wall. If you're at home, they have, with their marvelous machines, superimposed my picture looking at this green wall, and they've added to that wall Ike Pappas' picture from another circuit and blended the two. And what comes out in your home is a single picture that makes it look as if I were talking to Ike Pappas. Now, that bothers me. Technically, it's terrific, and it gives you some feeling that Ike and I are really talking and exchanging nifty notes. But that's fakery. It makes you feel that what you're doing is not reality, but you are succumbing to and participating in this slight, little fraud."

Mudd, who is nothing if not candid, quickly conceded that he uses a Teleprompter and make-up. In the 1950s and 1960s, he recalled, he had refused to use those aids, "because I thought it was all deceptive." Then, with a hearty laugh, he added, "I started getting lines in my face, and my eyesight began to go, so you make those little compromises." More soberly, he said: "But every one that you make leads to another one. That's disturbing. Once you allow yourself and your machinery and your management and all your money to begin to arrange stories and manipulate stories, then you become as important or more important than the story itself—because it's your presence that's making things pop around. And then we're in serious trouble."

(For the benefit of trivia addicts, the conversation with Mudd was conducted while he still was in the employ of CBS

News, which, in its New York studio, had a green wall behind the anchorman. When Dan Rather took over the job from Cronkite, the wall was repainted blue, reportedly to "soften" Rather's somewhat "harder" features.)

In light of the embarrassing revelations about major articles in *The Washington Post* and *The New York Daily News* having been fabricated, Mudd's criticism of "fakery" in television seems unduly harsh. What Mudd described is, after all, basically cosmetic; his print colleagues were engaged in substantive chicanery.

Televised deception, though, whatever its form, when compared with lapses in newspapers or magazines, geometrically increases misunderstanding. It is the "machinery" and "money" that Mudd mentioned that often lead to manipulation.

The Greatest Communications Network in the World

*T*HOSE OF US who still aren't quite sure how the telegraph works are thoroughly mystified by the science and technology that bring us live pictures from the moon, live scenes of mobs screaming at us from the front of the American Embassy in Tehran, instant replays of people shooting presidents and popes, and videotaped eavesdropping on congressmen being conned into taking bribes.

Most of us take for granted this visual wonderment, reminded of the technical wizardry behind it all only occasionally by baseball announcers like Joe Garagiola, who, when viewing an instant replay clearly demolishing an umpire's call, cries out to the camera crew and technical staff, "Great shot, guys!"

What none of us should take for granted, however, is how our thought processes may be overwhelmed by a surfeit of television's prodigious techniques when they are applied to news.

For that reason, it is worth reflecting on the staggering capabilities of television news, recognizing that some of its most potent tools only recently have become part of our daily viewing lives and therefore have only just begun adding to the impact television news has on our understanding of world events.

First and foremost, there is videotape, the elemental stuff of providing instant sound and pictures to a news-hungry world. Videotape, with its application to sports events and the slow-motion instant replay, has been with us at least since Howard Cosell and *Monday Night Football* invaded America in 1969.

In terms of news, however, the full impact of videotape came later. Videotape lent itself to news not only because of its immediacy, but because of its simplicity: it was harder to foul up by over- or underexposure; there was no risk of ruining it in the darkroom; it could be spliced electronically instead of manually. Because electronic splicing, or editing, equipment was big, bulky, and, for practical purposes, immovable, the use of videotape to cover news events in areas remote from a modern television news operation was limited.

Then portable electronic editing equipment was developed. The first use of portable tape-editing equipment with electronic cameras for a news event occurred during President Nixon's 1974 trip to Moscow. The first national political conventions in which the three major television network news organizations relied solely on videotape rather than film were held in 1976.

About that time, the networks started making full, regular use of the telecommunications satellites spinning around the globe. Technicians have been able to figure out how to get sound and pictures from anywhere, at any time, to the news capital of the networks, New York City.

At the end of the 1970s, new video inventions provided slick, electronically created graphics that could be "punched up" over pictures to reinforce them and the "voice-over" message of the newscaster.

The magic of telecommunications is not confined to the networks, of course. In fact, White House communications specialists often work closely with network technicians.

In 1978, when President Carter was about to travel to Nigeria, communications specialists representing the American government laid eight miles of cable and actually moved a satellite from one orbital pattern to another to ensure fast and uninterrupted communications between the President, while he was traveling in Nigeria, and Washington. The estimated cost was $5 million. The networks whose coverage would be affected were called in for advice on the project.

On the same trip, CBS News discovered that communications systems recently installed by the Nigerian government (apparently in anticipation of the American President's visit) were inadequate; the network decided it could use its own systems more efficiently. In a brilliant stroke of unofficial diplomacy, network representatives told Nigerian bureaucrats that they were delighted with the new equipment and would be happy to use it at whatever reasonable cost was involved. It was done, says David Buksbaum, then CBS News's deputy director of special events, "to assuage their national pride." Actually, he says, the network rented a ground station, by-passing government stations, to beam its signals to the communications satellite.

Television news has the money and the technology (plus the willingness to use both) to cover any story it chooses.

In 1979, the White House wanted to know whether the television network news organizations would and could cover the signing of the Camp David accords between Egypt and Israel if the ceremonies were conducted at the historic but remote Mount Saint Catherine Monastery in the Sinai. In the old "can do" spirit of the World War II Seabees (the Navy's Construction Battalion), the networks responded that they were prepared to cover the event wherever it took place. It wouldn't be easy, however, and the quality of pictures would not be as good as they would be closer to a "media center." The monastery is in the middle of the desert, and, as befits a non-media center, there are no ground lines to it and no transmitter to beam signals from the site to a satellite. The signals, then, would have to be beamed from the site to the nearest large transmitter in Tel Aviv, which meant that a series of small receiver-transmitters would have to be built between the monastery and Tel Aviv.

Television signals move only in a straight line from any point to the horizon; they don't follow the curvature of the earth. It was determined that beaming the microwave signals from the monastery to a large transmitter in Tel Aviv would require twelve "hops," a hop being the line-of-sight distance between transmitter-receivers. But quality begins to deteriorate after only three hops. In addition, the signal would have to be converted from the American standard television picture (525 lines per square inch) to the European standard (625 lines per square inch) for the Tel Aviv–to–London satellite transmission, and then back to 525 lines per square inch for the London–to–New York satellite transmission — another quality-reducer.

At any rate, that was the gist of the report the network technicians made to the White House: they could do it, but the quality would leave something to be desired. (It is worth noting that few print journalists had the foggiest notion that the Sinai site even was being considered.)

Shortly afterward, it was announced that the agreements would be signed in Washington. The White House denied that the decision had anything to do with television coverage of the event, but the pictures of Presidents Carter and Sadat and Prime Minister Begin were much sharper than they might have been otherwise.

When President Carter took a political vacation along the Snake and Mississippi rivers, each of the big three networks assigned fifty to sixty people to cover the story (correspondents, producers, cameramen, soundmen, lighting technicians, editors). That was stateside. Even overseas, the networks had full capability to tape, edit, and transmit material to the United States ready for home viewing. In Iran, during the hostage crisis, each network maintained thirty to forty representatives on the scene.

The investment a news organization makes in covering a story contributes to the amount of play the story receives. It is not often that a network will fail to expose a story fully after sending three dozen or so personnel and all their electronic gear great distances to the scene of an event, and underwriting for days or weeks the cost of their food, lodging, and other expenses.

The hardware that increases the rapidity and reach of remote television news transmissions concomitantly increases their cost. The resulting greater investment guarantees that once the decision is made to give blanket coverage to an event, we will be smothered by it, whether it turns out that we really ought to have been or not.

Television news reports of the takeover of the American Embassy in Iran exemplify both how news coverage tends to expand to meet the cost of that coverage, and how an understanding of the news technology "system" can ensure the widest possible attention to one's message. As it happened, Ayatollah Khomeini's minions were masters of the game.

60 Minutes, with Barry Lando as producer and Mike Wallace as correspondent, has reported extensively on Iran over the years. Lando believes television's impact on that nation's politics has been "tremendous."

"First of all," Lando said, "[there is] the fall of the Shah. A lot of that has to do with the feeling back here among the [Carter] administration, with pictures, with images of people on the streets, people being killed during demonstrations, being shot at, stories of brutality beginning to get out and then being transmitted to the United States...

"The holding of the hostages had an awful lot to do with television, in that the people who did it suddenly found out that, by having the hostages, they had this incredible audience.

"We gave them a ticket to being able to talk every night. I don't think they realized it until after they had the hostages, and the press was suddenly there. And you had guerrilla theater every night at the [American] Embassy. That's all we covered—and the militants knew that, and they arranged press conferences inside the embassy, carefully staged with the hostages paraded out to talk. But there were always preconditions that the militants had to be able to present their message unedited for five minutes or ten minutes. That was their ticket of admission: 'You let us present our message, we'll let you talk to the hostage'—you know, 'two boxtops and twenty-five cents'—and it worked. Americans might not have been prepared to listen to it, but from the militants' point of view, they got their message out. How many groups in this country have been able to do that? Six or seven minutes of unedited prime time? Access to twenty, thirty million Americans? And this went on month after month after month...

"The Iranian national press would go and do filmed interviews with the hostages and then turn around and sell them to the American media. We were all bidding with each other for interviews with the hostages.

"There were always propaganda packages tied in to the interviews, and because of the attention and importance given to them, they became incredibly important in Iran itself—much more so than they probably would have been, because what average Iranian could really care less if fifty Americans were stuck in the U.S. Embassy?

"Their life goes on very much [as usual] in Tehran, except when you get near the U.S. Embassy, but you'd never have known that by watching the television coverage. So you do your life-goes-on piece, but the next night your desk [in New York] is saying, 'All right, but last night NBC had on this incredible thing in front of the embassy. Where were we?'

"We devoted incredible resources to covering that story— I mean, twenty-five, thirty staff people from each network— that includes crew—week after week. There'd be at least a couple of editors; two, sometimes three editing set-ups, with complete ability to edit pieces [and] thirty, forty hotel rooms booked in the Intercontinental Hotel in Tehran, almost totally taken over by the foreign press. This huge hotel became like a broadcast center.

"[There were] three, four, five television crews for each network at any particular time in Tehran to cover this story. The embassy had to be covered on a sixteen-hour basis; dawn to dusk, you had to be in front of that embassy, no matter what, until the militants said, 'You can go home; there's not going to be anything more tonight.'

"And the cost of doing that—plus satellite transmissions day after day after day—you're talking about millions and millions of dollars for each of the networks.

"Then the images we're all getting back are the hostages, the militants—and not about what was going on in Iran, what was on the minds of the Iranians or the Iranian government...[There was] very little which explained why the situation in Iran was like it was, why the Shah had fallen...[and] virtually nothing about what should be done or what could be done. That we'd leave to *The New York Times*, *Washington Post* editorials."

CBS News's Sanford Socolow was not perturbed by the possibility that television news was "used" by Iranian militants, nor, in fact, by criticisms that there was excessive concentration on Tehran mob scenes that may have been organized primarily for the American news-consuming public.

"Using us?" Socolow asked, echoing the question. "We get used all the time. Presidential news conferences—we're used. Your question is premised on the fact that we did have some effect. I have no idea. Again, that is an immeasurable, unanswerable question. Whether we had an effect or not depends on your political orientation, where you come from. I don't think there's any bit of objective proof that we had any effect at all.

"Why do you cite, when you talk, those pictures of the mob scenes? You didn't cite the two or three stories we did within the first month of captivity of how life in Tehran went on as usual, including one story about the life of Americans who were out there teaching in the Iranian schools as civilians and living there and not being molested and were friendly with Iranians. And another story about how a block away from the embassy fruit vendors were still selling. . ."

I interrupted to ask why, if life was going on as usual, Americans had been inundated with daily scenes of anti-American demonstrators in Tehran?

"Because," Socolow replied, "that's what was happening in Iran — and we told you they were playing to the cameras [and] this was happening at the embassy. You are not seriously saying to me that we should have made an editorial decision to suppress pictures of the scene at the embassy? I feel there was an obligation to tell the American people, to the best of our ability, what was going on at the scene of [the hostages'] captivity."

Lando's view of the Iranian revolution is of a popular reaction to torture and repression by the Shah. He blames television, primarily, for doing "absolutely nothing to tell Americans when the Shah was there what was going on." He said, somewhat facetiously, that it might have helped us to understand the situation if Walter Cronkite had presented a kind of "tortured-of-the-week" series (my phrase, not Lando's).

"How many Americans have ever seen interviews with people who actually were tortured by the Shah? These guys are all over Iran now. They're available to the media." Lando thinks that if a Western journalist had told government officials in Tehran that he wanted to do a program on torture in Iran, he "would have had fifty, a hundred, two hundred people paraded up to [his] hotel suite or wherever you'd wanted them — armless, legless, still twitching — who could have given the most incredible kind of stories. Former Savak [Iranian secret police] torturers are there, and they're willing to be interviewed. They could talk about their tie to the United States. Did the U.S. teach them to torture or didn't they? What was the U.S. connection? What wasn't? No one tried to do it."

Including, it might be added, *60 Minutes*, which, several months before my conversation with Lando, had presented a segment entitled "Iran File." The segment, which was broadcast on March 2, 1980 (Day 120 of captivity for the American hostages), showed portions of earlier Mike Wallace interviews with the Shah and his ambassador to the United States, Ardeshir Zahedi, as well as current interviews with Americans and Iranians in a position to support reports of extensive torture under the Shah's rule.

"The American people, a fair number of them, didn't really understand the anger felt by the Iranian people generally," Mike Wallace said to me two months after "Iran File" had been aired. "This is a real revolution. This isn't a revolution by a handful of people fighting the system. If there are thirty-five to forty million people in Iran, I am willing to wager that twenty-five million of them, minimum, are with this revolution and, to varying degrees, angry—if not at the American people, at the American government. What is at the root of their anger? That's all this broadcast tried to tell."

The American government, in turn, was, to varying degrees, angry—if not at Mike Wallace, at *60 Minutes*.

"I have seldom seen..." Wallace said, helplessly searching for words to describe the Carter administration's efforts to discourage *60 Minutes* from broadcasting "Iran File."

"From Henry Precht at the State Department [the man who became a mini-hero when he told an Iranian envoy to his face that his nation's protestations about wanting to end the hostage crisis promptly were "bullshit"] to Cy Vance...to Jody Powell to [presidential counsel] Lloyd Cutler...I talked to all of these people about it. Everyone questioned my patriotism, with the exception of Cy Vance...Precht did. Powell did. Cutler more or less did...The President called [CBS News president William] Leonard and told him not to broadcast it."

"Great pressure from the White House," Don Hewitt recalled. "I mean, Jody and I went around and around on this phone. I mean, Jody said to me, 'What do you care about and what do you love?'

"And I said, 'Listen, you son of a bitch. If you're saying what I think you're saying, I loved and cared about this country before you were born. I think all you care about is the Massachusetts primary, if you must know.' It was vicious."

Hewitt, however, believed that too much television coverage was concentrated on the American Embassy in Tehran. "I think that's been overdone," he said when the takeover was entering its fifth month. "I'm a minority of one on that. I would pull out of there," he argued hypothetically — American reporters had been ordered out of Iran a few months earlier. "I would leave a reporter there, but I'd take all the cameras out early on because of the repetition of almost the same thing. I claim that the pictures over and over and over of the front of the embassy add nothing to anybody's sum of knowledge." Hardly anyone at CBS agreed with Hewitt.

Clearly, the reporters and editors concerned with the coverage in Iran devoted considerable attention to it. But their thoughts focused on the superficial — as journalism almost always demands: Who would be the first to interview Khomeini, and would it be exclusive? Are we taking too many pictures of the mobs at the embassy? Shouldn't we show the torture victims and the "reformed" purveyors of torture? Can we interview the hostages — and at what price?

The message had been — and millions of Americans will recall only — that repression by the Shah caused the revolution. The *60 Minutes* episode that unsettled the administration didn't really examine the root causes of the revolution, but, rather, asked: What did American officials know about the torture in Iran, and when did they know it? "And it was quite apparent after the broadcast," Wallace said, "that it didn't do one bit of harm."

His assessment probably is accurate, but it didn't do any good, either, in terms of explaining the causes of the revolution. The use of torture as a tool to dominate political foes, after all, is as ancient as Persia itself. It is likely that the Iranian revolution, not unlike those in other poverty-ridden countries in recent years, resulted more from the Shah's efforts to modernize his nation economically than from his methods of repression. Even the United States, with its broadly based, highly responsive, and deeply entrenched democratic institutions, has experienced social unrest when rising expectations have outrun reality. The Shah's attempts at industrialization, land reform, improved education, and the broadening of women's rights—hugely successful for that nation and the region—outstripped any concurrent modernization of political institutions equipped to maintain the loyalty of a people beginning to sense a better way of life.

Of necessity, journalism rarely operates in the realm of sweeping sociopolitical concepts, and it is foolish (and perhaps unwise) to suggest that it can or should. It would do well for journalism simply to recognize its limitations—and the power it has to influence us whether it stays within or strays beyond those limitations.

Understanding Iran in the context of hostages and mobs and twisted bodies is like understanding America in the context of the Boston Massacre. What receives a lot of attention and contributes to patriotic sloganeering rarely provides answers to questions about underlying reasons for these events.

Television news, however, provided precisely the outlet sought by Ayatollah Khomeini and his supporters. It was not merely a means to reach the outside world, though that was important. It was a means to excite internal support for what clearly was, and remained, a very shaky government.

What television news did was to put "the greatest communications network in the world. . .at the service of the government of Iran," according to former Undersecretary of State George Ball.

Barry Lando was instrumental in arranging the interview between Mike Wallace and Khomeini. "The interesting thing about the whole negotiation was, once again, we were using Khomeini—'*60 Minutes* Has an Interview with Khomeini'; terrific, big audience—and he was using us.

"He got, in the space of two hours, interviews with three American networks, the Japanese, and EuroVision—and [the Iranians] knew exactly what they were doing."

When Lando arrived in Iran, Sadegh Ghotbzadeh, whom he had known as Khomeini's aide and confidant before the revolution, was running Iranian television. Ghotbzadeh had promised Lando an exclusive interview with Khomeini.

"I see Robert MacNeil [of PBS] is there at the hotel. What the hell is MacNeil doing here? He's got an interview with Khomeini. How could he have an interview with Khomeini? So I go to see Ghotbzadeh's assistant—Ghotbzadeh refuses to see me. And he says, 'Lando, how are you? Have a cup of coffee. Sit down.' Young guy; he's been educated in England.

"And I say, 'We've got an exclusive interview, right?' He says, 'You've got the exclusive program interview.' I say, 'What do you mean, exclusive *program* interview?' 'Well, there's news interviews and program interviews, so we are also giving much shorter interviews to the networks as well. But you will get the first program interview.'

"I said, 'Just a minute,' and with that we start bargaining. We're trying to get the first interview with Khomeini for our own egotistical purposes, plus we want to get the story out first. And he frankly tells me, this. . .thirty-year-old Iranian, very sophisticated, he says, 'Look, look at the figures. I can get it on three networks—ABC, NBC, CBS. I can also get it on EuroVision, and I know if I feed it to EuroVision, Japan will pick it up.'

"He knew how the entire system worked, how news organizations pool, how they share, how EuroVision worked, how Japan is connected to EuroVision, and once it goes to Japan, how it can go out to Asia.

"So he said to me, 'Make me a better offer.'

"I must say, my jaws absolutely swung open. I couldn't believe the sophistication, the thinking that was going on. He was absolutely right. They wanted to get Khomeini's message out. They knew how to do it.

"You go to Khomeini's home in Qum. His little living room is about half the size [of a good-sized American living room], television lights all along the room. It's a studio. The lights have all been added since the revolution. There is a satellite antenna up on his roof. There's also a camera from Iranian television permanently there, so any time Khomeini decides he wants to talk, a crew from Iranian television walks in, the lights are switched on, and this twelfth-century figure from the past is talking to the nation of Iran. And when he decides to let the foreign press in, he's talking to the world—and he knows it...I don't think President Carter has such immediate access. They could have cared less about summoning an American diplomat to discuss [the crisis] with them. They're doing it all via television."

From the start of the hostage crisis to its incredibly dramatic, emotional close, television news provided a base on which the Iranian government could build domestic support and influence the shape of American policy toward Iran.

Writer and television critic Jeff Greenfield approached with thoughtful insight the way in which American policy has been influenced—even molded—by modern journalism.

"To put it most coldly," Greenfield said in a commentary on CBS's *Sunday Morning* in January 1981, "the national interest of this country may not...be the same as the freedom, even the safety, of fifty-two citizens. It is at least arguable that the seized Americans should never have become the centerpiece of our foreign policy, that competing interests may have required us to put their very safety at risk...

"But...what can television transmit that could possibly match the images of the families in whose homes we have lived week after week, whose members we have come to know and care about? What image can convey the argument that at times these good and innocent people may suffer, might even risk death, in the pursuit of other principles? It can't be done. . .

"How do you construct a national policy when each of us is bound so personally to individuals whose most urgent hopes and needs may not converge with the nation's?"

Indeed, Dorothea Morefield, the wife of one of the American hostages, threw open her doors to the media — and destroyed her family's privacy for the duration of her husband's captivity — expressly to personalize the crisis. So did other instinctively media-savvy relatives of hostages. The families knew what they were doing.

Khomeini and his supporters used international media to help weld Iranian factions against a common, alien foe. When reports of internal regional dissension and lack of governmental authority over the militants in the American Embassy became embarrassing, American reporters were expelled. Iranians knew what they were doing.

President Carter and Jody Powell, among other administration officials, tried to scotch a *60 Minutes* report on Iran that might have proved politically deleterious on the eve of the Massachusetts primary. A month later, forty minutes before the polls were to open in the Wisconsin and Kansas presidential primaries, the President and Powell summoned reporters to the Oval Office to announce a "positive development" concerning the hostages — a "development" that, sadly, dissipated after the polls closed.

As Jeff Greenfield pointed out, when Carter made the captives' release the keystone of his policy, television coverage was heavy; "when the Carter administration apparently ignored the hostages after [the April 1980] rescue attempt," he said, "TV coverage dropped noticeably." (Only a year later, El Salvador would become, first, a cause célèbre in America, and, later, when the Reagan administration determined it had overplayed the issue and directed its attention elsewhere, El Salvador virtually disappeared from our television screens—to return when it became a centerpiece of American policy again.) The administration—whether Carter's or Reagan's—knew what it was doing.

The families of hostages, Khomeini, the Iranian militants, Presidents Carter and Reagan and their advisers—all knew how to handle journalism; journalism, however, didn't seem up to handling them.

NBC's John Chancellor was quoted as saying, when referring to the growing sophistication in "using" American media, "We are becoming more vulnerable as they are becoming more skilled."

The vulnerability may be found in journalism's penchant to publish, photograph, videotape, and record anything and everything—particularly that which the competition is covering—with a maximum of manpower, money, and technological skill, but with a minimum of thoughtful selectivity.

The result is journalism that is not so much disinterested as it is promiscuous. The profligacy of both cameras and those directing them has demonstrated not an ability to "see all" in the interest of adding to public knowledge, but, rather, the tendency of a trained dog to leap blindly toward whatever is held aloft.

7

From One Media Center to Another

*A*N ARTICLE in the December 1979 issue of *Media People* was entitled "The Press Creates Its Candidate." The headline matter read:

Psst... Wanna hear the year's worst-kept secret? Even though he waited to announce his candidacy, the media had already named Teddy Kennedy the front-runner.

A headline in the January 30, 1980, issue of *The Washington Post* proclaimed THE ANTI-KENNEDY BIAS IN TV NEWS REPORTING. Television critic Tom Shales wrote that Kennedy was running not only against an incumbent President, but against all three television networks as well.

What happened between the media's anointment of Ted Kennedy as the Democratic nominee for President in 1980 and its consignment of him to the political scrap heap a month later was more media, especially a lengthy interview by Roger Mudd with the Massachusetts senator on national television.

The Mudd report on Kennedy, which was broadcast on November 4, 1979, three days before the senator formally announced his candidacy for President, was that rarest of all commodities in political reporting—a revealing portrait of a candidate drawn simply by allowing him, rather than the reporter, to do most of the talking.

To be sure, Mudd was well prepared to ask challenging questions on the events at Chappaquiddick. However, that segment of the hour-long *CBS Reports* ended, predictably, with Mudd concluding that Kennedy and his advisers "plan to volunteer nothing more on Chappaquiddick or make any attempt to clear away the lingering contradictions," suggesting, Mudd told us unrevealingly, that voters would believe him, not believe him, or wouldn't care. It was when Mudd asked what journalists call "softball" questions that the Senator was devastated, so much so that Kennedy's aides tried to spread the misinformation that the interview had been conducted in July, "before he'd even really thought about being President," Mudd said. The telling interview, though, had been conducted on October 12, 1979, only three weeks before he announced his candidacy—and fully two months after his rather ostentatious revelation that both his mother and estranged wife would approve should he decide to run.

The question that Mudd asked, effectively short-circuiting Kennedy's candidacy, was "Why do you want to be President?"

"You know," Mudd said in a conversation the following March, "it's kind of a laughable question, because when you're at a press conference [and the question is asked of a candidate], everybody groans." Using a baseball analogy in which a slugger is served up an easy pitch, Mudd said, "You know, the hang time on that [question] is at least nine and a half seconds. You can read the laces on that one.

"But the more I think about that question, the more I think [it] ought to be required of every candidate. The question is really mushy. But it reveals whether the candidate has ever really thought about it. And what that revealed with Teddy is that he hadn't."

For weeks after, the attitudes of journalists covering the

political campaign of Senator Kennedy changed; the focus was on whether he could articulate his views, on whether he could depart effectively from a prepared text, on whether he had a clear idea of what he expected to accomplish as President. Mudd concluded that Kennedy's "dispersed and diffused" answer to his question resulted from Kennedy's never having "really been to the mountain and [having] asked himself that question because his ascension to the presidency probably seemed so automatic."

It is worth repeating Kennedy's response as a reminder of how much can be learned from the news when reporters don't try to interject themselves in interviews to show us how knowledgeable or tough they are:

MUDD: Why do you want to be President?
KENNEDY: Well, I'm—were I to—to make the, the announcement and to run, the reasons that I would run is because I have a great belief in this country, that it is—has more natural resources than any nation in the world, has the greatest educated population in the world, the greatest technology of any country in the world, the greatest capacity for innovation in the world, and the greatest political system in the world. And yet, I see at the current time that most of the industrial nations in the world are exceeding us in terms of productivity, are doing better than us in meeting the problems of inflation, that they're dealing with their problems of energy and their problems of unemployment. And it just seems to me that this nation can cope and deal with its problems in a way that it has in the past. We're facing complex issues and problems in this nation at this time, but we have faced similar challenges at other times. And the energies and resourcefulness of this nation, I think, should be focused on these problems in a way that brings a sense of restoration in this country by its people to—in dealing with the problems that we face, primarily the issues on the economy, the problems of inflation, and the problems of energy. And I would basically feel that, that it's imperative for this country to either move forward, that it can't stand still, or otherwise it moves back.

MUDD: What would you do different from Carter?

KENNEDY: Well, in which particular areas?

MUDD: Well, just take the, the question of, of leadership.

KENNEDY: Well, it's a—on, on what, on—you know, you have to come to grips with the, the different issues that we're, we're facing. I mean, we can—we have to deal with each of the various questions that we're, we're talking about, whether it's in the questions of the economy, whether it's in, in the areas of energy.

Mudd tried again, pointing out that he had noticed some "sharp differences" between the two on national health, arms sales to the Middle East, and decontrol of oil and gas prices.

MUDD: But, really, to get from you to Carter doesn't take a huge leap. For a, a voter, why would he go from Carter to Kennedy?

KENNEDY: Well, well, you'd have to—you'd have to take the particular issues. I mean, if you want to—I mean, take on the issue of energy, and take the problems of inflation. Effectively, the decontrolling of crude oil prices has added anywhere from. . .three to four points on the inflation rate, let alone what it has done as a—in a multiplier effect on the inflation rate. That was an executive action. This was an executive action. The eliminations of, of, of controls on home heating oil is going to mean that the people in the colder climates, as well as in the warmer climates, are going to pay additional costs. That had an impact on the inflation rate. I would have specifically opposed the, the decontrol at— certainly at this time. I think it's one thing for OPEC countries to control the price of oil in the international market, but I find it unacceptable that the OPEC countries are going to control the price of oil here in the United States. And that has had a major impact on the rates of inflation, which are the number-one issues before the American people. That's a, a specific example.

In reflecting on Kennedy's vacuousness, Mudd concluded that the senator "never had to stop and say, 'Who are my enemies? Who do I want to get even with? Who do I want to help? What part of the government needs work? What will I

symbolize to America? Why am I in this, other than that I am
the surviving brother?' You can dump on the question all you
want—and I was in charge of the questions. I was not in
charge of the answers. I think it's valuable to see how those
guys [are] when you cut 'em loose from their press sec-
retaries, send 'em out in front of the public, and ask 'em that
question, and see what they come up with."

Mudd believes an asset of a television portrait is that it
reveals a person's composure. "This was not a high-pressure
interview," he said of the two one-hour sessions with
Kennedy, spaced two weeks apart. "I was not Torquemada; I
was not the Hanging Judge. I was a friend who nonetheless
had some worrisome things in the night to ask him. The
reason that broadcast came as such a shock to so many people
is that over the years, the 'television Teddy' we've all come to
know is the subcommittee chairman berating some corporate
bad guy who has slipped some sleazy formula into South
America; or it's the good-looking Teddy with the beautiful
children and the wife and the softball and the volleyball and
the Frisbee and the sailing—and all of that in clips [of] a
minute-fifteen, a minute-twenty: a rather romantic persona.
But rarely in the sixteen, seventeen years in the Senate has he
submitted himself to *Meet the Press,* or *Face the Nation,* or
Issues and Answers. . ." Until he announced his candidacy for
President, Kennedy had appeared three times each on those
programs in the nearly seventeen years he had been in the
Senate.

"[Almost] never putting himself into that unrehearsed,
uncontrolled environment," Mudd said. "[People heard] for
the first time all those 'uhs' and 'ahs.' All of us [reporters] sort
of knew about him up on [Capitol] Hill and at parties and on
the campaign—but it never got out on the public tube. That
was one of the things that was so arresting. People didn't
know that side of him. But a lot of newspaper people wrote,
'That's the way he is. We knew that.' But nobody *wrote* that
[before]. . . When you decide ahead of time to do an interview
like that, then the questioner becomes subordinate to the

answers. And we deliberately kept the camera on him. It made the broadcast more believable and authentic, because I didn't get in the middle of it and you didn't have a thirty-second question followed by a fast cutaway and a ten-second answer and back to a prosecutorial follow-up, followed by a tight shot and a three-word answer."

That is the exception to the rule in political reporting, especially on television. Every study (if the process of counting minutes and seconds constitutes a "study") of political reporting on television reaches the unsurprising conclusion, as did Thomas E. Patterson and Robert D. McClure in their 1976 study, that the networks "devote most of their election coverage to the trivia of political campaigning that make for flashy pictures — hecklers, crowds, motorcades, balloons, rallies, and gossip."

Print media, however, are no less the captives of the superficial in campaigns, with reporters devoting considerable amounts of time and energy to predicting the winners in any contest.

David Broder concedes that "people who read about political campaigns are less interested in what happened yesterday than what's going to happen tomorrow." Commenting on the dynamic by which most candidates are selected for "front-runner" status at one time or another during the marathon presidential campaign, Remer Tyson of *The Detroit Free Press* says the media are "victimized by an 'Andy Warhol syndrome' — everybody's going to be famous for fifteen minutes."

Kennedy was not the only candidate to be declared a winner, then a loser, then a potential winner again. John Connally was an early news magazine cover boy until it became clear he couldn't win anywhere; in the end, his campaign expenditures of about $10 million resulted in his winning one delegate at the Republican National Convention. Senator Howard Baker, unfortunately, ran against an unlisted candidate named "Expected" in a Republican Party straw poll in Maine. When he didn't draw as many votes as Expected, and Ambassador George Bush outpolled Expected, Baker was, to all intents and purposes, counted out of the presidential race.

When Bush, on the other hand, defeated Governor Ronald Reagan in a straw poll among Iowa Republicans in January 1980, NBC's Tom Pettit, among others, interred Reagan as politically "dead." (Most news reports gave Bush a comfortable margin of victory, 33 percent to 27 percent. It turned out that a computer malfunctioned; the real difference was 31.5 percent to 29.5 percent, giving Bush a margin of 2182 votes in 64,878 cast. An ABC–Lou Harris Poll a week later showed that because of his Iowa "landslide," Bush had captured the voters' fancy. Though Reagan held a seemingly insurmountable pre-Iowa popularity lead of 45 percent to Bush's 6 percent, the latter, now the news magazines' cover boy, had tied Reagan at 27 percent. People, polls, or both can be fickle.)

Later, John Anderson SHOCKS RIVALS, according to *The Chicago Tribune,* by doing so well in Massachusetts and Vermont; REAGAN STUNS BUSH, said *The Boston Globe,* by winning handily in New Hampshire; KENNEDY SCORES DOUBLE UPSET, reported *The Philadelphia Inquirer,* when he defeated Carter in New York and Connecticut. Quite obviously, all of the sound and fury of telling us who led whom by how much in what stage of the race signified very little.

The extent to which television and print journalism affect American voters has been the subject of a dizzying number of studies and analyses producing a dizzying variety of conclusions.

I, for one, believe that political reporting has almost no discernible effect on voters; else, how could they keep confounding the polls and pundits? Voters have an uncanny way of knowing when one politician or another best reflects their own interests or concerns. They also know when their vote won't make "a dime's worth of difference," to quote George Wallace, because of the candidates' similarities or, in recent years, because they consider no candidate worth a dime in the first place.

Political commentators Jack W. Germond and Jules Witcover, in one of their co-authored syndicated columns, fretted before the New Jersey gubernatorial primaries in the spring of 1981 that, because there was no commercial VHF television channel in the state, "the voters are clearly at some disadvantage in sorting out this huge field" of twenty-four candidates. "This lack also means," the authors intoned, "that candidates can exploit the audience...with their advertising [from] New York and Philadelphia [the cities that provide New Jersey with commercial television] by presenting pictures of themselves that are not likely to be contradicted by the intrusion of the real world" — meaning that there were no New Jersey–based television news programs in which journalists could criticize the candidates, the Germond-Witcover concept of "the real world" of politics.

They quoted public opinion analyst Peter Hart puzzling punningly over "how people straighten out something in a non-electronic state. I don't know how you crystallize it." (Living in a "non-electronic state" means living in a place like New Jersey, where there is no locally based commercial television; or perhaps it means a state of existence in which one is not "plugged in." In the current cant, the two meanings appear interchangeable.)

In addition to having no faith in either newspapers or radio, Germond and Witcover clearly were certain the voters would be fooled without a television journalist to show them the light and the truth. They even hinted that one rich neophyte might buy the nomination by outspending his opponents in the expensive New York and Philadelphia television markets on which New Jersey voters depended.

Somehow, New Jersey voters surmounted these alpine obstacles; *The New York Times* congratulated them editorially for selecting worthy candidates on both the Democratic and Republican tickets (including the man Germond and Witcover feared might be defeated by the rich neophyte). The

Times's complaint, quite properly, was with the New Jersey primary system, which allowed such a multitude of candidates, most with neither political experience nor party background, to qualify in the first place.

Even a candidate who is largely ignored by the media may be noticed by the voters, like Jimmy Carter in late 1975 and early 1976, and George McGovern in early 1972.

Television journalists like to claim that they don't influence voters very much. "I think we have much less power over people's minds than we are given credit for having," Sanford Socolow said. "We [journalists] are generally perceived as liberals. Well, if that were so, how do you explain Nixon's overriding victory over McGovern — I mean, the biggest win in American presidential politics? If we were in the business of trying to change people's minds, [supporting] one set of beliefs over another, then we were ignominious failures and we're a joke. I submit we weren't, and we couldn't, and we didn't."

I agree. Further, I don't think people learn a great deal from political news, other than the gossip, the gaffes, and the prognostications.

One of the more gifted observers of modern American life, Michael J. Arlen, wrote in *The New Yorker* in April 1980 that the news media, principally television news, "communicate politics preponderantly on a mythic level," making

> only occasional, dutiful attempts at interviewing candidates according to old-fashioned rationality (sitting them down and asking them logical questions about issues)...Thus, Senator Kennedy is shown embattled and pugnacious on the streets of Chicago; George Bush...is seen as a solitary type, seated by himself in an airplane, returning from the Southern primaries, or else perpetually jogging; and the television news about John Anderson is not...how he stands on nuclear power but how he shakes hands in Illinois (in a raincoat, in a friendly, modest, and somewhat startled manner, as befits the mythic underdog)...But recently the manufactured political commercials paid for by the candidates seem to be inclining more

and more to a presentation of the supposedly rational side of things — as if, with so much myth being communicated by the news, there were a danger that the candidates would lose all identifying... differences... unless they put down their money and spelled things out themselves and obviously *for* themselves. At least, there was Senator Kennedy pumping away about economics in a series of Illinois commercials, while the nightly news talked relentlessly about his "troubled personal history" and his "faltering campaign." And there was John Anderson... giving us some straight talk about the energy problem. And, strangest of all, there was Ronald Reagan... purveying his views on foreign relations and inflation by means of paid commercials.

Arlen's point was made by political scientists Patterson and McClure, again, in their 1976 book (*The Unseeing Eye: The Myth of Television Power in National Elections*):

> The only noticeable effect of network campaign news is an increased tendency among voters to view politics in the same trivial terms that the newscasts depict it. Regular viewers of network news are likely to describe an election campaign as a lot of nonsense rather than a choice between fundamental issues... But people do come to understand better where the candidates stand on election issues from watching televised political commercials [that]... make heavy use of hard issue information... In fact, during the short period of the general election campaign, presidential ads contain substantially more issue content than network newscasts.

It's worth repeating that line for emphasis: "Presidential ads contain substantially more issue content than network newscasts." Patterson and McClure's study showed a 28 percent increase in knowledge of candidates' positions among regular viewers of network news during the 1972 presidential campaign. Knowledge of the positions among those exposed to many campaign spots, by contrast, increased 36 percent; the figure was 35 percent among regular newspaper readers.

To which Sanford Socolow, who, in another context, supports the notion that television doesn't influence anyone, replied: "That is total, utter, fucking bullshit." It would seem the only thing worse than suggesting the news media have too much influence in our political system is asserting that they've got none at all. In any event, Socolow was just warming to his subject.

"That criticism comes from people who don't watch newscasts," he continued. "That's a fucking knee-jerk liberal, conservative, know-nothing criticism of television news. Read our transcripts. If anything, we give people *more* than they want to know. We *choke* people on issues and substantive stands on the issues.

"I'm sorry that. . . along with the voluminous, encyclopedic amounts of information we give you on substance and issues. . . we also feel obliged to talk about tactics every once in a while. And I'm sorry that they choke whenever we do tactics or a 'horse race.' It's a fact of life. You know, I'm sorry that it rained today, but it *did* rain today, and I'm ready to face it. Those guys aren't ready to face it.

"The criticism that we don't deal enough in substance or in candidates' positions is absolutely fraudulent and nefarious and mischievous — and doesn't do anybody any good." When Socolow paused to punctuate his remarks with a sharp nod, I couldn't resist noting, disingenuously, "I take it you think their conclusions were in error."

Whoever is right about the ratio of issues to fluff in campaign news, reporting about the Great Election Game is among the best things that American journalism does. Whether or not it succeeds in educating voters, campaign reporting doesn't appear to change many minds. Therefore, it can't be much of a danger — unless you think that if minds aren't changed to your particular understanding of truth, Armageddon is around the corner.

Though a number of reporters, unlike the Peter Finley Dunnes and H. L. Menckens of yore, insist on taking campaign politics (and themselves) very seriously, the Patterson-McClure study suggests that the voters do not. People tend to regard politics and campaigns as three-ring circuses and as a lot of nonsense. Political scientists often condemn campaign reporting for creating that state of mind rather than reflecting reality. They presume "reality" is considerably more dignified than history suggests. Political journalism — reporting the *process* by which people are nominated and elected, bills are passed, or legislators are influenced, rather than the issues themselves — is, for the most part, pure entertainment, mirroring the essential tomfoolery of campaign shenanigans and legislative infighting. When it plays for theater or for laughs, campaign reporting is peerless. It becomes noisome when reporters, not allowing candidates to explain themselves directly, interpolate their own notions of what "really" is meant.

Political campaigns provide American voters with the chance to sneer and snicker at candidates who, if elected, will command respect and wield considerable influence. Most candidates anticipate this leveling process, accept it, and even encourage it.

When Calvin Coolidge put on an Indian headdress for photographers and voters, it was a piece of vote-getting nonsense. When Andrew Jackson's supporters nearly tore down the White House during their drunken celebration of his inauguration, it resembled a democratic three-ring circus. Political campaigns, basically, are clownish. Nevertheless, the voters have managed to select some good Presidents, along with a fair sampling of lemons, with or without television, and whatever the substantive level of political journalism may have been at the time. If contemporary political reporting is to blame for producing a series of lesser lights as Presidents in recent years, it couldn't have been more assiduous when Chester Arthur or Warren Harding was elected. If journalism can't be blamed for bad Presidents, it can't take credit for the good ones. Voters work in mysterious ways their political wonders or blunders to perform. In 1932, candidate Franklin Delano Roosevelt promised to balance the federal budget. The nostalgically beloved Harry Truman had a popularity rating in 1952 rivaling that of Richard Nixon on the eve of the latter's resignation. Recent biographies of Dwight Eisenhower demonstrate that he was anything but the marionette the press portrayed him as being for most of his eight-year term in office. The basis on which voters made their decisions clearly did not rely on journalism alone, if at all.

On the other hand, people take notice when media focus on campaign frippery. We liked it when Truman gave 'em hell in 1948; we had a good leer when Jimmy Carter confessed to lust in his heart, refused to kiss Ted Kennedy's ass in 1976, and then promised to whip same in 1980 — all from a God-fearing born-again. We smirked when Richard Nixon delivered his teary, televised *mea culpa* in 1952, and when he stamped his foot petulantly at the press in 1962; we were smugly superior when we learned in 1968 that George Romney had been "brainwashed" some time earlier about events in Vietnam and therefore was pronounced too dumb to be President.

In their work, political reporters become part of the show. In his 1976 challenge to President Gerald Ford for the Republican presidential nomination, Ronald Reagan proposed slashing $90 billion from the federal budget, a proposal, ironically, that would be ridiculed and judged a political liability. Reporters traveling with the Reagan campaign quickly wrote a song (presciently, as it would turn out four years later) to the tune of "Give Me the Simple Life":

> Cut ninety billion, make it a trillion,
> Just call me "Ron the Knife";
> This old vaudevillian can save you a zillion,
> I'll give you the simple life.

During the general election campaign, reporters prepared an entertainment for the Carters on Jimmy's fifty-second birthday. Donning straw boaters provided, on request, by a Carter advance man, five reporters entertained the couple at a private party in a Pittsburgh hotel with this parody, to the tune of "Heart of My Heart," of Carter's *Playboy* interview:

> Lust in my heart, how I love adultery;
> Lust in my heart, that's my theology.
> When I was young, at the Plains First Baptist Church,
> I would preach and sermonize —
> But, oh, how I would fantasize...
>
> A bunch of women I did screw —
> But in my head, so no one knew...
>
> As *Playboy* said, I've got lust in my heart.

The acknowledged master reporter-comic of the 1980 campaign was Thomas Oliphant of *The Boston Globe,* who, as correspondent Waldo McPhee of KRAP-TV Action News, would entertain reporters and political aides on Ted Kennedy's campaign press plane with his nightly news reports. When Kennedy delivered a speech bearing no relationship to the advance text distributed to the media, Waldo, using the plane's public address system, announced that Kennedy "has revealed himself as a textual deviant." When Kennedy quoted an unnamed poet to conclude his standard political speech, Waldo identified the author as Edna St. Vincent Malaise, a reference to Carter's earlier scolding of America.

What could have been more entertaining than the on-again, off-again, right-again, wrong-again reporting of whether Ronald Reagan and Gerald Ford would emerge as a ticket from the 1980 Republican National Convention in Detroit? About 7:00 P.M. on the crucial night, Ford indicated in an interview with Walter Cronkite that he would accept the vice presidential nomination under certain circumstances. Apparently, that and subsequent interviews fueled discussions among Reagan's aides about whether such a political marriage could be arranged and, if so, how successful it might prove in the campaign. By about 10:00 P.M., Cronkite was announcing that Ford was, indeed, Reagan's choice; an early edition of *The Chicago Sun-Times* carried the headline IT'S REAGAN AND FORD. By midnight, Dan Rather was raising caution flags, and, just then, Chris Wallace broadcast the word that George Bush, not Ford, would be the vice presidential nominee.

Somewhere between, a new plateau in political-reporting farce was reached at what *The New York Time*'s Washington editor, Bill Kovach, called a journalistic "hall of mirrors": Albert Hunt of *The Wall Street Journal* was assured by a prominent governor that Reagan had, in fact, selected Ford; his source, the governor told Hunt, had been Dan Rather.

(The same phenomenon would occur the following spring in somewhat tragic circumstances. During the continuing coverage of the attempt on President Reagan's life, Rather reported—as did other network correspondents—that James Brady, the President's press secretary, had died. Rather even called for his viewers to observe a moment of prayer. Immediately, contradictory reports began to emerge. On ABC, anchorman Frank Reynolds shouted angrily on the air for his editors to get the correct information. On CBS, Rather switched to the White House, where Lesley Stahl was reporting. Stahl said she had almost confirmed the erroneous report of Brady's death. The reason, she explained, is that when she heard the announcement by Rather that Brady had died, she walked into the area of the press secretary's office. There, she saw two of Brady's assistants sobbing uncontrollably. That sight, she said, convinced her that the report must be true—until she realized they had heard of Brady's "death" the same way she had: by watching Dan Rather on television.)

At the Republican National Convention, there was no life-and-death issue; it all was harmless fun, with a fitting dénouement that kept millions of Americans awake into the wee hours. Reagan himself broke tradition by speaking to the convention before formally accepting its nomination. Because of the extraordinary coverage, he said it was necessary to announce to the convention—not to mention us bleary-eyed voters—that Bush, not Ford, would be his vice presidential selection.

Nothing less could have been expected, what with nearly

12,000 newspaper, magazine, radio, and television people to watch 1994 delegates ratify what had been already decided and everyone expected — Ronald Reagan's nomination as the Republican candidate for President. *Time* magazine, which keeps up with these things, reported that "the networks together spent some $30 million to send nearly 2000 staffers, along with more than 500 tons of office and technical equipment, ninety-plus cameras, and hundreds of miles of cable."

At the Democratic National Convention, where about 11,500 media-connected people were accredited to cover the deliberations of 3331 delegates, columnist Ellen Goodman recalled that, while she was writing, "I turned around and saw my colleague Curtis Wilkie writing a story...Behind him was *Time* magazine's Steve Smith writing a story about Curtis Wilkie...That same day, *The New York Times* carried a picture of *Time* magazine's Steve Smith writing about *The Boston Globe's* Curtis Wilkie...Now I am sitting here writing a story about a reporter who wrote a story about a reporter who wrote a story about a reporter who wrote a story. This should qualify me for the incestuous media story of the year, but I am not sure. The competition has been pretty heavy."

Heavy competition to cover the press covering politics, or to present primaries and conventions like hotly contested races or ball games, are amusing and harmless. An overlooked pol's pride may be hurt now and again, but the voters have shown that when they feel like it — whether because of ideology or just orneriness — they can propel a John Anderson into the headlines or breathe new (if brief) life into a Ted Kennedy campaign.

Heavy competition for heavy-handed revelation and punditry, however, is something else. When political reporters start to take themselves too seriously, believing, perhaps, that the very foundation of the nation is riding on their perspicacity, politicians and politics itself are affected mightily. That seminal year of journalism as intrusive giant — 1968 —

provides some examples of the way in which journalism makes politicians jump (often in the wrong direction), and, at the same time, embeds in our minds seeds of perception that grow, too often, into weeds of knowledge.

Journalism, especially on television, pumped into our heads so persistently that Senator Eugene McCarthy was the "real winner" of the New Hampshire Democratic primary of 1968 that most of us remember it that way. In fact, President Lyndon Johnson, who had decided to enter the primary so late that his name was not on the ballot, received 26,337 write-in votes (48.5 percent), and Senator McCarthy received 22,810 (42 percent). Further, the showing by McCarthy (better than "Expected"), was interpreted widely as an anti-Vietnam vote — and probably most of us remember it that way, too. Without question, that interpretation of events provided the impetus for Robert Kennedy to enter the presidential race; it likely hastened the decision by President Johnson to launch his own peace offensive in Vietnam — rather than waiting for an initial signal from Hanoi that might have facilitated a compromise and a quicker end to the war. Both were responding to what they *believed* the reaction of the American people would be to the reports that the Vietnam War was anathema.

Harry Reasoner, for one, remembers "the New Hampshire verdict" as part of "the final realization that basic Middle America did not believe in that war anymore."

The truth, though, is far different from media-impressed memories. By a margin of nearly three to one, according to polls conducted after the New Hampshire vote in March 1968, those who voted for McCarthy were dissatisfied with Johnson for not pushing a harder line in Vietnam. Of those who favored McCarthy in New Hampshire but switched to another candidate by November 1968, a plurality voted for George Wallace, one of the era's "superhawks."

When I ask people to name the city in which six people were killed during rioting in connection with a 1968 national political convention, invariably they reply, "Chicago." There were no deaths attributed to violence at the 1968 Democratic National Convention in Chicago; six people died during rioting in connection with the 1968 Republican National Convention in Miami Beach.

The reasons underlying the mediazation of the violence in Chicago but not the more profound violence the same year in Miami Beach remain the subject of controversy. Some columnists (Drew Pearson, Jack Anderson, Ernest B. Furgurson) suggested that the networks were angry with the Democrats because of their refusal to hold their convention, like the Republicans, in Miami Beach, thus costing them millions of dollars in moving expenses. Another theory is that a subtle racism was at work: most of the Miami Beach protesters were black, and their concerns were poverty and civil rights — not the dominant media issues at the time. The overwhelming majority of the Chicago protesters, in addition to being white and having planned and organized their actions more thoroughly than their Miami Beach counterparts, focused on the Vietnam issue — and that was the central issue gaining public attention.

Unquestionably, more raw drama surrounded the Democratic convention than the Republican. The Democrats had been in power and could, legitimately, be held accountable for previous Vietnam policy. Robert Kennedy had been murdered not long before, removing the only real challenger to Vice President Hubert Humphrey for the nomination. The "youth movement" supporting Senator McCarthy would make itself heard and felt, even though victory was beyond its grasp. Already, there was a political "boomlet" for Senator Ted Kennedy.

About the only drama at the Republican convention was the selection of Richard Nixon's vice presidential running mate.

In Chicago, too, resided hizzoner, Mayor Richard Daley. Daley clearly had no intention of making life any easier for the networks. He refused to exempt their large broadcasting trailers from parking regulations around the major hotels, limiting the amount of equipment the networks had available

at the locations where the major candidates for the nomina-
tions and key political operatives could be interviewed. A
telephone installers' strike made impossible the laying of the
lines necessary to permit "live" coverage of the protesters'
activities at sites remote from the convention hall.

Most network correspondents and producers remain convinced to this day that the strike was the handiwork of Daley
to prevent live coverage of any protest activity. Sanford
Socolow judged this an example "of where officialdom inter-
fered with an otherwise free process and, as far as I'm
concerned, brought disaster on themselves — deservedly so."

Prevented — whether or not by design — from transmitting
live pictures from the scenes of rioting, "we were constrained
to make do with film," Socolow recalled. Transported to the
convention hall by motorcycle, the film would be processed
by network technicians and rushed to the producers. "The
result," Socolow said, "was that the riots, which were mostly
daytime, late-afternoon, early-evening affairs, wound up on
prime time because of the lag. So [at] the height of the
convention, with all the ruckus that was going on in the hall,
over which we had no control... over those scenes we were
showing the rioting, an hour, two hours later than it was
happening (and telling you that), but that was the quickest we
could get it on the air... We just slammed it on the air when
it came through — as a result of which everything came
together.

"If you were at home and not paying close attention, if you
had one hand in the refrigerator and were opening a beer and
you were only listening with half an ear, it would not be a very
wrong conclusion to think that rioting was coincidental with
the convention."

That coincidence, according to *The Baltimore Sun*'s Ernest
Furgurson, writing a year after the convention, made "it seem
that the violence in the streets was simultaneous with the
nomination process in the hall — indeed, somehow, that
Humphrey was being nominated by the force of police clubs."

In *The Making of the President: 1968*, Theodore White

observed that just as Carl Stokes, then mayor of Cleveland, was about to second Humphrey's nomination at nearly 10:00 P.M., NBC ran a film of earlier street violence. "Stokes's face," White wrote of the black mayor, "is being wiped from the nation's view to show blood—Hubert Humphrey being nominated in a sea of blood."

Reasoner conceded that he was "distressed...concerned" when "a tremendous amount of mail" from viewers "ran eleven to one against our coverage. When it's eleven to one, maybe something was wrong. I think mabye there *was* something wrong. I was highly conscious afterwards that nobody was killed and that, under considerable provocation, the Chicago Police Department may not have always behaved as ideal policemen should behave, but they didn't kill anybody.

"I don't think it was television's finest hour—but I don't think it was America's finest hour, either. I think it was a crisis in 1968. I think it was a crisis of this country—not of television and not of journalism."

Reasoner is right about crisis in the country, and Socolow may be right about Daley "arranging" for a telephone installers' strike, but both observations are irrelevant to journalism's role at the conventions. Why wasn't there comparable coverage of people being killed—not merely clubbed, odious as that is, but *killed*—in Miami Beach? Did the crisis in the country begin after the Republican convention but before the Democratic convention? Isn't it possible that protesters, who went to great lengths to plan their activities well in advance of the convention, knew perfectly well how to time their confrontations so as to make prime time? Put another way, isn't it likely that if the networks had been able to transmit live pictures of battles between the police and the protesters, the riots would have been staged later in the day to coincide with convention activities?

Lawyer-diplomat Max M. Kampelman, once a close aide to Hubert Humphrey, wrote in *Policy Review* in 1978 that a few days before Richard Nixon's inauguration as President in

January 1969, "a world-famous network correspondent visited Vice President Humphrey in his White House office and tearfully apologized: 'We defeated you, Hubert,' was the confession."

The irony, of course, is that one can find as many journalists who will justify the coverage at Chicago either on grounds that reporters should report what's happening and not try to evaluate its impact (the Socolow school), or on the wholly conflicting basis that reporters should judge whether events reflect a larger problem and therefore deserve attention (the Reasoner concept).

Whether journalism is judgmental or mindless, the likelihood of its representing historical truth always has been a roll of the dice, or, more aptly, given journalism's potential for power, a live bomb or a dud.

The potential power of media may create legitimate concerns, but the perception of its power among politicians creates even more.

When President Carter was in the midst of his "noncampaign" campaign of 1979 in deference to the American hostages in Iran (not to mention his hope of improving his sagging ratings in the polls), he maintained in an interview with *The Des Moines Register* that, lest anyone get the wrong impression, he would be better off politically if he had not eschewed the campaign trail:

> It would be good for me to go from one media center to another, to have press conferences, town hall meetings, to be seen shaking hands with factory workers and visiting a farmer and looking at his livestock with him.

The key words are *media center*. That is what campaigning meant to the President and probably means to any major-party nominee.

"With this single statement," *The Washington Post* editorialized, "President Carter retires the cup for Candidate Candor...The President was frankly saying that he does not miss seeing Iowans quite as much as he misses Iowans seeing him in Iowa. Of course, Iowans, like other Americans, have been watching him virtually every night on the network news, but apparently the old campaign instinct — even in incumbent presidents — yearns for the real thing: the 'media center.'"

Because they place such store in the importance and influence of their own visibility, politicians infer that what people see — and what they are told they are seeing — will unalterably affect their actions and (as important) their votes. Thus, President Johnson believed his Vietnam policy must fail after Walter Cronkite stated it already had. Johnson thought he had lost the "center" in America, though, if the analysis of the New Hampshire vote is any indication, he miscalculated.

When George McGovern dumped Senator Thomas Eagleton from the Democratic ticket in 1972, he did so clearly because of the pressure of week-long news coverage that was intensified by the misfortune (for Eagleton) of an otherwise "slow" news week. There was no independent, reliable yardstick to indicate that McGovern's candidacy would be harmed by Eagleton's presence. (Considering the eventual outcome of the 1972 presidential election and the fate of the McGovern-Shriver ticket, the retention of Eagleton may be compared to giving chicken soup to an invalid: it might not have helped, but it surely wouldn't have hurt.)

In the first months of the crisis of the American hostages in Iran, President Carter adopted a policy of patience that relied on the eventual collapse of warring factions within Iran and the country's resulting, acute need to be welcomed back into the family of nations. Then, as columnist James Reston wrote in *The New York Times:*

> President Carter rejected this notion. He was being criticized for being indecisive and for letting time go on without "doing something" to liberate the hostages. Oddly, but seriously, one of the innocent villains in motivating Carter to want to "do something" was my old buddy, the Ayatollah Walter Cronkite.
>
> It seems slightly mad, but it happens to be true, that these

characters in the White House really felt some pressure from Uncle Walter's announcing every night the number of days of captivity of the hostages.

The polls, which have become the foundation of political reporting, plus the visibility accorded those polls by the media, have changed politics and politicians, causing them to react precipitately to what they believe to be the people's will.

"The evidence seems persuasive," Ernest Volkman wrote in the December 1979 issue of *Media People*, "that [polls] are being overused. What is their appeal to the media? First, they are easy and cheap. The certitude of numbers obviates any necessity to spend money and time finding out what's behind the figures. Second, they fulfill the long-standing American dream of quantifying everything. The weekly poll bulletins supposedly tell us all we need to know about how the people feel."

When he wrote the article, Volkman pointed out that a telephone survey of 1422 people underwritten by CBS News and *The New York Times* had recently asserted "with 95 percent certainty" of only a 3 percentage point error "that over 60 percent of the American voting population wants Teddy Kennedy as the next president of the United States."

Carter's public opinion analyst, Patrick Caddell, complained in a *Playboy* interview that "the American press lets the polls set its agenda. It'll quote any poll that comes along. The polls and television have in some ways been a great disaster for the political process...They have hastened the decline of the political parties. They have become the preselectors of who can run for office in this country. Modern technology overwhelmed the process and drove out some very good people who did not know how to adapt to it. We have produced a professional class of politicians who pose for TV cameras but never do anythng else and who are among the most gutless group of people I have ever seen."

It became abundantly clear that more than 60 percent of

the American people did *not* want Ted Kennedy to be
President; they may have said otherwise—and the scientific
sample may actually have represented accurately the opinions
of a hundred million American voters. Obviously, they didn't
mean what they said, or they changed their minds quickly and
often. Chances are, they simply wanted to inform the Carter
administration that they were mad as hell. That did not mean,
however, that they were ready to embrace Kennedy's politics
or forgive him Chappaquiddick.

Conversely, when they gave Ted Kennedy and John
Anderson victories late in the 1980 primary season, did they
really mean to derail Carter or Reagan—or, knowing by then
that neither Kennedy nor Anderson had a snowball's chance
in hell to win the nomination, did they simply want to remind
Carter and Reagan that they were less than overjoyed with
either?

Caddell's gloomy assessment of how the press and polls are
"preselectors of who can run for office" is not valid unless one
accepts the frequently expressed, rather elitist view that
voters' minds are easily addled. The *indirect* impact of the
press and polls—their influence not on the people but on the
politicians—is another story.

A convincing argument can be made that a precipitate
response by politicians to the galaxy of news stories assembled
under the rubric of "Watergate," and the subsequent orgy of
so-called investigative reporting that measured the relative
import of news by its content of revelation, not information,
have pressed the political system to the brink of chaos.

Public financing of elections and the proliferation of
primaries have resulted in a proliferation of candidates with
minimal party or political loyalties. Indeed, many of the new
slew are so-called one-issue candidates who would have had
trouble being entrusted by the now-passé county and precinct
party organizations with licking postage stamps. Meanwhile,
the extraordinary requirements for public disclosure of information once regarded as highly personal, plus laws subjecting
public officials to inquisitions if nearly anyone makes nearly

any sort of accusation against them, have depleted the number of talented people willing to participate actively in politics and government.

What that has done, in turn, is to separate the politics of getting nominated and elected from the politics of governance. As Jimmy Carter's presidency illustrated, when someone's nomination and election are exercises wholly removed from party participation and loyalty, one cannot expect the participation and loyalty of a party in one's government.

The thoughtless rush by Congress to enact the so-called post-Watergate reforms erupted amidst a media *rat-tat-tat* persuading lawmakers to restructure overnight a system that had worked well for the better part of two centuries. Here's why it happened:

☐ Journalism functions without memory, without a sense of the past. News is, by definition, a here-and-now commodity.

☐ Political scandals and corruption, past as well as present, are proclaimed by journalists to be the biggest and most colossal yet, much as hucksters herald the latest motion picture extravaganza: selling government commissions under Garfield, taking kickbacks under Grant, Teapot Dome under Harding, accepting a freezer under Truman, receiving a vicuña coat under Eisenhower, and, around the country, selling favors under Bosses Tweed, Curley, Crump, Pendergast, and others.

☐ Watergate, a series of disconnected governmental misdeeds, most of them minor, was presented as a unified whole, suggesting a pattern of corruption that was, somehow, unique in the annals of American politics.

☐ Television news reports evoked enough local response (most often, editorials in local newspapers and on local televison stations) to convince lawmakers that something should be done — not just to President Nixon, but to end forever what President Ford called our "long national nightmare."

Television news just hadn't been around before, and the system had therefore escaped the congressional meat cleaver.

The impact of massive journalism on a media-minded Congress is apparent in what its members chose to condemn during Watergate-related deliberations, and what they chose to overlook then and before.

In 1967, when President Johnson was escalating American participation in the undeclared war in Vietnam, Adam Clymer, then a reporter for *The Baltimore Sun*, asked Senator Birch Bayh, chairman of the Senate Constitutional Amendments Subcommittee, whether such American involvement was not, in fact, unconstitutional.

Senator Bayh merely shrugged. "It's a moot question," he said. "We're already there." Few—clearly not the chairman of the Senate committee closest to an understanding of the constitution of the United States—dreamed of suggesting that legal charges should be brought against a President who, in clear disregard of constitutional requirements, had committed the nation to a war costing billions of dollars and tens of thousands of American lives.

The House Judiciary Committee, in considering charges against President Nixon, deliberately omitted from the articles of impeachment Nixon's continued escalation of the war—including the massive bombing raids in Cambodia. The omission was not based on ideology; most committee members did not think that article of impeachment would pass.

The point is that, while the Vietnam War in its later stages was a visible and unpopular issue, media barely explored the question of its legality. Apparently because media hadn't questioned it, the House Judiciary Committee feared there was insufficient sentiment in Congress to pursue it.

Media—and therefore Congress—made very little of Nixon's assertion, on one of the White House tapes, that Lyndon Johnson had bugged Barry Goldwater during the 1964 presidential campaign, and had authorized bugging during Nixon's own 1968 campaign. As Theodore White wrote in *Breach of Faith: The Fall of Richard M. Nixon*, these activities must have seemed to Nixon to be part of his brief as President:

The clumsy break-in at Democratic headquarters...was technically criminal but of no uglier morality than the spying at Barry Goldwater's headquarters which Howard Hunt of the CIA had supervised for Lyndon Johnson in 1964. Their penchant for wire-tapping must certainly have been stimulated by the wire-tapping authorized by Johnson against the Nixon campaign of 1968. Their little early illegalities must have come naturally—and must have seemed only a step beyond those of their predecessors.

If media ignored, dealt lightly with, or even glorified actions that, in any other context, might have been viewed as unethical or illegal, Congress ignored, dealt lightly with, or even glorified them as well.

As David L. Altheide pointed out in his 1976 book, *Creating Reality,* Nixon and his aides were not the only people involved in Watergate who thought they had the right to break the rules:

> The journalists...Carl Bernstein and Bob Woodward illegally questioned a grand juror to get information for one of their reports. On another occasion, they blackmailed an FBI agent to have a report verified...Satisfied that the stone-walling defendants would crack under pressure, [Judge John] Sirica sentenced E. Howard Hunt to thirty-five years in prison.*

Because of its power to set the national agenda, journalism has imbued its practitioners with a sense of their own importance, resulting in a symbiotic relationship between politician and journalist. Each needs the other to survive, and each believes his or her own survival is vital to the nation. If one had a mean streak, one could liken this relationship to the mating dance of a couple of tarantulas. They circle one another for the longest time, but finally jump into a furry-legged embrace that they quite obviously enjoy—but that

---

*Woodward and Bernstein themselves described these actions in their book *All the President's Men.*

produces nothing except more tarantulas. Tarantulas look mean and scary and have a sharp bite, but, contrary to belief, they're not especially dangerous to man. Neither are most reporters — as long as they confine themselves to reporting, leaving the actions to the politicians and the inferences to their audiences. Reporters ought regularly remind themselves that theirs is, in the broadest sense, the business of entertainment. The word means "to interest" as well as "to divert," "to fascinate" and "to amuse." Entertainment encompasses William Shakespeare and Neil Simon; to both, however, the play and not the polemic was the thing.

Journalists, like actors and other entertainers, abjure responsibility for the impact of their product. They disavow any link to the policies or actions of those they interview and write about; they believe the motives of sources irrelevant to the newsworthiness of the information they provide. Indeed, First Amendment champions like Alan Barth maintained that the exercise of a free press meant reporters must have the "freedom to be irresponsible." As actors are only shadows of the characters they portray, journalists are only reflections of those with real influence and real authority. There is no more basis for expecting Walter Cronkite to behave responsibly because he has talked to Presidents than there is Henry Fonda because he has portrayed them.

It might be well for journalists, particularly in television, to remember whence their Herculean idols came. Edward R. Murrow may be enshrined in myth because of his 1954 broadcast attacking Senator Joseph McCarthy, but a year earlier, Murrow was host of the hokum, long-running interview program called *Person to Person*.

Once, he was quoted as snapping that he hated *Person to Person* as "damn demeaning. But," he added, "it really makes a lot of money." Gary Paul Gates, in his 1978 book, *Air Time*, quotes newsman Bill Downs accusing Murrow of "whoring" with *Person to Person*. "Yes," Murrow is quoted as replying, "but look at all those voyeurs." In 1959, when the program had been on the air for six years, Dr. Frank Stanton, later to become president of CBS, made a speech promising to eliminate the "hanky-panky" that had plagued television quiz programs. When he was asked afterward what he meant by hanky-panky, he singled out *Person to Person* for giving the false impression that the interviews were spontaneous when, in fact, they were all rehearsed. Murrow's reply, termed by Gates "a model of intemperance" (but also showing some defensiveness), was that Stanton had "revealed his ignorance both of news and of requirements of television production."

Walter Cronkite may be remembered by journalists as the all-time anchorman, starting with the national political conventions in 1952, but after the conventions, he spent most of his time interviewing characters like Brutus and Helen of Troy on *You Are There*. "We are standing outside the tent of Achilles," Cronkite started one program, according to Gates. "The place: the plains of Ilium outside the great walled city of Troy. The date: 1184 B.C. And—*you* are there!" Cronkite would slip a bit deeper. A year later, on CBS's newly minted *The Morning Show*, Cronkite was assigned gag writers so that he could challenge Dave Garroway on NBC's *Today*. Not only that; Cronkite spent a part of each program trading lines with a lion puppet named Charlemane.

The level of professionally accepted hucksterism varies from medium to medium. Television reporters won't read commercials, and, though they have "anchored" programs like *You Are There* or *Person to Person*, most disdain someone like John Cameron Swayze for leaving news to become a "watch salesman." Print reporters often deride the proximity of their television colleagues to the advertising side of journalism—but the better-known print reporters command (and readily accept) fees ranging upward of $7500 for addressing well-heeled business or professional groups about whose activities they may have reported or will report in the future.

Whether or not the activities of some reporters are hypocritical, a rigid, professional ethicality and morality, tinged with self-righteousness, can be carried too far. Many reporters worry themselves gray over whether the acceptance of a dinner invitation from a politician or a corporate lobbyist would constitute something akin to fraternizing with the enemy. Reporters who become public relations executives for substantial increases in their income are often described by their former colleagues as having sold out. Even within the profession, print reporters who have been drawn to television news by its greater money and glamour are denigrated by their print brethren, and sometimes even denigrate themselves. James Wooten, after moving from *The New York Times* to ABC News, where his reports were as informative, intelligent, and gracefully written as before, replied to a new acquaintance, who had asked him what he did for a living, "I used to be a reporter." Journalism is becoming a church of all-or-nothing purists, its preachers issuing harsh judgments, like Cotton Mather, on those in the congregation who view the religion of reporting as less than a life-or-death enterprise. That kind of intensity carries over into the content and style of much reporting, so that almost any major development is presented with ponderous gravity.

Charles Kuralt always has understood that we yearn for a bit of gossamer, a touch of whimsy, wit, and wistfulness somewhere amidst the disaster—not unlike what the ancient scholars must have considered when they inserted the Book of Ruth, a sad-sweet story of love and loyalty, between the unrelieved Old Testament tales of war and death and hatefulness.

In the fall of 1980, Kuralt had been substituting for Cronkite on *The CBS Evening News*—and he had had enough:

> I'm about to commit a public indiscretion. I could be wrong about this, but I've been wondering whether one of our problems might be that we know too much. A reporter expressing the thought that there might be too much news in the country is like a General Motors vice president saying there might be too many cars, but I'll tell you what brought

this on. I have been substituting for Walter Cronkite...so I've been spending every day working on it. I've learned that orders for durable goods rose 8.4 percent in July and that these new orders were valued at a seasonally adjusted $72.1 billion, up $5.6 billion from June's $66.5 billion. Things like that.

I've learned that the Muslim militants are reviving the Kashmir issue, and that a couple tried to swap their baby for a sports car. Just as I was getting used to the idea of Hua Guofeng as premier of China, I learned that the premier of China is going to be Zhao Ziyang. A little girl, after an argument with her parents, put a tarantula in their bed. Pullman, it appears, will merge with Wheelabrator-Frye. And Reggie Jackson struck out four times in one game. And France is going to build a 1200-megawatt prototype nuclear reactor. Pork bellies are up. Feeder cattle are down. Edward Gierek is out. Chris Evert is in. Abbie Hoffman is back. A bomb went off in Guatemala City.

You can't spend your time, day in, day out, learning things like that without beginning to brood about it. No wonder Walter Cronkite takes such long vacations.

Maybe we know too much, too fast. If Billy Carter testifies under oath that he is not a boob or a wacko, 200 million Americans have this weighty fact impressed upon them within the hour. Maybe we know too much about what is happening. I'm certain that I know too much. So, I'm going to go somewhere and see what I can learn about the mountains and sunsets. Durable goods are just going to have to rise or fall without me...for a while.

Kuralt's reporting is an indication of the kind of news we get when journalists tell a story at a leisurely pace, asking questions and making comments but rarely being intrusive and allowing their interview subjects to do most of the talking. Reporters like Kuralt, David Brinkley, and Roger Mudd understand the value of watching *with* the viewers, sharing our wonder, our concern, our care.

Of course, with some exceptions, Kuralt's way is rarely the way it is. Perhaps that's the way it ought to be. The most informative and entertaining campaign reporting is that way; it allows the candidates to display, without reportorial interference, their smiles, pompadours, jogging outfits, their views on taxes, their attitudes on the Middle East, and sometimes their ignorance.

Too often, however, modern reporting becomes so kinetic, so determined to root out evil, that it sweeps over American institutions much as a flash flood hits a town's bottom land: there isn't much warning, nearly everybody runs for cover, and when the water recedes, there's nothing to show for it but mud and debris. As any farmer will tell you, only a slow, steady rain will help the crops grow. A slow, steady rain of information, with a minimum of journalistic lightning, thunder, and river-swelling downpours, would help us *all* grow, with little needless destruction.

8

The Genius...
and the Menace

*I*F GOOD JOURNALISM is unhurried, informative, entertaining, revealing, then *60 Minutes* represents the very best in modern journalism. If bad journalism is breathless, misleading, ostentatiously confrontational, pretentiously designed to anger us, then *60 Minutes* represents the very worst in modern journalism.

Best and worst, *60 Minutes* represents the world's most popular modern journalism — and its most profitable.

From its inception in 1968, *60 Minutes,* which was aired on alternate Tuesdays in prime time, had critical acclaim but small audiences. (It began its life opposite the highly popular dramatic program *Marcus Welby, M.D.,* and survived mostly because CBS News executives Richard Salant and Bill Leonard argued that it gave the network sorely needed prestige.)

After three years, the network moved it into "dead time" — 6:00 P.M. on Sundays — where, despite frequent pre-empting for sports events, its weekly format began attracting an ever-growing audience. The audience multiplied at such a rate, in fact, that in 1976 CBS put *60 Minutes* back into prime time — 7:00 P.M. on Sundays — to challenge the redoubtable Walt Disney productions.

With eight years of development behind it, with five years' time to build up a loyal following, *60 Minutes* was more than ready for prime time. Before long, *60 Minutes* began attracting a large enough audience to propel it into television's select ten top-rated programs, a charmed circle never contemplated by or demanded of television news.

60 Minutes has been in that pantheon ever since, often attaining the number one spot. Its budget, according to Robert Chandler, who was the CBS News vice president in charge of the show, is a relatively low $150,000 to $200,000 a program. Meanwhile, its high ratings command enormous commercial advertising rates (as much as $215,000 per commercial minute). That makes *60 Minutes* the financial backbone of the network's news operations.

Usually, there are six commercial minutes sold by the network during *60 Minutes*. A little arithmetic indicates that *60 Minutes* nets — after salaries and expenses for some of journalism's highest-paid correspondents, reporters, editors, and technicians — more than $1 million a week.

"Unbelievable," news correspondent Daniel Schorr says, demonstrating the extraordinary reaction among television's sachems to *60 Minutes'* success. "No one ever dreamed that anything coming out of the [television] news area would ever be among the top ten, top twenty programs. It was just simply never to be believed. And yet it happened."

There may be various theories about why it happened, but there is no argument about who made it happen: a feisty competitor named Don Hewitt.

Hewitt arrived at CBS in 1948, when television was in its infancy. Before the year was out, he had become the principal force behind the rudimentary coverage of the national political conventions and was the first permanent director of the fifteen-minute, five-night-a-week network news with Douglas Edwards.

Hewitt, as a television director, was responsible for the technical production of the program. His fertile imagination and competitiveness drove him to develop the use of graphics, models, and globes to illustrate the news; he even discovered the concept of "mixing" news film with voice-over narratives (the two-projector system). Before that, when a reporter commented on film, the camera had to show him, not the action. Before long, Hewitt integrated the technical requirements of television with the editorial content of the program, using the medium to enhance the news while emphasizing those news developments best suited to the medium. The term "producer" in television was created to describe Hewitt's total control of the program, distinguishing him from "mere" directors. Hewitt has been described by ABC News executive Av Westin as "the guy who invented the wheel in this business."

For fourteen years, Edwards and Hewitt were a team. However, Edwards was replaced by Walter Cronkite in 1962 as part of an effort to stem the popularity of NBC's Chet Huntley and David Brinkley. Hewitt stayed on as top dog with the title of executive producer. *The Huntley-Brinkley Report* had captured the ratings lead in 1960 over the Edwards and Hewitt offering. By the fall of 1963, CBS had persuaded its affiliates to allow Hewitt and Cronkite to extend the evening news to a half-hour. NBC followed suit shortly, and it was the winter of 1967 before Cronkite and CBS achieved parity in the ratings with NBC. It was not until 1970, when Huntley retired, that *The CBS Evening News with Walter Cronkite* won undisputed possession of first place in the hearts and television sets of America's news-watchers.

By then, Hewitt was long gone. In 1964, Fred Friendly, then president of CBS News, took the evening news program away from Hewitt. Friendly believed the news should be more a forum for ideas than a showcase for events. Before that happened, though — before Don Hewitt was sentenced by Friendly to four years of exile, during which he retained his title, his income, and his perquisites, but lost his fief and vassals—Hewitt had established himself as a legend in television news innovation.

Tired of Douglas Edwards glancing too often at his notes during his daily telecast, Hewitt (before the development of Teleprompter and similar devices) urged Edwards to learn Braille. ("I still think it's a great idea," Hewitt remarked to a journalist about twenty-five years later.)

Gary Paul Gates quotes Hewitt, "I'm the original 'Smilin' Jack' of TV journalism. I fly by the seat of my pants. I operate by visceral reactions." When a film story he was editing did not open with a "punchy" lead, Gates wrote, Hewitt would yell, "How many times do I have to say it? You've got to get 'em into the fucking tent."

In 1962, when an airliner crashed in Jamaica Bay in New York, Hewitt couldn't resist rushing to the scene. There was a tugboat strike at the time, but Hewitt spotted one tied up at a dock, located the owner in Connecticut, offered him double the normal amount to hire the boat for a day, and, while his competition was shore-bound and could not get close to the downed airliner, Hewitt and a crew were chugging to the scene.

Around that time, Hewitt was on the scene of a prison "riot" in New Jersey. In fact, a rather minor disturbance had been quelled by the time he arrived with a camera crew. Officials did not want him to enter the compound for fear that the sight of the cameras would set off the prisoners again. However, Hewitt pleaded the First Amendment, and after pledging that neither he nor anyone in the crew would say a word to the prisoners, he was allowed to enter to take some pictures. Once inside, Hewitt looked up at the cell block and the inmates peering at him through the bars. He then slapped a hand into the crook of his other arm, jerked up his fist, and extended his middle finger—a combination of the Sicilian sign of contempt with the American signal to "shove it." The prisoners started clamoring in response—and Hewitt returned to the studio with "good footage." As Hewitt told writer Harry Stein more than two and a half decades later, "I used to think of myself as Hildy Johnson."

It was more as the impresario—the editor Walter Burns in *The Front Page*, not the aggressive reporter Hildy Johnson—that Hewitt conceived the idea of a televised news magazine and shaped it into *60 Minutes*.

Hewitt has his own ideas about why *60 Minutes* is a critical and popular success. Oddly, they are not particularly incisive, perhaps because he does operate viscerally rather than intellectually. But others seem to have a keener fix on what makes Hewitt and his *tick-tick-ticking* news program run so successfully.

"In a sense," Daniel Schorr recalled, "I was present at the birth of *60 Minutes*." Hewitt had come to the CBS News bureau in Washington, Schorr's base then, to explain the show. Schorr remembered Hewitt discussing the importance of visuals to the magazine format, and his reliance on New York reporters Harry Reasoner and Mike Wallace to do no more than three or four pieces during the sixty-minute program.

"And what he said was that he thought there was a bigger audience for information than [viewed] existing news broadcasts, but that they had to be brought in by using the methods borrowed from entertainment. It was clear that he thought in terms of confrontation as the chief value on television."

Schorr was familiar with what he calls Hewitt's "flamboyant approach to news, which managed sometimes to dramatize news." He recalled that in early 1960, when he was a CBS correspondent in Germany, Hewitt arrived in Berlin "I guess on some kind of junket; he was at loose ends, just traveling around." It was during "one of the recurring little flaps over closing of the autobahn and air corridors and all the rest—small, harassing things that were being done to us in those days. And we stood there together in Berlin at Checkpoint Bravo, where the East German police were making difficulties for Allied (and especially American) cars that wanted to travel through East Germany to get to West Germany."

Schorr and a crew had decided the correspondent would stand about a hundred yards from the checkpoint and turn to indicate it when the film started to roll. "And Don Hewitt said, 'What happens when you get up to the East German checkpoint? Do they stop you? They won't let you get through?' Hewitt turns to my cameraman and says, 'Do you people have a wireless microphone?'

"Yeah. It was part of their equipment. 'How far will it carry?' Depends, of course, on conditions—a hundred and fifty, two hundred, three hundred yards. 'Why don't you [Schorr] put a wireless microphone on, we follow you in your car as you go up there, and you try to get through, and we record—with the camera held here and the wireless microphone is on you, concealed, and you just say, "Why can't I go through? I'm an American. I want to go!" And they'll tell you whatever they say.'

"We did, and it was immensely successful. It made the story much more concrete. All the menace of East German troops with their guns and all the rest of it. Being stopped personally...I represented the whole United States. And that was the kind of eye he brings to these things.

"It isn't that he will necessarily distort the news, but that he will bring it down to a simple and concrete image which will make it much [easier] to sell to an undifferentiated audience."

The casting of the correspondent as a stalwart, facing down foes on behalf of the viewing audience (if not always of the United States), is an indelible image of *60 Minutes,* created, obviously, by Don Hewitt.

In fact, Hewitt maintains that the story is secondary to the reporter (although, I hasten to add, he does not mean that a reporter can please the viewers with a juggling act; he means that viewers identify with those correspondents who ask the questions they would ask and register the same kind of awe, disbelief, amusement, bemusement).

When Hewitt harks back to his directing duties on *See It Now* and suggests that people "weren't interested so much in the stories; they were interested in Murrow—what Murrow found out," he is twisting a knife slowly in the side of his former nemesis, Fred Friendly, Murrow's producer and a believer in dead earnestness in television news.

Friendly, to be sure, rarely misses an opportunity to return the favor.

"They're a good show, but they are now in the ratings business. They think if they slipped out of the top 10, they'd be in trouble," Friendly said in a *New York Times* magazine interview in 1979. "The show is excellent," he said in a 1980 interview in *The Los Angeles Times*. "But it could be so much more. It's got a lock now on one hour of prime time. No one in news had that kind of franchise before, not even Ed Murrow. They could do so much with it. You see that when they're at their best. I just expect more of them than they do of themselves." To which Hewitt replied to writer Harry Stein, "It may do something for Fred Friendly's ego to rap me. It does nothing for my ego to reply." (Too good to be spontaneous, I think; these two seem to have practiced over the years to reach their carefully calibrated level of mutual dislike.)

Attitudes toward *60 Minutes* obviously are shaped by general attitudes toward news. Hewitt told an interviewer that people are "less interested in the news of the last twenty-four hours than information about the times we live in. Besides, we have the six-thirty news on ahead of us."

Roger Mudd does not agree that *60 Minutes* necessarily provides information about the times we live in. "Generally," Mudd says, "the stories they go after are the stories that are revelatory or breath-sucking or confrontation-promoting, because they've found an audience there that really looks forward to that, likes to see the devils get their due. Occasionally they will have long and thoughtful interviews. But generally their stuff (and also *20/20* and NBC's *Magazine*) is—I don't want to say, 'a streak of yellow journalism'— confrontational journalism.

"It seems to me that when you have a broadcast like that—
60 Minutes in particular, with such an enormous audience
and one of the top-ten-rated every week—that you have
some obligation to take that audience and give it more than
simply various Perils of Pauline.

"'Here's our favorite reporter! Will he get past the
receptionist in the Medical Arts Building lobby? Will they
block the door? Will the irate blood technician come out and
hurl himself up against Mike Wallace?' All that sort of stuff
becomes kind of exciting. But that bothers me. That's not
reporting. That's an awful lot of acting going on there. And to
do that involves a deliberate decision on the part of the
management of these broadcasts to set up a camera, to say to
the reporter 'Now you walk along and we're gonna be right
behind you and we'll be shooting off the tailgate of the station
wagon. You walk along here, and then you turn left and you
ring the bell and then you face this way.' That's a stage-
managed operation. That's not journalism as I think it ought
to be. Tennessee Williams could block that one out: 'Stage
left.'"

Schorr believes that *60 Minutes* represents "a very large
thing that was happening in the whole field of television and
news." *60 Minutes*, he says, "clearly was a marriage of
entertainment values and news values. Just as news was
borrowing from show biz, the entertainment side of television
was finding that the raw material of history offered them
better plots than they could devise."

So-called docudramas became highly popular—*Raid at
Entebbe, Death of a Princess, Holocaust, Roots,* the Jean
Harris trial. Two advisers to President Carter—Hamilton
Jordan and Gerald Rafshoon—planned to tell the inside story
of the Iran crisis as a docudrama. "A certain kind of subtle
thing has begun to happen in the American mind as a result of
this crossover, in which people are really no longer sure what
is real and what is unreal," Schorr commented.

"Anybody who stands back and looks at what's been
happening in television in the past ten years will know that

the entertainment side and the news side have been slowly drawing closer together. News borrows entertainment techniques; entertainment borrows news plots and documentary techniques. And what nobody has thought about is the subliminal effect on the audience.

"Now, into this situation comes *60 Minutes*, with a producer who combines in himself this great instinct for dramatizing information. He knows that television is *par excellence* a medium for confrontation between two people. And so almost every important story is set up with a confrontational theme — it is something against something, somebody against somebody. If nothing else, it is his correspondent against somebody. And that is why Mike Wallace is so perfect for this thing. Mike Wallace easily slips into the confrontational mode."

Daniel Schorr should know. Long a Peck's Bad Boy to CBS, Schorr, early in 1976, had obtained a congressional report on activities of the CIA and had been excerpting portions of the classified findings in his news reports. But he also thought the entire, 340-page document (called the Pike Report, after Representative Otis Pike, the investigating committee's chairman) should be published by CBS. The network declined, and before long, the document appeared in *The Village Voice*, with an introduction by Aaron Latham, then the fiancé of CBS News Washington correspondent Lesley Stahl.

Shortly after the publication of the Pike Report, *The Washington Post* published a story suggesting that Schorr had given the report to *The Village Voice*. The House Ethics Committee summoned Schorr to testify; the committee wanted to know from whom Schorr had acquired the classified committee report. Meanwhile, Schorr had been suspended by CBS, ostensibly because the network thought the impending hearing might create a conflict of interest with his coverage of the Congress. Actually, an internal matter seems to have been at the root of his "temporary" suspension. After the report was published in *The Village Voice*, Schorr left the impression with several CBS News executives that he had not passed the report on for publication; instead, he seemed to imply that somehow Stahl may have obtained the report and passed it along to her fiancé, presumably to provide him with an important news beat.

Needless to say, the enmities created over this event have been long-lasting. Schorr, of course, had in fact given the report to *The Village Voice* (not in return for any money, as had been reported at the time, but for a contribution to the Reporters Committee for Freedom of the Press). He denies implying that Stahl took the report. Others, like Socolow, remember it quite differently. He maintains that Schorr specifically suggested there was a Stahl-Latham cabal to filch the material, thus deflecting corporate antagonism from Schorr for leaking material without CBS's express permission. Many former colleagues, including Stahl, rarely recall Schorr with unbridled affection.

Still, it was the publicity accompanying the leak of the entire report (as distinguished from portions of it, which had been leaked earlier to Schorr and other journalists) that set some Pike Committee members' teeth on edge. Some insisted on finding out who slipped the report to Schorr, and Schorr, claiming First Amendment privileges, didn't care to tell.

It was not the first time Schorr had been out of favor with his bosses. In 1964, shortly before the Republican National Convention, Schorr reported from Germany that, after his expected nomination, Barry Goldwater would vacation at Berchtesgaden, which, Schorr pointed out, had been Adolf Hitler's favorite retreat. (Schorr also mentioned that Goldwater would be the guest of Lieutenant General William Quinn, commander of the United States Seventh Army. According to a book by his daughter, the controversial CBS and *Washington Post* reporter Sally Quinn, the general was passed over for anticipated promotions because of the Schorr allusion, which seemed to cast him as a political ally of Goldwater.)

CBS president William Paley was outraged. A close friend of former President Eisenhower, who had made no secret of his antipathy toward a Goldwater nomination, Paley was embarrassed by charges from Goldwater's camp that the Schorr report represented part of an anti-Goldwater crusade by the network. Schorr was reprimanded.

A decade later, Schorr struck again. The occasion was a discussion with Duke University students in January 1975, five months after President Nixon had resigned from office as a result of imminent impeachment by Congress because of Watergate-related crimes. According to a report in the campus newspaper, Schorr told the students that CBS management had instructed Walter Cronkite, Eric Sevareid, and Dan Rather to avoid vindictiveness toward Nixon during a post–resignation speech analysis. The fourth member of the discussion group, Roger Mudd, had not received that official word, according to Schorr, and therefore had been more sharply critical of the disgraced President. Schorr himself had been excluded from the discussion, the story suggested, because he had refused to adhere to the company policy.

Indeed, the comments by CBS's intrepid reporters had been surprisingly gentle, perhaps because the reporters believed that one shouldn't kick a President when he's down. To Cronkite, the Nixon speech was "conciliatory"; to Sevareid, "magnanimous"; and Rather thought it contained "a touch of class — more than that, a touch of majesty." Through it all, Mudd wore the expression of a preacher at a county fair who, looking for the evening prayer meeting, had wandered into the girlie show: he was amazed by what he saw but was too transfixed to leave.

After what seemed like an eternity, Mudd observed that the speech "did not deal with the realities of why [Nixon] was leaving."

(Mudd said later that in his comments that night, he was trying to represent the likely reaction among congressmen on Capitol Hill, Mudd's principal beat. To that end, he described "the deficiencies and the elisions with the truth and the sliding over and the rounding of the corners and [his] not accounting for certain major factors in his departure.")

"What made it look 'uncool' and 'hot,'" Mudd recalled, using McLuhanesque terms to describe his memorable impact on viewers that night, "is that the other three went in a different direction. I think under any other circumstances my post-speech analysis would have been fairly ho-hum. It was not particularly startling. But it was a very emotional evening for the country. People wrote to me that they were throwing drinks at the television set. And then I came on, and they cheered. I think what I said was heard in a very high emotional state by the people of the country."

The report of Schorr's criticisms at Duke stirred the emotions of Cronkite, Sevareid, and Rather, who jointly sent a letter to *New York* magazine in response to a story about Schorr's allegations. The three charged that a "slander" had been committed against them and CBS executives in the accusation that they had conspired to "go soft on Nixon." The three, their letter said, merely "felt constrained from whipping an obviously beaten man."

Gary Paul Gates reported that Sevareid, who had interceded with Paley on Schorr's behalf during the 1964 Goldwater flap, was particularly outraged, snapping, "And this is the goddam thanks I get!"

Schorr maintained that he had not been critical of his colleagues, although he had made some remarks not flattering to management. He informed his superiors that his talk had been taped, and the CBS executives, Gates wrote, were eager to hear it and judge for themselves the gravity of the comments. Then one of the more bizarre phenomena involving modern journalistic infighting occurred. As CBS News executives were listening to the tape of Schorr's discussion at Duke, the tape reached the point where Schorr began to examine the network's coverage of Nixon's resignation — and went dead. Just as a year or so earlier, when Americans were incredulous over the claimed accidental eighteen-and-a-half-minute gap in a taped, potentially incriminating White House conversation, the Daniel Schorr tape contained a gap of its own. Though few network officials would comment on the coincidence, Gates reports that Sevareid said, "I'm sure the son of a bitch erased it himself."

By the time of his suspension in early 1976, then, Schorr would not have won many popularity contests around CBS. However, it was not until September that Schorr's conflict with the House Ethics Committee was resolved. By that time, antipathy toward him by the media in general (mostly because of the initial misapprehension that Schorr had sold the Pike Report) had turned to solid support. Here was a fraternity brother being threatened with prison for contempt of Congress unless he identified a source. Schorr, with attorney Joseph Califano at his side, dramatically refused to yield to the committee's entreaties; in the end, the committee averted a clash of constitutional rights by voting not to prosecute.

It was at that point that Daniel Schorr learned firsthand how devastating the confrontational style of Mike Wallace, coupled with Don Hewitt's instinct for the pith of any news event, could be — even for an old television hand who was no stranger to controversy. Daniel Schorr was about to become a guest on *60 Minutes*.

It is not a fond memory; at the beginning of our conversations, Schorr did not wish to talk about it. He was eager to discuss *60 Minutes* conceptually, however.

"In the case of *60 Minutes*," he said, "it is so important to maintain the dramatic effect that there is no question that as they shoot the material, the material is arranged in order to make a plot of it. That is both the genius of Don Hewitt and, of course, the menace of Don Hewitt. Nobody who has ever participated in a *60 Minutes* [segment] has come away without a feeling that there was something that wasn't quite [right]. I think some of it is done quite unconsciously. They have a formula—a successful formula. The formula consists of taking this raw material and building a piece somewhere on the borderline between drama and news.

"It has a powerful impact, but the impact comes partly from following the dramatic rhythm and rearranging the information to fit that dramatic rhythm. I am not condemning it. On one hand, it does manage to convey a certain amount of information to more people than have ever gotten information on television. On the other hand, I do sometimes worry about the nature of that information."

One of the times that Schorr had cause to worry about the nature of the information conveyed by a *60 Minutes* segment occurred on September 26, 1976. It was that Sunday evening that Daniel Schorr watched himself on television being interviewed by Mike Wallace; it was that night that Daniel Schorr learned how it felt to be the pursued, not the pursuer—and how television news could, overnight, erase a national image of Dan Schorr the media hero, and substitute the new image of Dan Schorr the media opportunist.

9

The Worst Brew
of Bad Taste

60 *Minutes* has a reputation of going for the jugular. At
the same time, it wraps itself firmly in protective armor.
Usually, it succeeds in subduing its victim while evading
serious harm. The reason it usually wins is a matter of basic
mathematics: when *60 Minutes* goes on the attack, as many as
forty million people are watching as it skewers its victim;
when *60 Minutes* is the target, the arena is most often a
publication with a circulation of a few hundred thousand, if
that. When a major television program did, in fact, examine
the journalistic ethics of *60 Minutes* in September 1981, that
program was (you guessed it) *60 Minutes*. However noble the
effort at self-appraisal, it was unlikely that *60 Minutes* would
provide the sort of information designed to knock it out of the
ten top-rated programs on television. Indeed, critic Tom
Shales described the program as an exercise in self-
exoneration.

Given its virtual imperviousness to criticism, it is not
surprising to discover that *60 Minutes* flies the Double
Standard from its antenna.

For instance, in May 1979, Harry Stein reported in *The*

New York Times magazine that Mike Wallace, when being interviewed, "is guarded; during one recent session, he snapped off the reporter's tape-recorder every time the conversation edged into what he deemed sensitive territory." Walter Anderson, managing editor of *Parade,* told Stein that Wallace, after an early 1979 interview, visited the publication's offices and asked to see the galleys in advance of publication. The request was refused. After the article appeared, however, Wallace discussed it with Anderson for more than an hour. "I was surprised," Anderson said to Stein, that "one of America's premier journalists would be worried about a magazine article."

In the fall of 1980, when writer Paul Good was questioning Wallace about a suit brought against *60 Minutes* that was settled out of court, Wallace took umbrage. "I am angry," Good quoted Wallace as saying. "You were not at the trial. You say we apologized and we did not. You don't know what you're talking about."

Good proceeded to quote from the transcript of the trial, and Wallace backed down. "Forgive me for being pissed," Good says Wallace told him.

In the spring of 1981, *60 Minutes* correspondent Morley Safer planned an update of a segment critical of Haiti that Wallace had broadcast nearly a decade earlier. The Wallace report had described the regime of François (Papa Doc) Duvalier as "bloody." Wallace's wife has relatives in Haiti and, Wallace recalled, "the story caused an infinite amount of distress to the family in Haiti. They asked me, candidly, not to do another one." Wallace heard of Safer's plan, went to Safer — at the suggestion of executive producer Don Hewitt — and asked him to kill the story. Safer agreed. Then someone leaked the story to muckraker Jack Anderson, forcing *60 Minutes* to eat crow.

"My motive, the safety of my family, was a decent one," Wallace explained in a statement. "Having said that, Hewitt shouldn't have told me to go to Morley and Morley shouldn't have said, 'Okay.'" ("My motive, the safety of our country, was a decent one," President Nixon might have said. "Having said that, I think the CIA shouldn't have agreed to ask the FBI to stay out of Watergate, and the FBI shouldn't have said, 'Okay.'") "Both Mike and I made a mistake," Safer said, "but I was caught off guard. This is the only time in my experience that someone tried to wave me off a story."

In an October 1980 article in *Time* examining so-called reality programing on television (like the show *That's Incredible!*), in which daredevils sometimes are injured while performing stunts for the cameras, Safer described such programs as "the worst brew of bad taste yet concocted by the network witches."

Yet a few months earlier, Safer was the correspondent on a *60 Minutes* segment portraying how a man, who had repeatedly threatened to murder his wife, was allowed to leave the premises of a psychiatric institution to which he had been confined by court order. It was the story of the murder of Eva Berwid by her husband, Adam. The story had appeared earlier in *The Village Voice*, written by Teresa Carpenter; it was one of the articles (the other was on the murder of Allard Lowenstein) honored with a Pulitzer Prize after Janet Cooke of *The Washington Post* was forced to return hers. What made it a *60 Minutes* story, even after it had been treated lengthily in a newspaper, was a passage in Carpenter's account referring to a frantic telephone call Eva Berwid made to a police emergency number. The life-and-death call had been recorded — and it was dramatic.

Safer and *60 Minutes'* cameras followed the trail of Adam Berwid from the institution to his wife's home.

> Eva Berwid now has only hours to live [Safer said, narrating the *60 Minutes* segment]. Shortly after breakfast, pass in hand, Adam Berwid walks off the hospital grounds. He boards a train and, within the hour, he is only blocks away from Eva Berwid's home... He goes to a sporting goods store and buys a hunting knife... He calls the hospital, tells them he's missed his train, he'll be back soon. What actually happened was he came to the house. He came around the back and looked in

the window and saw his wife and children. At the same moment, she saw him. As she dashed for the phone, he broke in. She did manage to dial 9-1-1, the police emergency number.

The scene shifted to a Nassau County, New York, police station, where Safer stood next to the machine that had recorded Eva Berwid's terror-stricken plea.

SAFER: At exactly 5:07, the Nassau County Police received a 9-1-1 call. It was from a woman — frightened, hysterical, screaming. Here's a tape of that call.
EVA BERWID (on tape): Olga! Call the police! Olga!
SAFER: She says, "Olga!" Olga's the name of the oldest child. "Olga! Call the police!" And then the 9-1-1 operator.
OPERATOR (on tape): Stop screaming and tell me where you are. Where are you?
EVA BERWID (on tape): [Indistinct; screaming.]
SAFER: The woman is shouting, "He's killing me!"
OPERATOR (on tape): Ma'am? [Eva screaming.] Lieutenant . . . Lieutenant, I have this woman on this line. She's hysterical. Something's wrong there, but I don't know what. She's calling some guy's name. He don't answer. [Eva says something.] Ma'am?
EVA BERWID (on tape): Oh! Oh, God!
OPERATOR (on tape): Ma'am?
SAFER: The police could not get a name or address out of her. If they had been able to, they say, they would have been there in three minutes. And then the line went dead. It was about ten or eleven minutes past five, the approximate time of death of Eva Berwid.

There are distinctions between the *60 Minutes* segment on Eva Berwid and concepts behind shows like *That's Incredible!*, but they are not necessarily redeeming ones. *60 Minutes* may argue that it is defensible to report an event that already has taken place but it is not supportable to arrange for a daredevil to risk life and limb for the diversion of the kind of audience that watches auto races in the perverse hope of seeing a smash-up. Further, the portion of the segment dealing with the murder of Mrs. Berwid was part of a larger story probing the security system of New York's psychiatric institutions.

It is doubtful, however, that *60 Minutes* would have considered the story had the blood-curdling tape recording of a woman being stabbed to death not been available. Remember, the story did not result from original sleuthing by *60 Minutes*, as many do; it had appeared earlier in *The Village Voice* and been reported and written about fully. More revealing, though, was the use of the Eva Berwid tape in the segment. It added no information that could not have been provided less shockingly. Grisly as it is to hear someone in the process of being murdered while screaming for help and appealing to God, it was even more chilling to realize this was happening in front of her children: the children watched as their father murdered their mother! (Safer didn't tell us what happened to the children. They were not harmed physically, according to the account in *The Village Voice*, though the story by Carpenter indicated that they subsequently needed psychological counseling.)

That's Incredible! pays performers to risk their necks; viewers know in advance why they are tuning in—thrills, spills, shock, perhaps even a touch of blood. Presumably, a viewer watches *60 Minutes* for somewhat different reasons—information, interest, the real-life confrontation between the good guys and the bad guys. Yet with the use of the Berwid tape, *60 Minutes* clearly was reaching for the same level of "entertainment" associated with the programs that Safer, for one, derogates.

At a 1979 television industry conference on docudramas, network executives and television critics generally condemned the genre because, they said, docudramas sacrificed accuracy in favor of dramatic impact, unlike news programs like *60 Minutes*. One of the participants, Art Buchwald (who had appeared on the first broadcast of *60 Minutes* and is a regular viewer), commented: "What makes you people think that television news and *60 Minutes* are not also 'docudramas'? I've been at congressional hearings that lasted for hours, and on the news they use one tiny snippet where the Senator screams at the witness, 'You are a blackguard and a liar, sir!' Is that an accurate picture of what went on there?"

Though Daniel Schorr's own *60 Minutes* docudrama contained nothing to rival the shock of hearing a murder in progress, it demonstrated how easily someone can be impaled by *60 Minutes* for the diversion of millions of viewers.

In late September 1976, after the House Ethics Committee voted not to prosecute him, Schorr received a call from *60 Minutes*. "Mike Wallace calls up and says, 'You're a hero,'" Schorr recalled, "'and — let's look at it objectively — you are a story from that point of view.' He invited me to be on [*60 Minutes*], [giving] the impression — which I should have suspected — that the purpose was one thing, when clearly the purpose was adversary.

"If anybody should know Mike Wallace's technique, it's somebody in the profession — myself. I felt a little bit conned. Mike denies that he meant any conning, but when he called me up, there was a lot of 'You're going to think this is awfully funny, me asking you to appear on *60 Minutes*,' but the fact of the matter is, I was feeling very high because we'd won."

After the committee had ended its Schorr investigation, CBS News president Richard Salant telephoned Schorr, asking him to be in New York on Monday, September 26, to discuss, as Schorr recalled it, his reinstatement. Schorr had been suspended (he used the word *fired*) by Salant seven months earlier. "Everything was looking very rosy in this situation," Schorr remembered.

Wallace arranged to interview Schorr on Saturday for the next evening's program; Schorr would meet with Salant the day after *60 Minutes* was on the air. Wallace, Schorr said, had been "briefed" on Schorr's planned meeting with Salant, a meeting Salant had instructed Schorr to keep confidential to avoid arousing interest among reporters.

"In the course of the interview, Mike Wallace says, 'I understand you're seeing Dick Salant on Monday,' and that's dirty pool, because it is not a reporter interviewing; it is the company person with company information interviewing. At that point he says, 'I understand you're going to be faced with three charges,' and I said, 'Well, that's more than I know.'

"While I think you've got to take your chances in these interviews, the one thing that happened to me that I don't think has ever happened to somebody else is being interviewed by a CBS correspondent for a CBS broadcast with material from inside the company being used to [put] me at a disadvantage — [information] which the company had asked me not to talk about."

Schorr said that Califano, his attorney, had warned him against agreeing to the interview. "You know what Mike Wallace is like," Schorr said Califano told him. "No one has ever come off well." I asked Schorr whether he thought the Shah had not "come off well" in his interviews over the years with Wallace. "Yeah," Schorr said, "until recently." Referring to the *60 Minutes* segment focusing on torture in Iran before the Shah's overthrow, Schorr said, "I thought his picking on the Shah now when he was down was a singularly graceless thing for Mike Wallace to do, having ridden all those years on the bounties of the Shah's interviews."

A comparison of the transcript of Wallace's interview with Schorr with the transcript of what appeared on the air shows Wallace's style, a style many journalists find advantageous in their work. It may be called the iron-fist-in-the-velvet-glove approach: soften 'em up, and then flatten 'em from the blind side.

The "charges" to which Wallace referred were that Schorr had accused the network of ordering correspondents Cronkite, Sevareid, and Rather to "go easy" on Nixon on resignation night; that Schorr had said during his suspension that television news should not be taken seriously; and that Schorr had wrongly implicated Lesley Stahl in the leak of the Pike Report to *The Village Voice*.

When Wallace began the interview with Schorr, there was no suggestion that any of those things would be discussed. On the contrary, Wallace set a tone indicating that Schorr was indeed a hero to journalists and that the situation was indeed rosy.

"Dan," Wallace opened when the cameras started to roll, "you have my profound admiration and that of your colleagues here and elsewhere, I know, for the eloquent and persuasive case that you made for the protection of a reporter's sources."

Wallace then asked Schorr what leaked material he would and would not publish, whether he would publish grand jury leaks and under what circumstances, the motives of those who leak information to the press about the CIA, the FBI, and the White House, whether the motives of leaks should be reported—questions that provoked lengthy, serious replies, none of which was included in the televised segment.

During that portion of the interview, there was a technical problem that interrupted the taping, and Wallace asked Don Hewitt whether he would have to start from the beginning. He turned to Schorr and said, humorously but prophetically, "I'm going to have this line about my 'profound admiration' down pat by the time. As a matter of fact, what I'm going to say [is] 'I think you are a shit, Schorr, and as most of your colleagues do, too, and...'"

At that point, Wallace was instructed to resume taping with a question he had asked about the use by reporters of grand jury leaks. That was on the seventh page of a seventy-five-page manuscript; on the twenty-first page, Wallace asked Schorr the first question that was used in the televised interview (which ran for thirteen minutes; the interview lasted more than an hour and a quarter). That question was why Schorr, over the years, had been in so many "flaps." Later, Wallace aimed his questions with precision at those issues of greater interest to CBS than to the general public: the flaps with his colleagues, the Stahl incident, and whether Schorr would prefer being a print journalist.

Nowhere was there any suggestion of admiration for Schorr on the part of Wallace or of Schorr's colleagues. This is the opening as broadcast:

WALLACE: What about Dan Schorr?

Almost every one of us in the news business has been asked that question the past few months. Since last February he's been on suspension from all reportorial assignments at CBS — although at full pay — until the end of congressional investigations into his leak to the newspaper *The Village Voice* of a secret, House committee report on the CIA.

Well, this past week, the House Ethics Committee voted not to punish Schorr, and their investigation ended. However, his differences with certain of his colleagues are still to be resolved — as [is] his future with CBS News.

Dan and I sat down to have a chat. It was not an easy chore. I didn't want the interview to be perceived either as making a case for CBS News, or for Dan Schorr.

It was on the second reel used to record the interview that Wallace first asked Schorr whether he wanted to come back to CBS and whether he was angry at his colleagues.

WALLACE: And do you want to come back to CBS?

SCHORR: It seems to me that after these seven months of...not talking to each other, that propriety dictates that questions like this first be discussed with bosses and not colleagues.

WALLACE: Are you angry with your colleagues?

SCHORR: No, I'm not angry at my colleagues. I think that partly because of mistakes that I made and partly because of a whole lot of other reasons, that I had a great deal of difficulty in making it understood to some of my colleagues what I had done and why. I think that, however, from the moment that a subpoena came from the House Ethics Committee, that kind of stripped away all the trivia and peripheral problems that had gone before...I thought that my colleagues, on the whole, were wonderfully supportive on the principle that I felt was really important.

WALLACE: And now that the confrontation between you and...the Congress is over, what about your colleagues? You and your colleagues?

SCHORR: My colleagues, in a very wide sense, not only go through CBS but have a lot to do with a lot of newspaper columnists and a lot of other people with whom I have problems of one sort or another.

WALLACE: But inside the family, inside the family—there is perhaps more urgency...Animosities have built to be resolved.

SCHORR: There were animosities. We are all rather a high-strung breed, aren't we? There were animosities that existed before any of this happened, animosities that may continue. I have never been able to conduct my life as a popularity contest and, oddly enough, popularity is not my immediate concern.

WALLACE: What's your immediate concern?

SCHORR: ...To come out of this with as much dignity as possible, to try as far as possible to get over the troubles...The time has come for some sort of healing...

Wallace wasn't having any. He came right back with a question about whether "the ball is in Dan Schorr's court," meaning the decision about his future with CBS News. Schorr said he didn't know. Wallace then asked whether Schorr would apologize "for what you've characterized as trivia." Schorr said he wanted to clear up misunderstandings, and where he may have done something less than honorable, he would apologize.

None of that—absolutely none of it—got into the ten pages that constituted the entire televised segment. Watching at home, a viewer would not have sensed the slightest hint of contrition in Schorr. He would have heard Wallace's description of Schorr as "cocky"; the admission that, for Schorr, "there has never been a red carpet within CBS, as everybody in CBS well knows"; and mention of Schorr's flaps, including the one over the news analysis on the night of Nixon's resignation. Schorr suggested defensively that CBS management had "manipulated" his colleagues to attack him.

Wallace then asserted that Schorr was suspended because he leaked the Pike Report to *The Village Voice*, denied it for "a number of hours at least," and then "permitted your colleague Lesley Stahl to be implicated as the person who had leaked the Pike papers."

The final question of the televised segment was one that, during the taping, had been shouted to Wallace from outside the booth—apparently by Don Hewitt.

Hewitt or someone had called out, "I would like to know, all things being equal, if Dan had to pursue his career in journalism in print rather than broadcasting after the sensible things he said."

"Well, I think he's answered that," Wallace said, probably unaware that his response sounded, ironically, like a lawyer's objection during an adversarial court proceeding. "But," he went on, "I'll ask that again. 'On balance, Dan, would you rather now be a print journalist than a broadcast journalist?'" That question and Schorr's answer ended the televised segment. Schorr responded thoughtfully, but closed, unfortunately for him, with the observation that "I don't need broadcasting as much as I thought I did."

"The prosecution rests," Wallace might have added.

When Harry Stein interviewed Wallace in the spring of 1979 about the Schorr segment, about two and a half years after it had been aired, Wallace "was obviously annoyed by [Schorr's] complaint." "Listen," Stein quoted Wallace as saying, "I'd heard Dan Schorr on freedom of the press at B'nai B'rith dinners, in the newsroom, and Sigma Delta Chi luncheons a million times. I was after a totally different story. It reminds me of Henry Kissinger. Kissinger doesn't like to be edited, either."

I talked to Wallace about the Schorr segment a year later, in the spring of 1980, and the tone of his response was gentler, even mournful—but his message was not. "First of all," Wallace said to me, "I had the greatest admiration for Schorr. Still have the greatest admiration for Schorr. Liked him when he was in our Washington bureau, think we miss him now. He was a maverick, and we needed a maverick in the Washington bureau. Dan is sore at me because I caught him out. It's as simple as that. I treated him like I would have treated anybody else...I don't regret that it was done that way; I regret that he *feels* that way...Dan and I were friends; Dan and I, I guess, are not friends anymore...My admiration for him remains absolutely undiminished. He, for whatever reason and for however long, decided that he was going to tell less than the truth about Lesley Stahl...And we interviewed him for, I guess, an hour and we used ten or twelve minutes of it. That's pretty good; that's only six to one. Frequently, we'll go twenty to one on a piece. You're gonna go maybe twenty to one or fifty to one on your book...

"We seldom work with this kind of a deadline, but because it was Yom Kippur, because he didn't want to do the interview before sundown, we had to do it late in the afternoon. It turned out to be a Saturday afternoon...and we had to stay there until two, three o'clock Sunday morning to get it edited [for Sunday] evening's broadcast...The tack which I took with him, and it was hardly an investigative piece, and it was just nothing in the world but an interview, was a fellow who is that important this week or this month, who has just testified before the Congress, who is wrapping himself in the First Amendment, he would be the last person in the world who should not be questioned closely about the kind of an individual he is.

"What is his morality? Where does he come from, this guy Schorr...this man who takes it upon himself to ask all kinds of questions of virtually anybody? Joe Califano, his attorney, told him not to do it. It was hilarious, really, because he sat there—Don [Hewitt] will tell you, because Don and I went down to do the broadcast together."*

Told that Schorr had criticized him as "graceless" for doing a negative segment on the Shah after he had profited from access to the Shah, Wallace replied, "'Graceless' would be the wrong word...Biting the hand that fed us? Is that what

*In its September 1981 "self-examination," *60 Minutes'* guest host, Jeff Greenfield, wrung from Mike Wallace the admission he would not like to be the target of a *60 Minutes*–style adversarial inquiry.

Dan suggests? I think... Forgive me. Really, I'm astonished, 'cause I really do respect Dan. He is a good reporter. He is my kind of reporter, and I really am surprised that he still is bitter and that's too bad."

Schorr might be angry, I suggested, because Wallace had used inside information about the Lesley Stahl incident that the general public had not known. "I would certainly hope I use inside information in every interview I do," Wallace responded. "What in the world are you in business to do as a reporter if you're not gonna use inside information? This was an effort to draw a kind of character sketch of Schorr and to face him with, conceivably, some... contradictions in his own personality, if you will, or in his own background."

I asked whether there had not been some interest expressed by CBS officials in having Wallace conduct the interview. "On the contrary," Wallace said; "they deplored my doing it." Wallace said the idea for a Schorr segment occurred to him when he saw Schorr interviewed on *The CBS Evening News* the day he had testified. Schorr was asked by a CBS reporter whether he intended to remain with the network, "and he said something about the ball is now in CBS's court...

"'Jesus,' I said. 'My, that's a wonderful idea! Let me interview Schorr.' Didn't call Salant. Didn't call any of the people in the front office. I called Hewitt. He says [Wallace smacked his hands together], 'Great! Call Dan.' I called Dan. I said, 'Listen, I would love to do you on *60 Minutes* this Sunday. The only thing that I have in mind is if you're gonna be all over the air between now and then, no. But if you're not, and we can have your reaction exclusively, I would like to talk to you about this whole experience.'

"... Then he said, 'Well, I'm gonna be on a local show in Washington tonight and then I'm gonna be on *Good Morning America* tomorrow.'

"And then I said, 'Well, look, Dan, I can't see the local show in Washington, but I will take a look at *Good Morning America* the next day and if [my] questions... have not been already answered—and I'm sure that I have other questions that you're not going to be asked—then I'll call you.' I saw the show. He wasn't asked the questions. And then we began to go to work and did a little research. Sure I had inside information...I'd talked to people in the Cronkite news who said that he had—I don't want to go through the whole drama again."

Wallace then smiled and said he thought the complaint from Schorr would center on Wallace's opening remarks at the interview. "It really was funny," Wallace said, "'cause we said, 'I have nothing but admiration for what you...'—he probably told you about this or, if not, 'I have nothing but admiration...'—and it didn't work and Don came on the talk-back, 'cause we did it in some kind of a makeshift studio up on the third floor; for some reason, the studio wasn't available. And it happened three times. He [Schorr] couldn't understand why that wasn't in the broadcast.

"Well, I did have great admiration for him. But as we were trying to put...Ordinarily we have a transcript of a total piece and then you work off the transcript and you put that together. We didn't have time for a transcript or anything. We had to edit it as we went. And it simply...was not part of the piece, because we were going in the ten minutes or eleven minutes, whatever it was; we were going in a different direction...And so Dan was upset about that. But I think [he] always has understood...He saw himself doing perhaps the same thing in years past when people said to him, 'Hey, Dan, that's what you had to take out of an hour's interview? That's what you had to take?'

"And that is not special with television. That's true with print and with what you're going to do with the material that I'm giving you now."

Whatever his intention may have been, Schorr was "dissembling," to use his own word, in his actions following the leaking of the Pike Report. In his approach to the Schorr interview, it is obvious that Wallace was dissembling as well. That is nothing new to journalism; a reporter is not likely to extract important information from an interview if he starts out by browbeating his subject.

What is more important is whether the general public could possibly care if Dan Schorr preferred print journalism to broadcast journalism, or whether his colleagues liked him or he they, or whether he fibbed or dissembled or even lied to some CBS editors about who leaked the Pike Report. Those issues were of immediate interest only to CBS News officials. The day after the interview portraying Daniel Schorr as a slippery eel who tried to get himself off the hook by implicating an innocent reporter, and who implied he didn't care much for CBS or broadcast news anyway, CBS planned to negotiate with Schorr on the terms of his separation from the network.

Among the millions who watched the program — but who had missed the B'nai B'rith or Sigma Delta Chi dinners at which Schorr had, according to Wallace, discussed his views of the First Amendment and why he was willing to risk imprisonment rather than reveal a source — it is likely that there would have been considerable interest in who leaks information, why they leak it, whether reporters should report it, and in what circumstances.

Substance, however, wasn't on the mind of Hewitt, Wallace, or, in all probability, CBS News executives. Instead, they offered a segment whose effect rivaled the morbid fascination that grips us when watching someone pull the wings from a fly. The program didn't tax the mind, didn't really concern us, and wouldn't affect the scheme of things, but the spectacle was riveting just the same. Not so coincidentally, it seemed, the purposes of CBS News management were served.

The day after *60 Minutes* presented Daniel Schorr to its millions of viewers, the erstwhile knight in shining armor was battered. For CBS, there would be fewer public problems from shrugging off an unworthy than there would have been from trying to unhorse a hero.

10

Reality Competitive with Make-Believe

*D*OCUDRAMAS—the wedding of news and entertainment—are censured regularly by the journalistic community. Commenting on *Death of a Princess,* a docudrama about Saudi Arabian justice, *The New York Times* wrote, "Its dramatized form exalts entertainment at the expense of information." *The Washington Post,* criticizing the same program, complained that "it obviously mixed reality and fiction in a way that no one can entirely sort out." Karl E. Meyer, writing in *The New York Times,* referred to a docudrama on the trial of Jean Harris as "regrettably superior" because it was "a clever counterfeit, a form of pseudo-journalism."

In *Death of a Princess, The Washington Post* complained, "there was at least as much 'drama' as 'docu'...and that is at once what made it entertaining to watch and questionable as journalism. There is a subtlety, some would say a corruption, in this technique."

Meyer maintained that a "reasonable case for docudramas can be made when a subject is seen at a historical distance...but it is a different matter when the medium seizes on yesterday's news for tonight's prime-time entertainment."

The fundamental arrogance in journalistic condemnation of docudramas is the implication that unless Dan Rather or Roger Mudd is on hand to narrate the action or conduct the interviews, Americans by the zillions are going to be fooled, misled, misinformed, duped, and God-knows-what-all about how the Saudis treat adultery, how a jury judged Jean Harris, or, on *Holocaust* and *Roots*, how the Nazis dealt with the Jews and how plantation owners mistreated their slaves.

The hauteur of journalism is twofold. The first assumption is that most of us are incapable of making reasonable inferences or exercising reasonable skepticism on our own; the second, that journalism succeeds in separating fact from fiction. Daniel Schorr perceives that news has borrowed from drama as well as the other way around — and that he, for one, was victimized by the genre.

The condescension of journalists toward the general public is sometimes monumental. "Because TV is a prime source of information and news as well as entertainment," Meyer wrote, "audiences are easily led to believe that docudramas are in fact documentaries." At least as strong an argument is that the converse is true: people are more likely to be misled by the intrinsic distortions of journalism than by material they know has been dramatized. Orson Welles's famous radio broadcast about an invasion from Mars fooled and frightened thousands of Americans because it was presented not as docudrama (notwithstanding a few easily missed announcements about its being a dramatization) but as a live news report.

The docudrama about Jean Harris, Meyer maintained, was not justified, even though its entire content was drawn from the trial transcript. "Choosing lines involves a judgment," he said. Anyone reading about the Harris trial or the Patty Hearst trial or the Calley trial or any other "sensational" trial in more than one publication would agree. Harris in *The New York Times*, for instance, struck me as much more sympathetic than Harris in *The Washington Post*. But when "lines" are chosen by a reporter, rather than by a dramatist or by a television producer, what makes them more reflective of reality? Why is one a better judge than the other?

The use of docudrama techniques is the rule in the presentation of news, particularly television news. When Mike Wallace squats on the floor with Ayatollah Khomeini, confronts him with a question that was not submitted to the ayatollah in advance, and grimaces in disgust when Khomeini refuses to listen to the question, there are elements of drama as well as of news. When a State Department correspondent for a major television network arrives in El Salvador for the first time and, while still at the airport, presents his "stand-up" analysis of the situation in that troubled nation, there are elements of fiction and imagination as well as of news. When Soma Golden of *The New York Times,* as a panelist at a 1980 presidential campaign debate, "felt under enormous pressure to try framing a single question that would somehow catch the well-briefed candidates by surprise on a subject of impor-tance," as she wrote, there are elements of plot contrivance as well as of news.

To the Italian journalist Oriana Fallaci, reporters posing questions to the presidential candidates didn't contrive nearly enough. "I would have given a finger of my hand to be one of the persons who put the questions," Fallaci told an inter-viewer for *Playboy.* "I would have done so much!" Complain-ing that the reporters did "nothing, nothing," Fallaci denounced them as "traitors...bastards...parasite[s] of powers" who "betrayed" the American people. Demonstrat-ing the schizophrenia abounding among journalists, however, Fallaci said moments earlier in the same interview that journalists—especially television journalists—had grown "arrogant...because they have the power, they have this tremendous pull in their hands, and they cannot be con-trolled...It seemed to me that the [1980] campaign was not really done by politicians; it was done by the American TV. The most important guy in America in those days was not

Reagan or Carter—it was Cronkite...You have a monarchy in America. You have TV...We write so much about the abuse of power, and we are among those who commit most abuse of power."

Documentaries or news presentations in general rely no less than fiction on the shaping of ideas and information. That which reporters and editors select as news; those portions of events they choose to emphasize; the quotes, the interviews, the "experts" they decide to include as representative of a situation; the settings, the graphics, the sounds, even the background music—all these will determine the shape and meaning of the "facts" we read, see, and hear. They reflect reality only to the extent of the reporter's understanding of that reality; they will convey "truth" only within the limits of the reporter's ability to communicate and within the severe constraints of time and space—not to mention, in the case of television news, how the availability or absence of "good footage" often dictates what and how information is presented to viewers. In July 1980, a launch carrying an NBC camera crew on assignment collided with a smaller yacht carrying four passengers. The yacht, its hull severed, began to capsize, with its passengers trapped inside. With NBC cameras rolling, some of the trapped men, clearly visible on film, desperately—and unsuccessfully—tried to escape by breaking sealed, interior windows. All four died. Ordinarily, a boating accident claiming four lives might not have rated even a mention on a network evening news program. But *The NBC Nightly News* devoted a full segment to the story, treating nearly twenty million viewers to the spectacle of men trapped like rats about to drown. NBC, after all, possessed some good footage.

Mini-docudramas are regularly scheduled on news programs, and Don Hewitt of *60 Minutes* is television news's impresario-in-chief. "Our purpose," he said in an interview in the September 1980 issue of *Panorama* magazine, "is to make information more palatable and to make reality competitive with make-believe. There are shows on TV about doctors, cowboys, cops. This is a show about four journalists. But instead of four actors playing these four guys, they are themselves. Of course, there is a line separating show biz from news biz. You walk up to that line, touch it with your toe, and do not cross it."

Dan Rather's daring and strenuous escapade into a war zone in Afghanistan, though clearly a made-for-television event, didn't deserve the snickers it drew from television critics, including Tom Shales. "Rather wore peasant togs that made him look like an extra out of *Doctor Zhivago...*" Shales wrote of the April 1980 segment of *60 Minutes*. "Perhaps Barbara Walters is right now wondering how she'll look in mufti or having a designer disguise prepared. Geraldo Rivera may be trying on caftans at this very moment." An anonymous headline writer at *The Washington Post* dubbed Rather "Gunga Dan." Art Buchwald, in mock horror, lashed out at CBS management for "permitting Walter Cronkite's successor to risk his neck in the Khyber Pass...What would have happened if he had been captured by the Soviets? No major power can sit idly by if one of its anchormen is being held as a prisoner of war."

(The Soviet newspaper *Literaturnaya Gazeta* also criticized Rather—but less humorously—maintaining that he "repeated standard lies fabricated" in Washington about the use of poison gas by the Russians and about their objective of genocide. Grigory Organov wrote that the switch in CBS anchorman from Cronkite to Rather reflected a switch to an "adventuristic" foreign policy by the United States government.)

The segment was undeniably histrionic: Rather's disguise, his freshly grown beard, his breathless, whispered commentary from a ridge overlooking a battle while he was filmed silhouetted against a darkening sky. "I would've preferred not to be breathless," Rather explained defensively in a *Los Angeles Times* interview, "but we'd talked about twelve hours and then had a two-and-a-half-hour climb. I would've preferred to rest an hour and collect my thoughts. But light was going fast, and the rebels told us to be quick...This wasn't a scene from *Patton*...I can't do any better. If you didn't like this one, stick it in your ear."

CBS News's David Buksbaum, in strongly supporting the Rather segment from Afghanistan, struck at the heart of the reason that television news is subjected to more criticism than any other form of journalism: "Our biggest competition is from our biggest critic. Print [newspapers and magazines] fights us for news and the advertising dollar. These guys piss the hell out me with their 'Gunga Dan' lines. How the hell would Shales have gone in [to Afghanistan]? With a Pierre Cardin safari jacket and Gucci shoes?

"What Rather did took initiative. How many guys in Vietnam covered that war from the bar at the Caravelle and then got their news at 'The Five O'Clock Follies' [the daily official news briefing in Saigon]? Television has to be *there*. Rather had to be *there*, not in Peshawar [a Pakistani city close to the border], to do the story for television. No one had seen what that war was all about. He took that war to the viewer and let him see that war firsthand."

Buksbaum added an obvious truth unmentioned by print critics of the Rather–*60 Minutes* adventure: "Any print guy who could have gotten there would have gone; if he saw what Rather saw, he would have written just about the same story."

60 Minutes is the epitome of news as docudrama. It stars intrepid reporters ferreting out information in the public interest. Its reporters once opened a phony clinic in Chicago as bait for laboratory representatives to offer kickbacks in return for referral of Medicaid patients. Dan Rather faced down a meatpacking company official with charges of improper grading. A reporter admittedly "broke the law" to show how easy it was to acquire phony identification used later to cash bad checks. Hidden cameras caught Georgia gas station attendants puncturing tires on the cars of tourists in order to make tire sales. "I think what we've done," Don Hewitt says, "is, we've brought back the era of the by-line. We went through the era of the heyday of the reporter, most of whom today are nameless, faceless guys except for the fact that you see them on *Agronsky and Company* and *Face the Nation*. So the emphasis shifted from the reporter to the organization he worked for...This broadcast sort of brought back the cult of the reporter. I mean, I've been fighting for years against the title *CBS Reports*. What the hell does that mean? Nobody cares what CBS reports. They care what Mike Wallace reports and what Dan Rather reports and what Walter Cronkite reports and what Jack Chancellor reports — but they don't care what CBS reports or what *NBC White Paper* has to say. That's faceless, nameless...That's part of the times in which we live. You know, go fight with the Bloomingdale's computer about your bill. There's nobody there."

(In 1980, Hewitt received an award from the Consumer Federation of America. "They told me that they think *60 Minutes* has done more than their whole outfit has done for consumerism. It isn't that I'm looking to be a consumer advocate. It's just that those are good stories, and they're stories that are interesting to do and can be told well on television." Hewitt added with a smile, "My favorite consumer story: I went into a store the other day and a guy had a [sign] on the counter: 'An informed consumer is a pain in the ass.'")

In March 1980, Mike Wallace explored the reasons that the drug DMSO (dimethyl sulfoxide) had not been approved for general use by the Food and Drug Administration. DMSO is a widely used industrial solvent derived from lignin, the material that binds cellulose fibers in wood. Since the early 1940s, DMSO has been touted by some as a miracle drug that kills pain and promotes the healing process. Its supporters claim it has not been marketed because the Food and Drug Administration has not undertaken the kind of testing required for approval, and because drug companies aren't interested in marketing the product, since it is available already, for industrial and other nonmedicinal uses, and is too cheap to return a good profit.

Wallace began his investigation of DMSO by interviewing a second-string quarterback for the Atlanta Falcons who rubbed the liquid on his sore shoulder—and started to smell. "That's one small special characteristic of DMSO," Wallace explained. "It smells like garlic and tastes like oysters."

Wallace interviewed a young mother who, "when we first met her...was in agony. No painkiller, no therapy, no doctor, it seemed, could help." Then she went to see Dr. Stanley Jacob, an associate professor of surgery at the University of Oregon. (The use of DMSO as a drug has been legalized in Oregon and Florida.) "For fifteen years," Mike Wallace explained, "this man [Jacob]—some would say this zealot—has been pushing DMSO because he believes so deeply...in what DMSO can do." Two months after her visit to Dr. Jacob, the young mother reported that "the pain is totally, completely gone from my neck."

Wallace confronted Dr. Richard Crout, head of the Bureau of Drugs in the Food and Drug Administration. Crout maintained that, though the agency was "rooting for the drug...rooting for the investigators to come through," they had not yet provided "the right kind of evidence that stands up under scientific scrutiny."

"So," Wallace said, "I put a sampling of apparently credible scientific evidence before Dr. Crout."

WALLACE: Are you familiar with "Dimethyl Sulfoxide in Muscular Skeletal Disorders"—*Journal of American Medical Association?* [Wallace handed Crout the magazine.]
CROUT: Yes.
WALLACE: "Topical Pharmacology and Toxicology of DMSO"—*Journal of American Medical Association?* [Wallace handed him the publication.]
CROUT: Correct. Right. Uh-hmmm.
WALLACE: "A Double-Blind Clinical Study for Acute Injuries and Inflammations"—DMSO—*Current Therapeutic Research.* [Wallace handed him the magazine.]
CROUT: Yes.
WALLACE: "Treatment of Aerotitis and Aerosinusitis with

Topical DMSO." An entire book on the subject of dimethyl sulfoxide by D. Martin and H. G. Hauthal. [Wallace kept handing Crout the publications.] So it's not as though this is some quack remedy that a few people have used and swear by. There is a considerable body of scientific investigation undertaken...

CROUT: That's right, with some very key holes in that body of evidence...Controlled trials demonstrating that it really works for some of the claims that it's touted for.

Wallace concluded by saying that DMSO was available for treatment "of assorted ailments in Western Europe, the Soviet Union, Japan, and Latin America. And tomorrow morning in Washington, the House Committee on Aging begins an inquiry into why DMSO is not available to all Americans for any appropriate ailment, including plain and simple pain." The response was overwhelming. According to an article in *TV Guide*, "After the broadcast, ads for DMSO and DMSO clinics began appearing in newspapers, and Dr. Jacob reported an average of 10,000 letters and phone contacts per week."

Representative Claude Pepper, chairman of the House Select Committee on Aging, sent a letter of congratulations to Wallace for looking into the DMSO question; the committee counsel hailed the broadcast as a "tremendous service."

TV Guide even reported that "in the wake of the *60 Minutes* report," the Arthritis Foundation did "an about-face...Where it had previously denounced the drug, it now endorsed DMSO as a 'local analgesic' that 'might be useful in a host of conditions causing pain.'"

What Wallace and *60 Minutes* did *not* relate, however, provides instruction on the nature of journalism. First, Wallace did not report that the young mother used in the dramatic experiment had been selected by Dr. Jacob. *60 Minutes* went along for the ride. Wallace did not report that, since 1972, arthritis "clinics" along the Mexican border with the United States—particularly one in Piedras Negras—have had "enormous success," according to Charles C.

Bennett of the Arthritis Foundation, "in luring [arthritis] sufferers to receive what is alleged to be DMSO...According to one report, treatment fees and travel cost a Florida woman $1400 each time she visited the clinic. They are getting help for their arthritis, but the switch here is that it's not DMSO that's doing it. Investigation has shown that patients actually get other medication which is generally available in the U.S., but prescribed with caution because of risks." Some sufferers, Bennett testified before Representative Pepper's committee, "became desperate and willing to try *anything* for relief, at any risk, at any cost."

Wallace explains that *60 Minutes* spent time and money in Piedras Negras but did not use the material it gathered because the clinic was not administering DMSO. Here, it seemed, was an opportunity for an exposé by *60 Minutes*—a story more scandalous, perhaps, than an examination of why the Food and Drug Administration insisted that DMSO required additional testing. Wallace says only that the piece about the Mexican rip-off "didn't seem to be a part of our— had it been DMSO, we would have put it in, but it wasn't DMSO. If we'd been doing a print piece, it could have been a sidebar...but in our time constriction, that three- or four-minute segment, that ten or fifteen thousand dollars had to go out the window simply to go from beginning to end of our story without that unnecessary digression."

Unnecessary? Digression? According to Wallace, patients were paying ten times what they would pay in the United States for a drug that, the Arthritis Foundation averred, is available in America, helps arthritis victims, but is risky. Bennett testified that "there's no telling how many thousands of arthritis sufferers have gone this Mexican route and are now DMSO disciples. To what extent was this false public image of DMSO a factor influencing the action...to legalize DMSO...?" It would appear that the reputation of DMSO could have suffered by the disclosure that another drug, overpriced and risky, may have been helping arthritis victims while DMSO was getting the credit.

Wallace did not report that Dr. Jacob, the man who believed so deeply in the efficaciousness of DMSO, had paid $325,000 for stock in Research Industries Corporation, supplier of DMSO for an approved use in the treatment of a bladder disease. Four months after the *60 Minutes* report on DMSO, Dr. Jacob testified at a congressional hearing that his stock was then worth about $600,000. Wallace could not report that, after the broadcast, some officials of the Bureau of Drugs prohibited a Food and Drug Administration medical officer from disclosing evidence of grave flaws in the two studies on which the FDA had based its approval of DMSO for use in the treatment of the bladder disorder. The officer testified at the hearing he had been told that DMSO was "politically sensitive" and that Dr. Jacob had "political clout." The company in which Dr. Jacob holds stock, Research Industries Corporation, did not, as the law requires, notify the FDA of a May 1977 finding by a researcher retained by the company that eye problems were developing in DMSO patients. A random check on one of the two company-financed studies submitted to the FDA as part of the company's application for approval of DMSO showed, according to the FDA medical officer, that eye and other safety tests on patients either had not been performed or had been performed improperly. Efficacy data, the medical officer told the congressional committee, "appeared to be little more than testimonials."

There was more that might have been reported, but wasn't. In August 1980, commissioner Jere E. Goyan told a Senate subcommittee chaired by Senator Edward M. Kennedy that the drug DMSO often causes irreversible eye damage in five species of laboratory animals when the animals are given doses proportional to those administered to people. That particular "small special characteristic of DMSO" was mentioned by neither Wallace nor, surprisingly, the FDA's Dr. Crout during the *60 Minutes* segment. Could Dr. Crout have been disoriented by the lights, the cameras, the action, and Mike Wallace? Or, perhaps, could he have known less about

DMSO than others in the agency whom Wallace might have interviewed? Wallace, however, who had done all that reading about DMSO, surely had come across the evidence of eye damage in animals resulting from applications of the drug; much of that evidence had been gathered and published in 1965. Wallace also might have related how Dr. Crout had put his career on the line in 1975 and 1977 by supporting, despite highly publicized congressional opposition, the use of drugs known as beta-blockers. When the drugs finally were approved in November 1981, there was considerable fanfare over the fact that they had been saving the lives of numerous heart attack victims outside the United States since the mid-1970s.

Goyan charged that the *60 Minutes* program, which had been broadcast in March 1980 and was repeated the following July, had led directly to the use by hundreds of thousands of people of types of DMSO not intended for them but for industry or, in some cases, for animals.

ABC News has provided its share of docudramas on its answer to CBS's *60 Minutes*, *20/20*. *20/20*'s principal journalistic sleuth, Geraldo Rivera, was chided as "Geraldo Revolver" by *The Akron Beacon Journal* when he led a television crew into the Ohio industrial town in April 1980 to expose what he described as a "big local scandal." A *Beacon Journal* reporter was assigned to cover *20/20*'s activities, not the alleged scandal, on which it had reported little. He wrote a front-page story on how the television reporters had held secret meetings, badgered local residents, and threatened to stake out a prominent citizen. "It's generally a sleazy operation," a *Beacon Journal* editor concluded. A producer of the *20/20* segment charged, in turn, that the newspaper had "suppressed the news in this town." What was shown to viewers was described by Tom Shales as taking news "into the realm of Mondo Bizarro":

> Rivera could be seen chasing, with his camera crew at full gallop, a man Rivera claimed was a pimp...through the streets of Akron. Rivera was screaming accusations at the man

as the chase continued...It was like a parody of the Mike
Wallace confrontation technique [but]...considerably sillier.
Nowadays some TV reporters don't just ask intimidating
questions: they shout out incriminations.

The foot race between Rivera and his subject was more
ludicrous than exciting. Another scene, in which a prostitute
claimed that the county probate judge, James V. Barbuto, the
principal target of the *20/20* segment, enjoyed wearing her
panties when they were together, was irrelevant and need-
lessly salacious. By what standard, however, was the segment
"an electronic extension of vaudeville," as Shales wrote? How
was it unrepresentative of modern journalism, which, more
often than not, is judged, like the Canadian Mounties, on
whether it gets its man? In its attack on Judge Barbuto, *20/20*
turned out to be absolutely right in most of its allegations.
Largely because of the revelations of that program, the judge,
described by *The Cleveland Plain Dealer* as a "political
kingpin," was imprisoned. Three other local officials, including the sheriff, pleaded guilty to crimes first exposed during
the program. Newspapers win Pulitzer Prizes for that sort of
exposé. Why, then, were Rivera and *20/20* castigated by
many of their colleagues? The probable explanation is that
Rivera pursued investigative reporting to its logical conclusion — and fellow reporters weren't enamored by what only
television could make them see: the fundamental foolishness
and unfairness of much of what they do for a living. Just as
surely, Louis IX of France never believed there was anything
holy in the Holy Crusades; he not only resisted identification
with wanton looting and rape, but did it adroitly enough to
end up being elevated to sainthood.

Although fellow journalists were less than avid admirers of
Rivera's technique, an ardent fan of his is police Lieutenant
Ed Duval of Akron. Had it not been for *20/20*, Duval
maintained, the official chicanery would have gone unpun-
ished. "In conventional police work," Duval told me, "like a
homicide between two whorelane lovers, it doesn't affect
anybody. But here the players involved were high and

powerful. These weren't street crimes. In this case, the people in the system you normally have good relations with are closing doors on you. Normally, if a reporter wanted inside information on an investigation, I'd tell him to go buff his nuts. In this case, I'd build a statue to Rivera."

Hero or buffoon, Rivera was performing his journalistic chores. He was chasing someone who allegedly had been arranging sexual favors for Judge Barbuto in return for special treatment; the pimp also was allegedly the judge's contact for reselling weapons that the judge and the sheriff had impounded from criminals. The judge was found guilty of both those charges. Were Rivera's actions more opprobrious or silly than those of a reporter meeting a mysterious source called, of all things, Deep Throat in the shadowed bowels of a parking garage? Or a reporter "confirming" (incorrectly) an allegation against one of the nation's highest officials by counting to ten over the telephone and assuming its truth when the other party didn't respond?

Just a year later, in April 1981, Rivera used similar techniques in a story about an alleged arson-for-profit operation in Chicago. When the target of the news report walked to his car, he was accosted unexpectedly by an ABC News camera crew and by Rivera, who asked him, in effect, whether he was in the arson business. A Chicago television station, owned by CBS, then televised a one-hour report condemning *20/20*'s techniques. ABC News, for its part, answered the allegations with a detailed statement. The ABC response "casts considerable doubt" on the charges made by Chicago's WBBM-TV, concluded television critic Tony Schwartz in *The New York Times*. "WBBM may have been guilty of using some of the same investigative techniques that its documentary criticizes," Schwartz added.

(This wasn't the first time that journalism's attempts to condemn its own excesses proved excessive. Rival networks vilified NBC for permitting an Iranian terrorist to make an unedited statement on the network in return for allowing NBC reporters to conduct an interview, with no Iranian interference, of an American hostage. Next day, both rival networks rushed on the air with film that had been produced under the full control of Iranians with no American correspondents even present.)

"I think it's a self-conscious device," Mike Wallace said of staking out a subject who does not want to answer questions. "...What I'm against is heat for heat's sake. When it's heat for light's sake, that's a different story."

Whatever the story—and whatever the eventual outcome—only the reporter and his editor decide when and if heat will produce light. Whether created by Rivera or Wallace, whether self-conscious or not, whether or not they generate information of value, filmed dramatic confrontations are undeniably memorable. That is the power of television news. Though all reporting is subject to the same limitations and the same degree of error, the astonishing immediacy of television news—its all-encompassing reach, the dizzying impact of its message—endow it with incalculable influence on many events and what we remember of those events.

What Rivera does—and, despite his disclaimers, Wallace as well—is to apply himself to television's remarkable technology rather than to apply the technology to a more sedate form of reporting. "The technology has improved tremendously," Dan Rather said, "and keeps on improving. The technological curve in this business is almost right straight up. The difficulty is how to harness the technology to a well-trained reportorial mind. The young people coming into the business get taken up with the technology and the appearance aspect, everything from how your hair looks, what kind of suit you wear...The premium goes on people who understand the technology and have a good appearance."

It is like the story of the emperor's new clothes, but in reverse. Television's remarkable raiment is real enough, but it is the reporter who, too often, has no substance. Journalism's glittering, technological suit allows newsmen and newswomen to dazzle millions with reports of events half an hour old and half a world away. Too often, their reports resemble flash bulbs popping in a dark room, blinding us for a moment with their brilliance, but leaving us blinking at formless, fading patterns that we see but cannot grasp.

"Abscam," the Federal Bureau of Investigation's stinglike operation to persuade members of Congress to accept bribes, was the news media's ultimate docudrama — docudrama compounded, docudrama meeting itself coming and going.

Ordinarily, docudrama results when a reporter or dramatist reconstructs an event — supplying dialogue, motives, likely dénouements from his imagination or by ascribing them to a "knowledgeable source." The event itself, however — even a contrived one like a pro-abortion demonstration or a political rally — is real enough; the identities, goals, and roles of demonstrators, journalists, and public (as actors, authors, and audience) are well defined. Before a large Washington demonstration in 1980 by the so-called born-again Christian movement, editors considered whether the event deserved news coverage. "We try to be alert," Dan Rather recalled, "to the potential for manipulation by anyone with a special pleading who can put together somebody with posters and some semblance of a protest. Now, granted, if you can get 250,000 on the Mall in Washington, it says to a reporter that 'Yes, it's staged, well organized, and well planned,' but if that many people are willing to take their day out to come and stand on the Mall, maybe they do represent something that's worthy of note."

With Abscam, however, docudrama entered a new dimension. Its "real-life" manifestation was a blend of fact and fiction centered on made-for-television movies that, when replayed through a journalistic strainer which filtered out all but the most essential, exciting, eyebrow-raising details, resulted in a purée of dramatic hyperbole.

From first to last, Abscam was a media-oriented operation that turned reality upside down. It was planned around a basic fiction: FBI agents portrayed a sheik, the sheik's entourage, and his American associates; videotape cameras and sound equipment, hidden in strategic locations, recorded the performances; the *dramatis personae* included Melvin Weinberg, a convicted swindler, hired by the government to play the role of a well-connected businessman whose friend, the sheik, needed a favor from Congress and was willing to pay for it. The plan was to seduce public officials, on camera, into accepting bribes for helping the sheik emigrate to the United States should he be forced to flee his homeland.

Thus, a criminal, paid with tax dollars, delivered previously law-abiding, elected officials into a snare devised by men who were sworn to uphold the law and who, with the aid of costumes, lies, and bribe money—furnished with additional tax dollars—would do their best to persuade the officials to violate the law.

Congressmen who refused to help the agent-sheik were cut from the cast of this double-dip docudrama; those who agreed to assist (even if they initially refused an offer of money) were selected for additional screen tests. Representative Frank Thompson of New Jersey, for instance, at first refused an offer of money; the FBI agents continued to press a bribe on him until, apparently, he accepted. The episode was reminiscent of a motion picture director instructing his actors in a scene and filming it over and over until they got it right.

At some point in the investigation, several of those connected with it decided to inform the media. Although the first public reports of the operation were aired on Saturday, February 2, 1980, two NBC News reporters said they had known of the probe for two months and had shared the secret with NBC News president William Small. Several print media representatives—reporters for *Newsday, The New York Times,* and *The Washington Post*—seem to have been notified at least as early.

(Why the media were informed remains a mystery. When the story first was "leaked," my own reaction was that someone among the investigators feared that the politically potent among the operation's targets might escape prosecution and wanted to use the news organs as a lever. When the NBC television reporters conceded, however, that they had been on the story—and had been planning for the day they could break it—for two months, it seemed more likely that several investigators had considered early publicity an intrinsic and essential part of the operation: whatever else might happen, the targets of the investigation would be convicted in the press.)

Two weeks before the story broke, according to *Washington Post* television reporter John Carmody, the two NBC reporters were notified that "federal agents were about to move on the targets of the allegations." The network rented two large Winnebago vans and equipped them with cameras with special night-vision lenses, capable of amplifying available light thirty thousand times. One van was parked at each end of Washington's W Street, a short street on which a fashionable house rented by the FBI and outfitted with hidden video and sound equipment was situated. The house was the "set" for Abscam, and congressmen and others were invited to it for meetings with the sheik or his representatives. Round-the-clock surveillance by NBC cameramen of the comings and goings at the house resulted in what the rival CBS News Washington bureau chief conceded were "some sexy pictures. Some of that stuff done at night was pretty good."

When NBC reporters were notified that the authorities were about to close in, the Washington staff was buttressed by six additional correspondents from other bureaus—permitting "stakeouts" to be located at the homes of all congressmen about to be notified that they were targets of an official investigation.

If authorities were not aware of media's advance knowledge of Abscam, their ineptitude would rival that of Inspector Jacques Clouseau of *The Pink Panther* films. How could FBI agents be unmindful of two nearly identical Winnebago vans parked at either end of a short street for several days and nights, a street on which the FBI was conducting a continuing operation? Reporters pounced on congressmen as soon as agents, giving the elected officials the bad news, walked from their front doors. The Sunday editions of *Newsday, The New*

York Times, and *The Washington Post* carried full reports on
the investigation — material that was unlikely to appear if the
publications had not had at least a few days to prepare it. On
Monday, February 4, *Newsday* Washington bureau chief
Anthony Marro wrote a detailed account of the secret
videotape showing a congressman, Representative Richard
Kelly of Florida, accepting $25,000 in return for using his
influence to help the phony sheik arrange for political asylum
in the United States in the event of political upheavals in his
own country:

> While hidden FBI cameras filmed the scene [Marro wrote], an
> undercover agent laid out a total of $25,000 — $20,000 of it in
> $100 bills, and $5000 in $20 bills. The videotapes show him
> first stuffing bills into his pants pockets, then into the outside
> pockets of his jacket, and then finally into the inside breast
> pockets of his jacket.
>
> Four hundred and fifty bills can be a bit bulky, and Kelly
> kept patting his jacket to smooth out the bulges. Finally, he
> pirouetted, turned to the undercover agent, and asked: "Does
> it show?"

Before long, media provided us with more tidbits — in
many cases, before any criminal charges were leveled at those
already tried and convicted by the glare of publicity. We
learned that Representative Michael (Ozzie) Myers of Pennsylvania, in explaining to the sheik's aide how to use influence
in high places, commented, "Money talks, shit walks" — a
crudity that must have left the FBI as perplexed as any sheik
as to its precise meaning. Representative Frank Thompson
supposedly engaged in an ungentlemanly tug of war over an
attaché case filled with the bribe money. Senator Harrison
Williams bragged shamelessly about his influence in
government.

The episode was shocking on several levels: that so many
congressmen willingly peddled their influence for a substantial payoff; that attorneys in the Department of Justice
charged, tried, and convicted their suspects through the
media; that the media could be procured so easily into playing

the harlot in return for a fee in the form of lip-smacking news.

Burke Marshall, a Yale Law School professor who had served in the Kennedy administration as assistant attorney general for civil rights, was "shocked by the indifference of the press, the radio, and television networks to their use by the FBI for the enlargement of its own reputation."

The *American Spectator*'s editor, R. Emmett Tyrrell, Jr., wrote:

> Leaks have become a vice. Those who rely on them often are corrupted by them. Too often, leaks turn a reporter into a mere public relations agent for causes neither he nor the public fully understands. In reading the "Abscam" stories, the casual reader does not really know if a crime has been committed or who committed it. The careful reader does not know if [the leaks were]. . . meant to close down an investigation, preserve [its] integrity. . . insure the eventual acquittal of the alleged culprits, or what. Most likely the journalists. . . are not much clearer about the motivation of the leaker. . .
>
> More often than one would think, the fabled investigative reporter is only a simple hack sitting around waiting for the telephone to ring. When it does, he becomes a dutiful stenographer for sources whose intentions he either does not understand or will not speculate upon publicly.

Newsday's editor, Anthony Insolia, was miffed by such deprecations. "To use the pejorative 'leak' is a disservice to the tremendous work that went into getting this story," he said.

Joseph Kraft, however, was convinced that "the detailed character of the 'Abscam' leaks leaves no doubt that some accounts, at least, were handed out wholesale, not merely pieced together by diligent reporters." Almost always, Kraft asserted, leaks contain information that will become public through adversarial procedures. The "fix"—stifling governmental or judicial oversight functions that, generally, ensure the investigation and prosecution of a wrongdoer—is "so rare," Kraft maintained, "that it would be appropriate for all journalists to forswear pretrial publicity as a general rule." The kind of media "enterprise" that motivates the search for the "exclusive" may do wonders for self-esteem but "should be used with discretion — not loosely, and certainly not self-righteously in the spirit of the conceit that what's good for the media is good for America."

The conceit is omnipresent in American journalism. The very idea that authorities should express concern over the sources of potentially prejudicial leaks is repugnant to most journalists. When the Department of Justice launched an internal investigation into the Abscam leaks, *The Washington Post* ran this headline over its story about the man placed in charge of the probe: SUPER PLUMBER OF THE "AB-SCAM" LEAKS. Consciously or not, the language implied kinship with the distasteful "plumbers" operation of the Nixon White House.

Whatever qualms editors may have had over the ethical problems of publishing Abscam stories were short-lived; they were swept aside by the obviously more pressing consideration of competition. "The press was not unaware of the ethical problems," Anthony Lewis wrote in *The New York Times*. "Some editors worried about the fairness of publishing the names. But so many people knew by then, that the story could not be withheld." Lewis did not point out that these "people" were all journalists. *The Washington Post*'s William Greider was more to the point. If one publication holds back on a story while another prints it, he says, "all you're going to do is leave egg all over your face. If we'd had a firm notice that this was our call alone, I'd have pondered the question more."

Journalistic ethics, therefore, cannot be practiced — only preached about at professional conferences and award banquets to enhance the general deception that, by and large, the decisions of editors are motivated by considerations other than the demands of the marketplace.

In Abscam, those who offered the bribes, those who accepted them, those who prematurely divulged the scandalous information, and those who published it with scarcely a thought about the possibility of ruining the careers of innocent people, were all ethically culpable. The one person who acknowledged the consequences of his actions (and who openly relished his role) was the convicted con artist, Melvin Weinberg. Within hours of the FBI's formal notification of congressmen who were under criminal investigation, Weinberg—stout, mostly bald, cigar-chomping, possessor of a gravelly Bronx accent—telephoned an editor of *Newsday* to trumpet his role in the operation. "I'm a swindler," he told *Newsday*'s Robert Greene. "The only difference between me and the congressmen I met on this case is that the public pays *them* a salary for stealing...I keep saying you can't con an honest man. That's what happened here—these congress-men...got trapped in their greed. They came to us with their hands out...I'm going to be delighted to...let the people of this country know what their politicians are really like." Weinberg also was paid by the public—handsomely, according to his subsequent interview with Mike Wallace. Whether that constituted "stealing" at taxpayers' expense depends on one's attitude toward entrapment, which, though extremely narrow in its legal definition, is crystal clear in its dictionary meaning: "to lure into a compromising statement or act." Representative James Florio of New Jersey, for instance, reported that he was approached in his Capitol Hill office by Joseph Silvestri, an Atlantic City real estate consultant. Silvestri asked the congressman whether he would be interested in meeting his "friends," among them, a rich Arab sheik. Florio declined, but Silvestri persisted, even calling him at home and inviting him out for "a good time"—adding that his "friends" were "very, very generous." Florio, who was not implicated in Abscam, said he hung up on Silvestri. Some congressmen who, like Senator Larry Pressler of South Dakota, went as far as meeting the "sheik" or his money men but resisted temptation received congratulatory telephone calls from FBI director William Webster. Presumably, they had passed what *Time* called the agency's "bribery test." Another who "passed," Representative William Hughes of New Jersey, wondered whether it was "proper for the executive branch to pose a litmus test for the legislature."

Lost in the drama—at least in terms of the ability to reflect on Abscam's meaning in the midst of the cacophony—was what the bribery was all about in the first place. Had congressmen sold out to the Russians? Had our elected representatives placed special interests before the needs of their constituents? Had democracy been threatened?

What, in fact, the guilty parties had agreed to do was help welcome a friendly sheik into the United States if his government fell into the hands of anti-American forces. It was left to the British journalist Henry Fairlie to remind us that "the services asked in return for these [bribes] are of such insignificance that they threaten neither the prosperity nor the peaceableness of the nation. We are not in the middle of one of the historic ages of corruption which have formerly brought great republics to the dust." Fairlie pointed out that since World War II, forty members of Congress had been "indicted, convicted, punished, or in some way disciplined for various forms of peculation and other criminal or ethical misconduct...This figure would make most foreigners wonder that any nation can achieve such purity."

But for most journalists such considerations are beside the point when a front-page story beckons. In such circumstances, reporters respond like hungry lions that, guided by cunning and an instinctive sense of coordination, attack whatever prey is proximate and vulnerable.

In an assessment of *60 Minutes*, that prototype of docudrama masquerading as investigative news, Michael J. Arlen wrote that "clearly much of what sustains the popularity of the program is the thrill of the chase: the excitement that comes from watching a quarry being pursued and brought down by aggressive questioning on the air." As a result, Arlen wrote, there is an "increasing tendency to have prosecutorial indignation do the work of actual investigative reporting."

Other than government, the juiciest target for modern, confrontational reporting is big business. Recently, ABC News, in another of the innovations introduced by its president, Roone Arledge, aired a program entitled *View-*

point, which permitted those with complaints about news coverage to reply—albeit in circumstances controlled by ABC News. Reporters who may have offended a target of a news broadcast were included in the program, permitted to hear the complaints, and to parry them.

Kaiser Aluminum, which had been accused on a *20/20* segment of knowingly marketing hazardous aluminum wiring, was given an opportunity to respond—but, of course, not without the chief antagonist, correspondent Geraldo Rivera, on hand to respond to the response. Asked why he thought Kaiser should not have been permitted to respond, without editing, to *20/20*'s allegations, Rivera said it would have destroyed "the responsibility of responsible journalists"— bringing to mind Walter Lippmann's observation that "responsible journalism is journalism responsible in the last analysis to the editor's own conviction of what, whether interesting or only important, is in the public interest." Richard Salant, when president of CBS News, shamelessly (and absurdly, judging by the network news wars over ratings) maintained that "I take a very flat elitist position. Our job is to give people not what they want, but what we decide they ought to have. That depends on our accumulated news judgment of what they need."

Whether editors provide viewers and readers with what people want or need or, as is likely, a reasonable portion of each, the key fact is that their only qualification for doing so is that they work for an employer who owns a printing press or a network or has a license to operate a television station. (Salant, for one, is a lawyer who never had any journalistic experience until he became an executive of CBS News.) There is no standard, other than experience and instinct, for determining what makes news. Reporters and editors generally believe that what interests them probably will interest others. It is a long way, though, from believing that a story may be interesting to believing that a cause should be advocated as right or good, or a company or an individual attacked or confronted.

When that happens, those on the receiving end don't have much defense. Thus, even when he was given an opportunity to respond to serious allegations against his firm, the Kaiser Aluminum official, Steve Hutchcraft, was confronted with additional allegations by Geraldo Rivera. Rivera believed that Kaiser was being less than candid in its defense of the previous allegations.

"What we have missed here tonight," Hutchcraft said at the close of his exchanges with Rivera, "is...the issue of trial by television...where the accuser is also the judge, the jury, and the prosecutor, and the only way that the defense can make its point is through the voice of the accuser."

11

Someone Nailed
Those Guys

*I*N THE CONFRONTATION between big government, big business, big unions, and big special interests on one side, and media on the other, Don Hewitt thinks there's no contest.

"When people say, 'You are unfair...because you are only telling one side of a story,' I say, 'Oh, no, no! Madison Avenue tells the other side of the story for them and their PR people tell the other side of the story'...The biggest change I've seen in the years I've been in the news business is the layer upon layer of PR that now surrounds every government agency, every corporation, so that the job of a journalist is to see if he can't pierce the armor of the PR that is built up around [them]."

Hewitt says he first encountered the "problem" when he decided to have *60 Minutes* do a story on how movie-makers and military brass used one another in making war films — at the public's expense. "We called Twentieth Century–Fox and said, 'We'd like to do a story about the making of *Tora! Tora! Tora!* [a film about the Japanese attack on Pearl Harbor].' And we did. And Twentieth Century called me and they were furious. And they said, 'You didn't tell us what you were gonna do.' I said, 'Oh, yes I did. I said we were gonna do a story about the making of *Tora! Tora! Tora!* I wasn't about to tell you how Darryl Zanuck was using the Navy. I don't feel any obligation to do that.' The PR people assume, when you say you're gonna do a story about the making of *Tora! Tora! Tora!*, that you're gonna come out and do a Hedda Hopper, Rona Barrett kind of a Hollywood story.

"So I think if they think that journalists are arrayed against them — that is, corporations, Hollywood, government — boy, they've got more troops than we have. They've got more people trying to insulate and isolate them from the public under the guise of public relations than we have trying to pierce that protective armor."

Hewitt believes the reason for the protective armor is "to make it more difficult for the public to find out what they don't want them to find out. So that every time I hear that we are unfair because they say, 'Ah, *60 Minutes* brings up all these big guns'. . . you don't know how many sandbags you're gonna get through to get what you're trying to find out. If they say it's not a fair fight, it *is* a fair fight. . .

"Government and business and labor unions have retreated behind a phalanx of PR people and. . .in our quest to find out, and sometimes in their determination not to have us find out, I think we're outgunned, outmaneuvered, and outmanned."

The issues on which *60 Minutes* attempts to pierce the protective armor of its targets, however — like "exposing" coziness between movie-makers and the Pentagon — frequently are not concerns on which the future of civilized society hangs. "I think we do sometimes overplay the 'national disgrace' stories," Morley Safer conceded to an interviewer from *The New York Times* magazine. "There are times we do national disgraces that are only small disgraces, localized disgraces." Safer then smiled, his interviewer wrote, and snatched a ball-point pen from his desk. "Ball-point pens!" he said with mock gravity. "A national disgrace!"

Despite Hewitt's protestations, *60 Minutes* possesses the one weapon that guarantees it will snare its quarry every time — access to, and total editorial control over, one hour of prime-time network television each week. In addition, Hewitt's bravado notwithstanding, few among *60 Minutes'* prey are endowed with the resources with which to counter-attack; no one, certainly, can reach the forty million people before whom he or she may have been humbled, or worse, by *60 Minutes.*

For example, on October 2, 1976, as part of a *60 Minutes* segment on dealing with "diet doctors," Mike Wallace interviewed a woman named Barbara Goldstein, who discussed having been treated by a Great Neck, New York, physician, Joseph Greenberg.

> GOLDSTEIN: I could not determine where I ended and where you began for two years after that time [she said on the segment that was aired on November 7, 1976]. I walked around holding my hands, because I did not know that they were attached to my body.
> WALLACE: And when you said that to Dr. Greenberg, he said what to you?
> GOLDSTEIN: Nothing. He said everyone feels that way.

The woman told Wallace that Greenberg had given her eighty pills a day, four to six of which were "amphetamine-type drugs."

Wallace neglected to mention that Goldstein had last been Dr. Greenberg's patient in 1966, ten years before the interview for *60 Minutes.* Wallace never asked Greenberg to respond to the allegations. A few weeks after the segment was broadcast, drug investigators interviewed Greenberg and a druggist who had filled several of Greenberg's patients' prescriptions. None was for amphetamines. A few months later, a New York State narcotics investigator filed a report concluding that Greenberg had done nothing unlawful, and the case was closed. In an ensuing civil action, which was ended when CBS stated that it "regrets any embarrassment that Dr. Greenberg feels he sustained," Wallace testified that, other than his brief conversation with Greenberg and his on-camera interviews, he had done no research for the segment. In connection with the Greenberg interview, Wallace was asked, "How long did the interview last?" "Not very long," he replied.

> QUESTION: Did you tell him in the course of that telephone interview that he was to be named by a person appearing on your broadcast as having dispensed medication to her?
> WALLACE: No, I did not.
> QUESTION: Did you at any time tell Dr. Greenberg that in the course of your exposé of these amphetamine-abusers he was to be included in that description?
> WALLACE: No.

Wallace said he had relied for his information solely on research done by the segment's producer and her assistants.

> QUESTION: Mr. Wallace, did you take any independent action of your own, not relying on anyone else, did you personally take any independent action to verify the information given you by [researchers]?
> WALLACE: No.
> QUESTION: . . . Did you personally, as the correspondent who appeared on camera, take any independent action of any kind whatsoever to interview any other persons to do any formal research prior to the presentation of that telecast?
> WALLACE: No.

Don Hewitt, characteristically, saw no need for apologies. "We need more stories like that," he testified. Other testimony suggested that because Greenberg was not the primary subject of the segment—another doctor, who ultimately went to jail, was—it was not necessary to mention that the patient who denounced him publicly had not been seen by the physician for a decade. Further, no one checked with any authorities to determine whether Greenberg had prescribed amphetamines, wrongfully or otherwise. "It would never occur to me to check [with the authorities] when his patients were telling me what he was prescribing," a researcher-producer testified.

When Hewitt's troops marched on the Illinois Power Company in October 1979, however, its reputation preceded it. Although producer Paul Loewenwarter "assured us," company spokesman Howard Rowe recalled, "...that CBS was going to produce a balanced, factual presentation of the economics of building nuclear power plants," the company agreed to cooperate, with one stipulation: whenever CBS filmed anything on its property, a camera crew hired by the company would film *60 Minutes*. Clearly, Illinois Power did not confuse *60 Minutes* with Hedda Hopper or Rona Barrett.

Illinois Power had been locked in a controversy over its rates for nearly a year when *60 Minutes* appeared on the scene. The company had filed for a rate increase with the Illinois Commerce Commission in January 1979. Because the cost of construction of the company's nuclear power plant had been growing ever since the plant was begun, in 1973 — from $430 million to $1.3 billion — several of the company's customers, as well as members of the commission itself, were concerned about how well plant construction was being managed and the extent to which possible mismanagement was contributing to the proposed raise in utility rates.

Among those seeking to testify before the commission in connection with the proposed increase were citizens groups, environmentalists, major corporations like Jones & Laughlin Steel Corporation and Olin Corporation, and even the United States Departments of Defense and the Air Force.

The commission had maintained that, while Illinois Power's nuclear plant construction costs had climbed by 200 percent over the previous years, an identical plant being constructed in downstate Illinois had risen by "only" little more than 100 percent. Illinois Power maintained that the plants were not really comparable. In any event, by the time producer

Loewenwarter and *60 Minutes* correspondent Harry Reasoner arrived in Clinton, Illinois, the controversy was being well laundered in public—and the state's regulator of utilities was vigorously demanding answers to reasonable questions. No one was rolling over and playing dead for a corporate giant.

Nonetheless, some people resented the notion that at least some of Illinois Power's requested rate increase would be approved through a democratic process. Among them were two cost engineers, David Berg and Steve Radcliff. It was Radcliff who wrote to *60 Minutes,* suggesting that it do a piece on Illinois Power.

The *60 Minutes* crew and Reasoner interviewed Illinois Power officials for more than two hours; the company's side of the nuclear plant cost story was presented in the resulting *60 Minutes* segment in two and a half minutes.

Any disinterested critic watching the segment would have concluded that the cost of nuclear power surely was to be far greater than its proponents had estimated. Further, if Illinois Power served as an example, a good deal of the higher cost could be blamed on corporate mismanagement. If any evidence were needed that Illinois Power, deservedly or not, got a black eye when the segment was shown on Sunday, November 25, 1979, it may be found in the records of the New York Stock Exchange on Monday, November 26, 1979. On that day, Illinois Power stock was traded at a rate three times greater than on any other day in the company's history. The stock, which had been selling in the low twenties, closed the day off a full point. A few weeks later, the stock had dropped to fifteen, and had not fully recovered by mid-1981.

Within seconds of the opening of the segment, Illinois Power Company officials knew they were in for a bad time:

REASONER: The American nuclear power program is in trouble—and not only because of Three Mile Island...It's in trouble because the cost of building the plants has gone crazy—a China syndrome of cost. Take Illinois Power...

Whew! Reasoner packed a wallop into those few words: "trouble," "Three Mile Island," "gone crazy," "China syndrome," "Illinois Power."

Illinois Power struck back. It took the film it had shot of *60 Minutes* conducting interviews, combined it with the final *60 Minutes* segment, and produced a point-by-point rebuttal of the program's allegations. Since then, hundreds of newspapers and magazines have written about Illinois Power's project. Dozens of companies have borrowed the tactic and have produced similar filmed messages of their own.* Members of Congress point to the film as indication of the excesses of media. In all, Illinois Power reports that it has distributed some three thousand cassette videotapes of its film, entitled *60 Minutes/Our Reply*. Illinois Power produced and began distributing its reply within a week of the *60 Minutes* presentation in late 1979. Oddly, nearly a year later, Don Hewitt maintained that he still had not seen the tape. He did not, however, hesitate to comment on it.

"It's a very clever PR ploy," Hewitt said, "because it has obscured the fact that Illinois Power will probably have a much bigger cost overrun than we ever said they were gonna have. That's exactly what it's doing."

Could the company, I asked, put its reply on the same "loudspeaker" that is available to *60 Minutes*?

"Yes, they can," Hewitt replied. "Yes, they can... For years, statements and the public posture of corporations and labor and government have gone unchallenged, because they were judge and jury of what they said or did. They bought the time, they bought the space, and they said it. They put out brochures. They have lobbyists in Washington to tell their

*This development proved embarrassing to Mike Wallace during an interview with a San Diego bank official in March 1981. While the *60 Minutes* camera crew was changing film, Wallace made some remarks interpreted as racial slurs. The incident became public because the bank had hired its own camera crew—and it had continued filming during the break in the interview.

story...not that CBS doesn't have a lobbyist in Washington...But that is how the people [who] I think it is our responsibility to examine get their case across...

"I would say that, in the overall scale of whether Illinois Power has come out on the credit or debit side of the ledger after the *6o Minutes* story, with the people they care about, I would say right now they're on the credit side of the ledger, because they have tailored a response specifically to the kind of people that can make a real difference in their corporate reputation.

"But everybody has recourse to anything...Anything we say can be refuted. [I think Hewitt meant to say "disputed."] There's a perfect example. I mean, I'm kinda glad that happened, that somebody decided to show that 'Hey, we're not powerless if somebody says something about us.' Now, what they've argued with is our techniques more than the facts. The facts, when the dust settles, may very well show that their cost-overrun situation and the possibility of mismanagement was even greater than we hinted it might be.

"Having brought up these howitzers and fired all these salvos, they may be preparing the ground..."

Indeed, in March 1981, Morley Safer closed a *6o Minutes* program with an update:

SAFER: A little more than a year ago, we broadcast a report on the problems being encountered by the Illinois Power Company in building its first nuclear plant...Our report included charges of mismanagement, denied by the company, as well as predictions of future cost overruns and delays, also denied by the company. Illinois Power even went so far as to prepare and distribute a videotaped rebuttal to the *6o Minutes* story, charging distortion, inaccuracies, and insisting everything was under control. Well, less than a year after our report, the company went back to the Illinois Commerce Commission to ask for another rate increase...And just last week, Illinois Power announced new cost overruns and delays...

The essential issue of the *6o Minutes* segment and the company's reply, however, was not merely cost overruns—

many of which, obviously, resulted from governmental red tape and inflation—but the extent to which waste and mismanagement contributed to increased costs. The company's reply concentrated on those aspects of the *60 Minutes* segment which went to the heart of journalistic style. "The journalistic techniques used were what we protested all along," company spokesman Al Adams told me. "We vividly documented the general grievance against this type of journalism. Very few of these cases end up in court. It's the first time someone nailed those guys."

Although Illinois Power did protest some errors of fact, the errors were almost beside the point. Instead, its videotaped reply portrayed just how and why *60 Minutes* became involved with Illinois Power, how it chose its principal on-camera interview subjects, and just how the extraordinary capacity to sift and select available information guarantees that the "facts" will lead inexorably to a predetermined conclusion.

In his introduction to the segment, Reasoner said that Illinois Power "wants its customers to help pay for a nuclear power plant...before they can light a bulb or toast a piece of bread with electricity" from the plant. "...Critics say part of the blame lies with the 'cost-plus' contracts that govern most nuclear construction—and that here at Clinton, noboby had any incentive to hold costs down." Reasoner then introduced David Berg, "who was a cost engineer for the contractor in 1977 and 1978."

> BERG: Why did they have two guys on the wall and seven guys standing down below watching them, including two foremen? Why did one shift tear down the previous shift's work and rebuild it, and the first shift do the same thing at the second shift? We weren't getting concrete answers to these problems.

The scene shifted immediately to a man whose face was shadowed and whose voice was electronically disguised.

> MAN: I was never approached any time I was out there to

work on decreasing my costs or getting some of my costs under control or doing an operation more efficiently.

REASONER: This man was a construction superintendent at Clinton. Has a crack reputation. Works elsewhere now, but fears retribution if his identity becomes known.

MAN: Any time I came up with, ah, what I thought was a valid point to reduce costs or do an operation more efficiently, I was usually put down for it, ah, told, "forget it," that there was people above me that were paid to do the thinking. I was there to do the work.

At this point, Berg was back on camera, being interviewed by producer Loewenwarter.

LOEWENWARTER: Is this something that adds up to thousands of dollars? Millions of dollars? Conceivably, tens of millions of dollars?

BERG: In my areas, I would say that I increased the estimate tens of millions of dollars myself.

Reasoner popped back on screen:

REASONER: The company's sharpest critic is Steve Radcliff, who had been hired by Illinois Power in 1976 as a cost engineer to try to get construction dollars under control.

RADCLIFF: It's like Watergate. They've got themselves committed, they went into it, and all of a sudden they've got a bear by the tail and they don't know how to let go. And they don't have the moxie to say "We've made a big screw-up here and we don't know what to do about it."

REASONER: And when you talk to the company's executive vice president, Bill Gerstner, it's as though there's no problem at all.

GERSTNER: The job is going very well currently. We're on schedule and on budget.

Gerstner went on to say that the project had its "ups and downs" and that the rise in cost "is considerably more than the original estimate." He added the cost increases were "very little different" from other major utility construction projects in the country. He never suggested that there was "no problem at all," or that there would not be future problems. Essentially, he was responding then — and would, as well, in replying to later questions by Reasoner — to the allegations made by Berg, Radcliff, and the unidentified man.

Later, Radcliff claimed that before he was hired, the company "never had a written report on schedule status or cost status on any of their projects — coal plants or anything else. And after my four reports, they have not had any written reports to top management since."

Reasoner reported that Radcliff had demonstrated to management that the schedule at Clinton was running behind other nuclear construction projects and was costing more. So, Radcliff said, he was fired on August 1, 1977 (more than two years before the interview was conducted). Gerstner explained in some detail why Radcliff was fired; on the program itself he was shown saying simply that Radcliff wasn't doing his job. "Whatever the facts of the firing," Reasoner said, resuming the segment, "Steve Radcliff and the other former employees agree on the charges of mismanagement at Clinton."

LOEWENWARTER: Why were you asked to...leave?
MAN: ...I was making some people nervous...If you run out of something to do, just waste the rest of your day — just don't bring it up to anybody, don't take it to anybody above you that you're not working efficiently or anything.

We didn't learn much about Berg, Radcliff, or the unidentified workman from the *60 Minutes* segment. But the company's reply provided a few more intimate details that might have been of interest to viewers.

First, there was David Berg, the cost engineer who worked for the project's contractor. Berg told the story about a wall being erected and then torn down, apparently for no reason, while lots of workmen stood around watching. Berg, it turned out, had been hired by the contractor in June 1977. Nine months later, he injured his back ("while picking up a book," a company spokesman points out rather airily) and drew workmen's compensation pay for the next fourteen and a half weeks. When he returned to work, he was dissatisfied with a 7 percent pay increase, so he quit. Berg then started working with Prairie Alliance, an antinuclear organization whose principal objective is to stop the Clinton nuclear plant. Berg's connection with this group wasn't mentioned on the program.

Next, the man whose face and voice were disguised because he "fears retribution." His identity, a company spokesman claims on the videotape, "was fairly obvious." He was hired on July 17, 1978, and fired three months later. "During his brief. . . employment, he was warned twice about [his] amount of work. . . and [his] priorities." The spokesman added, "On his termination paper, Mr. X's supervisor wrote, 'Does not follow day-shift instructions.'"

Radcliff is the most interesting fellow of all. In August 1979, two years after he had been fired by Illinois Power, Radcliff appeared before the Illinois Commerce Commission as an expert witness on the nuclear plant. Representing a group called Citizens for a Better Environment, Radcliff submitted as credentials entries in the 1972–1973 edition of *Who's Who in the East* and the 1975–1976 edition of *Who's Who in Finance.* They listed Radcliff as having earned a B.S. degree from the Georgia Institute of Technology in 1957, a Ph.D. from Walden University at Clearwater, Florida (1974), and as having been a professor at Fairleigh Dickinson University. With Radcliff under oath, this exchange took place between him and a hearing examiner:

QUESTION: Mr. Radcliff, did you graduate from the Georgia Institute of Technology in 1957 with a bachelor of science degree?
RADCLIFF: No. That was a major mistake I made on my part. . .
QUESTION: Mr. Radcliff, if you would please, did you in fact receive a Ph.D. from Walden University in 1974?
RADCLIFF: No, I did not. . .
QUESTION: Did you ever undertake any studies with Walden University?

RADCLIFF: No, no. [Radcliff had applied for admission there in 1975.]

Later in the hearings, Radcliff admitted that, though he had lectured to some students at Fairleigh Dickinson, he had never been a professor there.

It was three days after his public humiliation that Radcliff wrote to *60 Minutes*, urging its editors to do a story on Illinois Power.

Obviously, when *60 Minutes* became involved, hearings before the Illinois Commerce Commission already were in full swing. The nuclear plant, the commission would say later, was "unquestionably the driving force for the requested electric rate increase." The company wanted (and would receive) some of the proposed rate increase to be dedicated to the building of the nuclear plant. When the commission issued its ruling (three days after the *60 Minutes* segment had been broadcast), about a third of its report was devoted to the Clinton nuclear unit controversy. It said that "testimony by staff, intervenors [outside interests], and the company contain much discussion, both generically and as it relates to the specific issues of these proceedings, favoring and opposing the inclusion of construction-work-in-progress in the rate base."

Two of the seven staff members assigned to investigating the Illinois Power rate-increase request were outspoken in their criticism of the Clinton project. They maintained that the project compared unfavorably with cost overruns elsewhere, and the commission agreed. The company took sharp exception. The commission also did not believe the company's current cost estimates would hold, and so required monthly estimates thereafter.

The elements existed for a sound story filled with furious and significant disagreement among company officials, commissioners, majority and dissenting staff members, environmentalists, antinuclear activists, citizens groups, and others. Instead, *60 Minutes* brought in the sound and fury, all right, but it signified just what you might expect. Neither Berg nor

Radcliff was identified as representing activist organizations opposed to the construction of a nuclear power plant; Reasoner's only reference to a possible connection was that "some of the anticompany forces have been the antinuclear groups... This time, their arguments were about dollars, not safety."

Instead of relying on the elements already existing for a reasonably spirited exchange about the economics of nuclear power, *60 Minutes* contrived to produce a segment more fundamentally confrontational: a man fearing retribution if he was identified (who turned out to have worked at the plant for three months); a man who claimed with a straight face that a major corporation was building its nuclear power plant without requiring written reports from staff (a charge the company termed "incredible")—and that particular fellow was known to *60 Minutes* as the nuclear industry's version of Janet Cooke; and a man who said he had witnessed waste amounting to tens of millions of dollars (all in the nine months he was on the job).

As to Berg's allegations about walls being built and torn down in rapid succession to no apparent purpose, the company's videotaped reply said that Berg, who had repeated those charges over a long period of time, had "never ...produced any evidence."

In quoting Radcliff and the others, *60 Minutes* laid the groundwork for maintaining that the Clinton plant was costing far more than other plants of its type. Reasoner put the icing on the cake when he commented that company executive Gerstner, when asserting that the Clinton project was little different from similar projects in terms of cost increases, was selecting "his own favorite nuclear projects for comparison. Our own comparisons show that, against other plants of similar design, Clinton cost overruns are well ahead of the pack."

Reasoner's assertion was defended later by Robert Chandler, vice president of CBS News, on the grounds that the Illinois Commerce Commission agreed that a plant of "identical vintage" elsewhere in Illinois was increasing at half the rate as Clinton. That evaded the issue. For one thing, Gerstner spelled out for Reasoner, on camera (an explanation included in the company's videotape, though not on *60 Minutes*), how Clinton compared with a half-dozen other boiling-water reactors, whose cost overruns were between 255 percent and 494 percent. The reactor the commission compared Clinton with is a pressurized-water reactor and was part of a four-unit construction package that, like anything bought in quantity, "afforded an extraordinary advantage in pricing versus a single unit," a company spokesman said. Most important, however, is that *60 Minutes* never revealed its "own comparisons" of nuclear construction costs; the basis on which Reasoner concluded that Clinton was "well ahead of the pack" on cost overruns remains a mystery.

Reasoner presented on the segment "the latest report provided by Illinois Power to the Nuclear Regulatory Commission" regarding whether a "nuclear plant is on schedule...But with the help of some experts, we found some questionable claims here." Reasoner went through the chart, showing at one point that Illinois Power would take only two weeks to perform certain tests, though "the median time for all nuclear plants for these tests is fourteen months."

Steve Radcliff, apparently one of Reasoner's "experts," appeared on camera to say that "if they are able to do it, they should be written up in Ripley's *Believe It or Not.*"

Reasoner asked Gerstner about that. His answer was not included in the program, though Gerstner explained at length that what Reasoner was talking about was a milestone, rather than a construction, schedule.

GERSTNER [being interviewed by Reasoner]: The diagram you refer to is called a milestone schedule...It's not...what we would call a schedule. It's more a coordinating tool between the utility builder and the NRC...One of the basic ideas of this is so the NRC can schedule its time to be there to make the specific checks that they make at those milestone points.

Gerstner used a specific example to explain the difference: setting the reactor pressure vessel, which had just been done the previous weekend. He said that it took a day and a half to move the vessel from a silo six hundred feet from the containment building and then lower it into the center of that building. The firm that specializes in moving the vessel had come on the site six weeks earlier, however, to prepare for the move and conduct its tests. It would be there a week following the move, Gerstner said, "cleaning up and moving their equipment out. So maybe you could say, then, that's seven weeks." The company, however, "began doing the planning and work necessary for this move" two months before, "when we had to excavate the dirt between the silo and the containment vessel, replace it with a special fill and compact it, because we were going to roll that 620-ton monster over it." Gerstner said that on the milestone schedule, "we chose to report to the NRC that the lift would be one week." In other words, the lift would occur within that week, so the NRC could plan to observe it; it did not mean that from start to finish, the entire planning, preparation, and execution of the move could be accomplished in a week.

Subsequently, the company contended that "the point which Illinois Power finds most disturbing about this...is the chronology in which CBS put it together. Mr. Reasoner's [televised] performance with the milestone chart was filmed in Springfield on Monday, October 8. His interview with Mr. Gerstner took place on Tuesday, October 9. In other words, the *60 Minutes* conclusion on this issue was already in the can before the question was even asked of Illinois Power."

Reasoner thought the Illinois Power Company officials "were very nice people and they were very cooperative with us...They were very upset about the broadcast...I think it was a fair enough piece. If I have any reservations about it...we did take one company. Obviously, in a fifteen-minute piece, you can't take the forty or fifty companies that are struggling through nuclear construction...Inflation and cost overruns are horrific—and they are particularly horrific in nuclear construction for all kinds of reasons, including changing government standards, and red tape, and resentment, and antinuclear people making delays, and so on. . . .

"We took one [company]. I think that's fair, but it's also a little hard on that company. I think they were a pretty good example of bad practice but, still, you are singling out one operation.

"In all fairness to us, you can't get it all in fifteen minutes. . . The basic body of evidence that we had that led to whatever tone was in the piece was very strong. We were not twisting anything. And in their reply, they were very slick — and I don't blame them for being very slick. They were very sore.

"But they picked a case that they used of the man who we gave a couple of minutes to, Steve Radcliff, and they pointed out that he had. . . claimed a degree that he didn't have. They didn't point out that he never claimed that to them. He was hired by them exactly as what he was. . .

"The essential point on the question of how long it takes to do the final tests can get so confused in technical terms, and all I can say is we were right, and the guy. . . for the Nuclear Regulatory Commission said we were right.

"It was not an unfair piece, because. . . our basic theme was: here's a facility which has had full approval, does not have any substantial opposition in its home community area, started by a company which has an excellent record as a utility but which has gotten involved in this — a project that admittedly is costing three or four times the initial cost estimate.

"I think we had a perfectly legitimate piece of journalism about a major American problem. . . My conscience is clear on it."

12

The Media
Made the Case

ST. MARYS is a small town tucked in Georgia's extreme southeastern corner on glistening Cumberland Sound, just over the state line from Jacksonville, Florida. Local historians say the town, in sprawling Camden County, is America's second-oldest settlement, after St. Augustine, Florida; and, despite more than forty years of pollution from Gilman Paper Company, which dominates St. Marys, its natural beauty, enhanced by an abundance of arching, moss-laden oaks, stately pines, and rich magnolias, remains soft and gentle to the eye and spirit.

Nothing else is soft and gentle about St. Marys. Its political intrigues over the past decades have been characterized by enough cunning, duplicity, and unscrupulousness to make Niccolò Machiavelli uncomfortable. Its people could proclaim, with Lear, "Machinations, hollowness, treachery, and all ruinous disorders, follow us disquietly to our graves"; or, with Jim Talley, a Gilman Paper Company executive, "In St. Marys, I suppose somebody's lying about everything, or everybody's lying about something."

For a fleeting moment in the spring of 1972, national

media, including *60 Minutes*, shone their blinding light on St. Marys and, more like a Grade B Western than the even-handed appraisal of Jim Talley, found good guys and bad guys, white hats and black hats. As they almost always do, the media championed the "little man" against the "giant." In so doing, they set off a chain reaction that not only resulted in what a federal appeals court found to be an unconscionably unfair conviction of three executives (on charges relating to a conspiracy to commit murder), but elevated to martyrdom some who, on closer examination, appear undeserving.

However, the media left the scene as quickly as they had appeared, never telling us how it all came out, never determining whether their revelations stood the test of time. I was among the media representatives who, in 1972, were drawn to St. Marys. Nearly a decade later, I decided to re-examine what I and the others had reported, and to compare the story that was relayed then to millions of viewers and readers with the truth of the matter today.

As in most Southern mill towns, nearly everything good or bad that has ever happened in St. Marys can be traced, in some fashion, to the "company." St. Marys was a dying town at the onset of World War II; it contained three hundred residents, a burned-out sawmill, and a shut-down porgy fishery. That's when the Gilman family decided to open a paper mill there, initially employing 125 people. The town grew with the mill, which now employs a third of St. Marys' five thousand-plus population, the overwhelming majority of all wage-earners. Largely because of the paper company's paternalistic beneficence, St. Marys boasts a well-equipped hospital, a large public swimming pool, a well-stocked public library, a diverse public recreation program, and—even taking into account the less-citified seven thousand souls who make up the remainder of Camden County's population— the highest per-family annual income of all Georgia's 159 counties.

On the debit side, the mill, like most in the South, had been a wanton polluter and, before undertaking a $60 million expansion in the 1960s, had negotiated an agreement with the town fathers (most of whom are employed by Gilman) to limit city taxes to less than $50,000 a year. Presiding over the town's economic and social life was George Brumley, who was installed as the mill's executive vice president in 1948 and remained there until his retirement in the mid-1970s. Brumley was the key figure in organizing the city's first bank; he controlled the nine-member hospital board; he owned large tracts of choice real estate; he and his wife even presided over meetings of St. Marys' bridge club. The mill's lawyer, Robert Harrison, was city attorney, hospital board attorney, county attorney, housing authority attorney, and, between 1966 and 1970, the area's member in the Georgia House of Representatives, where, among other acts of fealty, he once tried to push through the legislature a bill allowing a land company owned by one of his clients to develop protected state land. Brumley's son was vice president of the land-developing firm.

"Of course, through the years," Brumley once conceded, "all the civic and governmental bodies in the area had Gilman employees, often in a majority. If you start with the assumption that the presence of Gilman employees means company control, then, sure, we run everything." The mill's suzerainty seemed widely accepted.

Gilman ran St. Marys—but it by no means controlled Camden County. For years, a fierce political rivalry existed between the county's so-called North End, populated by owners of extensive woodland plantations and their workers, nearly all of them black, and the Gilman-dominated southern portion of the county. Until the mill's growth drew more and more workers to St. Marys—both by natural flow and by an overt mill policy that workers had to live in or near the town—the North End dominated county politics. For instance, while Gilman pays limited taxes in St. Marys, it pays ten times as much to the county. Although St. Marys was usually overlooked by the county in its road-building program, the thinly populated North End is laced with good roads, many built especially to provide access to the homes of individual landowners. Yet taxes on woodlands in Camden County are lower than in most Georgia counties, and during the 1960s three attempts by the county school board to issue bonds to improve dilapidated county high schools (which would have required higher property taxes) were defeated because of overwhelming opposition by the North End voters.

The mill's policy of demanding that its workers live in St. Marys was designed specifically to try to offset the land-owners' control of county politics. By the late 1960s, the Gilman-controlled hospital board voted to build a convales-cent center in St. Marys rather than in the North End, which had wanted it there. In 1968, a Gilman-dominated school board again proposed a bond issue; it wanted a new, consolidated county high school—and it wanted it in St. Marys.

With this bond issue the troubles in St. Marys began.

The county's two existing high schools were old and ill-equipped. Still, they were centrally located in a large county and, perhaps more important to rural Georgians, they were segregated: one for blacks, the other for whites. The courts had ordered Camden County to desegregate. If the new bond issue passed, there would be a single high school for all students, and it would be located in St. Marys. If the bond issue failed, the existing schools would be "paired"—that is, some students from each school would be exchanged for an equal number from the other school. A number of North End landowners, however, knew that with pairing, the court ruling could be skirted. The rule in the rural South was that only a few blacks wanted to integrate previously all-white schools, and most black families developed fierce loyalties to previously all-black schools. With integration, many blacks feared (with reason) that fewer of their sons and daughters would hold school offices, be elected to school clubs, be chosen as cheerleaders, make the athletic squads, play in the school band. The result was that pairing of two rural schools usually meant that a few blacks would enter the all-white school, but the all-black school would remain black. With a single, consolidated high school, however, there could be only one outcome: full integration.

Into this emotionally charged issue stepped a young, athletic physician, two years out of medical school, who had moved to St. Marys in 1966, when he received his diploma. Carl Drury, then twenty-eight, started speaking out against the school bond issue on the grounds that it would result in extraordinarily long bus rides for North End children — up to three hours each way, in fact. Those opposing the bond issue welcomed the support of a young, charming, articulate professional man. Many urged him to run against Robert Harrison for the legislature, but he declined. The mill and most of its workers labored mightily for passage of the bond issue. Gilman executive Talley was chairman of the school board. He claimed that Drury was fighting the bond issue because he opposed integration. Drury denied it.

The day of the special bond-issue election was in April 1968, shortly after the assassination of Martin Luther King, Jr. Dr. Drury had been activated by the National Guard. According to three affidavits, sworn to more than two years later (in the midst of a vigorously contested campaign by Drury for Harrison's legislative seat), the armed, khaki-clad Drury stormed toward city hall, where the American flag was flying at half-staff in memory of King's death. "He was threatening to shoot the flag of the United States down," swore Hayman B. Brown, a black part-time St. Marys policeman, "unless city officials took it down or raised it to full mast, and...he was also threatening to shoot all blacks involved in the balloting for a new consolidated and integrated school." Drury later pointed out that all three who swore to the alleged incident were connected with the mill, that the affidavits were sworn out in the midst of his campaign to unseat Harrison, and that for Harrison to win, he would have had to draw black votes from rural areas that usually were cast against the candidate from St. Marys. "Show something like that around to black people," he said, "and who do you think they'd vote for?"

The school bond issue passed as a result of prodigious support in St. Marys, and a two-year construction program was begun. Racial animosities flared now and again, but quickly were extinguished. In 1970, Drury decided to challenge Harrison for the district's seat in the Georgia legislature. The feisty young physician launched a campaign filled with acrimony: he attacked the mill for not paying a fair share of city taxes (but failed to mention the mill's heavy county-tax load); he accused Harrison of being Brumley's lackey in the legislature (an allegation with some foundation of truth); he attacked the mill head-on for its pollution of the air and of the St. Marys River, which threatened nearby estuaries and their life-giving plankton; he claimed Harrison was antilabor (though he was supported by most of the state's labor leaders); he charged that Harrison had sponsored a bill that would lead to a local payroll tax (which Drury himself later conceded was political hyperbole).

Just before the election, the new consolidated high school opened its doors. Immediately, resentment over integration (blacks made up 40 percent of the student population) and extensive busing swept through Camden County. Drury made the new school the central issue of the campaign. He won Harrison's seat with the combined support of the North End, Gilman's growing contingent of unionized workers, residents of outlying counties who resented St. Marys, and environmentalists from elsewhere in the state who volunteered services and contributed money. The bitter fruit of the campaign rotted in the wake of the election.

"I've lived in this town over thirty years," Brumley said angrily after the balloting. "I raised my family here. Along comes this man who calls me a fraud, holds me up to ridicule in front of the employees and the town. Am I supposed to take all this lying down?"

Clearly, he did not. During the campaign, the mill was involved in producing the affidavits charging Drury with racial hatred. After the election, three teen-age girls and a young housewife swore in affidavits that Drury had committed statutory rape and sexual assault. Drury's medical license was suspended; the legislature held up awarding him his seat; a grand jury was convened to investigate the allegations. The stories told by the housewife and teen-agers were contradictory. One charge—that Drury had sexual relations with a sixteen-year-old, shortly after he removed her tonsils, while her fifteen-year-old girl friend looked on— strained belief. The sixteen-year-old, Susanne Bloodworth, claimed that she continued the affair with Drury even after the hospital incident. Drury was cleared of all charges, his license was restored, and he was seated in the legislature. (After the charges were made, Drury asserted that Dr. George Barker called on him in the mill's behalf; Barker, an elderly physician, supposedly said that if Drury gave up his legislative seat and left town, the charges would be dropped. When I questioned Dr. Barker about it in 1972, he said the actual events were reversed: Drury approached Barker before the affidavits were sworn out, offering to leave town if the women could be restrained.)

After Drury was cleared, Henry Bloodworth, a mill employee and Susanne's father, attacked Drury with a metal pipe. At his trial, Bloodworth claimed he had gone to see Drury to demand that he stop telephoning his daughter at the school for girls to which she had been shipped. Bloodworth swore that as he pursued the agile Drury, the doctor repeatedly fell down and hurt himself. The jury acquitted Bloodworth after Drury admitted that he was well enough to play in a golf tournament (where he shot in the low seventies) a week after the attack. (The county grand jury, which had cleared Drury of the charges that he molested Susanne Bloodworth, had been dominated by Drury supporters; most of the members of the city trial jury, which acquitted Henry Bloodworth of conking Drury on the head, were Gilman employees. It appeared to be a tit-for-tat verdict.)

In the spring of 1972, the national media's attention was

drawn to the Byzantine struggles of St. Marys. In its May 1972 issue, *Harper's* presented a lengthy article by Harrison Wellford, former executive director of Ralph Nader's Center for the Study of Responsive Law, and Peter Schuck, a consultant to the center. The article condemned the mill, its politicking, and its seeming to be the instigator of the several attacks on Drury's integrity and person. On May 7, 1972, *60 Minutes* presented its version of the story. Barry Lando, the segment's producer, did most of the initial reporting, and Mike Wallace did the interviewing.

> WALLACE: Well, Drury defeated Harrison, defeated the mill. And that angered George Brumley. . .who feared that Drury, as state representative, would introduce legislation hostile to the mill. . .He accused Drury of waging a personal vendetta.

Brumley then appeared on camera; he was shown refusing three times to respond to Wallace's questions about the nature of Drury's vendetta. Wallace next interviewed a policeman who had been fired; the ex-cop stated that the mill virtually owned the police force. Wallace then mentioned the allegations of rape:

> WALLACE: Susanne's affidavit was drawn up in the office of lawyer Robert Harrison. But there were one or two strange things about Susanne's story. Though the rape allegedly took place in March of 1970, she told no one about it until the following November. And after she got out of the hospital, it turned out that Susanne had gone back to Dr. Drury for postoperative treatment.

Wallace then interviewed Susanne's father, whose testimony obviously didn't play well:

> BLOODWORTH: Mr. Wallace, I went by there. . .to see about him leaving my daughter alone.
> WALLACE: You did not attack him?
> BLOODWORTH: I did not attack him, no.
> WALLACE: How did he get hurt?
> BLOODWORTH: He fell, running.
> WALLACE: Running?

BLOODWORTH: It rained that night. And he ran out on the gravel. And I don't know whether he had leather shoes on or what, but every time he'd make a cut, he'd fall in the gravel and he'd roll and get up and run again.
WALLACE: You were chasing him?
BLOODWORTH: Oh, sure...
WALLACE: Why—I mean, he's a big, tough fellow. Why would he want to run away from a little fellow like you?
BLOODWORTH: Far as I'm concerned, when it comes to my daughter, there's nobody too tough, hear?

Wallace interviewed a friend of Drury's who had been fired from the mill; Brumley came back on camera, again refusing to answer Wallace's questions; Harrison was interviewed about the rape charges, which he had helped to draw up, and about the company's special tax rate in St. Marys. Wallace's comments clarified any doubts viewers may have had about who was in the wrong:

WALLACE: There are those who suggest that living in a company town means that...in a certain sense your mind and heart, your political affiliation, is bought by the company...We found that fear of taking an "anticompany" position was common among Gilman employees, both executives and workers. They're afraid to speak out on politics, pollution, or taxes. One of the city's three tax assessors told us that he'd lose his job at the mill if he tried to challenge the Gilman Company's low tax [payment] of only $45,000. Paranoia is so widespread among Drury's supporters that some are even reluctant to use their telephones for fear they're tapped.

Wallace closed the program by announcing that the Justice Department in Washington and a federal grand jury in Savannah had "begun to look into what's happening in St. Marys. They're trying to determine if Carl Drury's civil rights have been infringed upon."

When I saw the *Harper's* article a few days before the *60 Minutes* segment was broadcast, I telephoned Wellford. (At the time, I was a correspondent in *Newsweek*'s Atlanta bureau, and I had been searching for an interesting story to revive my morale. It had been waning since my editors decided that George Wallace's presidential campaign, which I had been observing from Florida to Indiana the previous few months, no longer required my day-to-day attention; the Little Judge's campaigns in the Michigan and Maryland primaries were not likely, they thought, to produce significant news.)

Wellford gave me the names of several people in St. Marys who he thought would be helpful. My best source, he assured me, would be Wyman Westberry, a millwright at Gilman, an active union member, and a staunch political supporter of Drury's. Westberry, twenty-nine, had been mentioned only in passing in the article, but according to Wellford, he was the man who had tipped off the Nader group to the situation in St. Marys. Wellford also suggested that I speak to Barry Lando of *60 Minutes*. The CBS program would present its own report on St. Marys in a few days, Wellford told me, but Lando and Wallace had come across additional startling information, which, for reasons of possible libel, they had decided to omit from their segment. I telephoned Lando, who informed me that he had explored a tip that George Brumley, Robert Harrison, and a mill executive named William T. (Tommy) Thomas had tried to hire a man to murder Westberry. It would be a good idea, Lando suggested, if I pursued the lead. I agreed.

When I arrived in St. Marys, I had several preconceptions about its people and institutions—a journalistic theory of prosecution. I imagined Drury as an embattled hero, fighting pollution and political domination by the mill; Westberry was a "common man" providing uncommon support to those who would champion the causes of justice; Brumley symbolized the company that owned the town and its people—and might even murder to retain its totalitarian control. Clearly, pinning down the "murder" plot was the key to my reporting; it would provide *Newsweek* with a fresh angle on a story that had been reported already by *60 Minutes* and *Harper's*. As it turned out, the week I spent in St. Marys proved to be the turning point of the entire, bizarre confrontation between the mill and its antagonists. Before the week was out, Lawrence E. Brown, a part-time mill employee who previously had told a federal district attorney and the Georgia Bureau of Investigation—as well as Barry Lando and Mike Wallace—that he had been approached by mill executives to murder Westberry, signed a sworn statement that Westberry and a friend, George Beaver, had offered him money to make up the story about the assassination plot.

Within hours of my arrival in St. Marys, I realized that my ability to separate heroes from villains was not as well developed as Wellford's, Schuck's, Lando's, or Wallace's. In the story that appeared in *Newsweek* a week after the *60 Minutes* broadcast, I reported that "the picture of St. Marys is a puzzling shade of gray." Very little of what I discovered there could be presented in *Newsweek*'s eight-hundred-word article; much more was contained in my seven-thousand-word file, from which my editors in New York extracted the obviously radically condensed published report. A great deal more than that happened subsequently, but the national media, as is their wont, ignored it. (The very day on which the issue of *Newsweek* appeared containing my St. Marys report, George Wallace was shot at a shopping center in Laurel, Maryland. My editors ordered me to the scene immediately; from that day through the Democratic National Convention that summer, I did little other than cover Wallace and the impact of his candidacy and martyrdom on political affairs in 1972. I gave St. Marys no further thought until I began writing this book. My purpose was to find out, with the benefit of years of hindsight, the extent to which the brief but intense attention devoted to St. Marys by national media had reflected—and affected—reality.)

My preconceptions began crumbling when George Brumley, whom I had expected to be cool and taciturn, greeted me warmly and was communicative. Perhaps he had realized, from watching *60 Minutes* the day before I arrived in St.

Marys, that, though keeping one's counsel may be viewed as
wisdom in business circles, it looked like flat-out evasion on
television. The exchanges between Wallace and Brumley, as
telecast on *60 Minutes,* could not have excited any sympathy
for the mill.

WALLACE: What's in it for [Drury] to conduct this personal
vendetta that you allege?
BRUMLEY: Mike, I have no other comment on the point.
WALLACE: It's just that he's out to get George Brumley or
Bob Harrison or whomever?
BRUMLEY: I have no other comment.
WALLACE: Well, you say—I mean you charge that it's a
personal vendetta, but then you don't want to say why it's a
personal vendetta.
BRUMLEY: I'm not interested in becoming involved in a
detailed discussion with regard to personal relations with Dr.
Carl Drury.

Brumley reappeared later in the segment, after Wallace
had interviewed Brian Lynn, a friend of Drury's who was
fired by the mill after Drury's election victory. Wallace said
Brumley told him Lynn was let go when business was slack;
Wallace asked why Lynn, who had worked for Gilman for a
dozen years, had not been rehired when business picked up.

BRUMLEY: Well, Mike, I really have no interest in discussing
personalities and why we chose not to rehire.
WALLACE: But he was laid off purely for economic reasons
and not for political reasons?
BRUMLEY: That is correct.
WALLACE: Well, I confess, then, I find it difficult to
understand. If he was laid off for economic and not political
reasons, then he ought to be rehired, one might think, for
economic and not for political reasons.
BRUMLEY: Well, once again I say that I'm not interested in
discussing that particular point.
WALLACE: What sort of loyalty do you expect from your
executives, as far as politics are concerned? Candidly.
BRUMLEY: The principal loyalty that we expect from our
executives is not to adopt or take an anticompany position.

WALLACE: What does that mean?
BRUMLEY: Just what I said.
WALLACE: Well, then, what is an anticompany position that you would not find acceptable from one of your executives?
BRUMLEY: Well, an anticompany position would be a position of publicly being for people who are anticompany and taking an anticompany position.
WALLACE: Is Carl Drury anticompany?
BRUMLEY: He has been, yes.

The implication that pro-Drury executives would not be welcome at Gilman is obvious, although it isn't obvious whether Lynn was an "executive" (he had been a shift supervisor in the mill's sealing tape department), nor was the question asked directly whether supporting Drury would mean being fired. Whatever the likelihood of the matter, neither Gilman nor Brumley is alone among companies and their executive officers who frown on their employees publicly taking anticompany positions. (CBS News, for one, sharply rebuked correspondent Roger Mudd after he criticized television news in a speech given at a university in December 1970. He could salvage his career, he was warned by a superior, if he learned "to keep his mouth shut.")

In *Harper's*, Brumley was described as "icily formal and aloof, with a penchant for elegant brocade shirts and *ex cathedra* pronouncements." My file to *Newsweek* described Brumley as a "courtly, carefully groomed, soft-spoken man." (It may well have been that Brumley treated Wellford and Schuck frigidly; both had been instrumental in the preparation of the Nader organization's widely publicized denunciation of paper mills along the Georgia coast.)

Westberry sounded brave in the Wellford-Schuck article: "We work hard. The mill is not down here out of charity. They're not giving us anything we haven't earned. I don't like to see the little man pushed around. Why should he have to leave his home town just so he can speak his mind and be his own man?" The Westberry I met used the epithet "nigger" a good bit in his conversation, until I told him it offended me.

Drury's affluence, reported by *60 Minutes*, seemed out of place with the beleagured defender whose life is in danger; when I learned he had played in a golf tournament a week after he had been "beaten with a blunt instrument" by Bloodworth, as *Harper's* described it, the incident seemed less than menacing.

When I talked to Jim Talley, the mill's safety director, and Bob Smith, who had worked under Talley, I received my first major shock. Wellford and Schuck had written that "each election year, [Smith] had to set aside his other work in order to...do other campaign work...According to Smith, Talley directed the campaigns...from [his] office and would call on Smith at all hours to run political errands." Quoting Smith, the article said that Talley ordered him to "spend all the time and money [he] needed" to learn who in the plant was voting for Drury. "All the men who were Drury supporters would be terminated." Smith said he refused to spy on his friends; he found a new job after he was ordered to "get that damned list or that's it."

Although Smith was not included on the *60 Minutes* program, he related substantially the same story to CBS reporters and to me. He told me that after the *Harper's* article appeared and the *60 Minutes* segment was broadcast, Talley had telephoned him at the mill in Dover, Georgia, to which Smith had moved in October 1970. He said he avoided Talley's calls for four days, but accepted a call on the fifth day, when he was told Talley wanted to speak to Smith's boss. Smith recalled that Talley "told me it was going to court and asked if I planned to testify to the grand jury the way I'd been telling it. I told him I was, that I could tell a lot worse things. And he said, 'If you do, we're gonna burn you up. You're dead here in St. Marys.' He doesn't know it, but I've got it on tape." Smith said he would play the tape for me over the telephone if I called him at home next evening.

Jim Talley, however, appeared to be the antithesis of the political boss. He recently had returned from Spain, where he and his wife had been painting landscapes; about fifteen of his paintings had been purchased when his work was exhibited in Jacksonville museums. But Jim Talley, despite his soft, south Georgia drawl and his artistic avocation, is no naïf. Smith obviously was unaware that Talley also had a tape of the conversation, which he played for me. On the tape, I heard Talley tell Smith, "Well, boy, it's hit the fan." Talley proceeded to mention the *Harper's* article, which Smith said he hadn't seen. Talley read him the section quoting Smith.

"Where would they get that from?...Where in the world would they have gotten that?"

"Well, they're really after our butts," Talley said. Smith went on to say that he had talked to no one except Barry Lando of CBS and that he had told Talley about that in an earlier conversation.

"What did you tell them?" Talley asked.

"Nothin'," Smith replied firmly. "...I don't know where they got it, but they're not gonna get me in any court...As far as I'm concerned, they can go to hell because I'm not gonna get involved in anything I don't know anything about...I've told you the way it was."

The taped conversation started precisely as Smith had described it to me. From that point on, though, there was no similarity between his recollection and reality. I reached Smith that night, told him about the tape, and asked whether he could explain the discrepancy between it and his memory—a memory that included grave threats against him and his own steely resolve to resist any threats. He hung up; for the next two days, when I telephoned, either there was no answer, or a busy signal sounded. (The operator reported that the phone was out of order.)

I encountered other discrepancies. According to the Wellford-Schuck article, a Chevrolet dealer lost $52,000 of mill business "overnight" when his support of Drury became known. The dealer, Colquitt G. Russell, had sold Gilman twelve vehicles a year, which, before the Drury-Harrison campaign, had amounted to $52,000. During the campaign, Russell told me, union workers at Gilman struck over provisions of a pension plan. Mill officials believed that Drury, who was supported by the local unions, had encouraged the strike. Russell said that Perry Whetstone, a mill executive, came to his showroom in the midst of the strike. "The mill doesn't feel like it can do business with anyone who helps prolong this strike," Russell recalled Whetstone telling him. "We feel that anyone helping Dr. Drury is helping prolong this strike." The mill started buying its cars and pickups at Coastal Chevrolet in Brunswick, Georgia. "What we need," Russell said, "is another pulp mill... Have you ever known a town with one big company where the company didn't have too much influence? What can you do unless there's competition?" When I questioned Russell closely, he conceded that his markup on the cars he sold Gilman was so small that he hadn't lost much in terms of profit. In addition, less than a year after the mill failed to renew its contract with Russell, he sold new automobiles to Thaddeus Smith, George Brumley's son-in-law — and to none other than Perry Whetstone, the man who is supposed to have told Russell the mill was canceling its business with him because of his politics. Russell's loss of business may also have had something to do with his having been chairman of the Camden County Commission at that time, and a long-time political foe of the St. Marys–based mill.

After his election in 1970, Drury demonstrated that he knew a bit about power politics. He persuaded the county commission to fire Harrison as its attorney. Harrison's replacement was Drury's friend and personal attorney, Blynn Taylor. Shortly after the election, Drury purchased Laurel Island, a pristine, coastal island just off St. Marys. He told me he had paid $100,000 for it. The island was sold to Drury by Rayonier, a paper mill in the nearby town of Fernandina Beach, Florida. I was unable to confirm what Drury had, in fact, paid for the island; he agreed, however, that $100,000 was a "reasonable price." It appeared contradictory that a man who so recently had run a political campaign condemning the pollution of Gilman and other paper mills in the area would enter into a business deal with one of those polluters. While the media were focusing on Drury's difficulties in St. Marys, he had hired his friend Brian Lynn (who had been depicted by *Harper's* as unable to get work) to clear areas of the island that Drury maintained he would turn into a wildlife preserve (and take the tax benefits) or develop for vacation homes.

What neither *Harper's* nor *60 Minutes* reported—although both knew of it—was the story of the alleged plot to murder Wyman Westberry. The story, in its initial form, went this way:

In April, Lawrence Brown, the part-time black employee in Gilman's laboratory division, approached George Beaver, a friend of Westberry's who worked in the lab. Brown, according to Beaver, said that a mill executive, Tommy Thomas, arranged a meeting with Brown at Ralph Bunche School in the nearby town of Woodbine. Thomas, whose duties included scheduling part-time workers, knew that Brown—deeply in debt and the father of six—was in desperate financial straits. His house had just burned to the ground. According to the story Beaver told me, Brown said that Thomas arrived at the school accompanied by George Brumley and Robert Harrison. Thomas offered Brown $1500 to kill Westberry. Brumley, Harrison, and Thomas outlined a plan, and Brown said he would think about it. On April 14, 1972, Beaver arranged for Brown to tell his story to a U.S. Attorney. On April 18, Brown met with Mike Wallace and Barry Lando in Jacksonville; the next morning, he returned and told the story again, this time on film for *60 Minutes*. On April 21, Brown went to Savannah, where an agent of the Georgia Bureau of Investigation administered a lie-detector test. A GBI spokesman in Atlanta told me at the time that Brown had "passed" the test and that the case was "active." He added, "What can we do? It's one man's word against three men and we'd have to try it down there [in St. Marys]. We wouldn't have a chance."

Two days after Beaver told me this story, Brown, accompanied by Tommy Thomas, signed a sworn statement before the Camden County sheriff, the county district attorney, and a GBI representative. He said that he had made up the earlier story; that Beaver had promised him $10,000 to make it up; that over a period of weeks he had received help in financing a new car. I looked into that last assertion and found that on April 19, the day he had filmed for *60 Minutes,* Brown, who had been broke, wrote a check for $593 as a down payment on a year-old car; the balance came from a bank in St. Marys whose president was a friend and supporter of Carl Drury's.

It had taken me less than a week to determine that in St. Marys there were no clear-cut heroes — only villains. Two weeks after my article appeared in *Newsweek,* Brown testified to a federal grand jury that he had made up the story about the mill executives meeting him to persuade him to murder Westberry. Two weeks after that, George Beaver swore in an affidavit that he had indeed bribed Brown to make up the story. A month later, Beaver recanted; he said the company had bribed him to back up the story Brown had told the grand jury.

Why kill Wyman Westberry? The motive, supposedly, was media. Although neither *Harper's* nor *60 Minutes* made any mention of it, Wyman Westberry had alerted the national media, whose attention cast Gilman Paper Company's reputation in such questionable light. In fact, Wellford and his Nader's Raiders had known Westberry and Drury since the 1970 Drury-Harrison campaign — and had worked in behalf of Drury's election.

At the time of the campaign, Wellford was director of Nader's Savannah River Project, a study of the effect of pollution from Savannah's Union Camp and other nearby paper mills on the river and the life of the communities that depended on it. Westberry had read of the project and, according to Wellford, "he showed up on our doorstep one night out of the blue." To Wellford and to his assistant, James Fallows, Westberry, in the summer of 1970, "gushed out his story" about pollution from the mill. Fallows knew Drury and introduced him to Westberry. During the campaign, Wellford told me, the Nader organization "provided environmental analysis and information that helped make Drury's case against the mill."

After the election, Wellford told me, "Wyman said the situation became much worse. He called week in and week out. He wanted us to do something—to study the situation and call it to the attention of people in Washington." Wellford was hesitant to involve the Nader group further in the politics of St. Marys: "We didn't control the situation and we didn't know if we could help...Then Drury was assaulted by Bloodworth." Because it seemed to be a matter of life and death, Wellford and his colleague, Schuck, sought help from the Department of Justice in Washington while, at about that time, Westberry called on Governor Jimmy Carter (whom Drury had supported). Neither effort paid off—at least, not right away.

But Westberry was persistent. Again, he asked the Nader team for help. This time, Wellford and Schuck adopted a new course of action. They decided to probe the situation, write an article, and encourage other media to investigate. By October 1971, Wellford and Schuck completed their own reporting. Wellford said he approached *60 Minutes;* Barry Lando, who had joined *60 Minutes* a short time before, expressed interest. Lando's initial effort for *60 Minutes* had been a failure—a "fiasco," Lando characterized it—and he was eager to embark on a project that would establish his credentials with Don Hewitt and the correspondent with whom he worked, Mike Wallace. As he had been for Wellford and Schuck (and as he would be for me later), Westberry became the media's primary "contact man" in St. Marys.

Events rapidly came to a head. In late April 1972, *Harper's* May issue hit the street with the Wellford-Schuck article, "Democracy and the Good Life in a Company Town: The Case of St. Marys, Georgia."

On Sunday, May 7, *60 Minutes* broadcast the Wallace-Lando segment, entitled "Company Town." On Monday,

May 15, *Newsweek* published (in its issue dated May 22) my report under the headline "Company Town: The Agony of St. Marys." Both *60 Minutes* and *Newsweek* reported that a federal grand jury would meet in Savannah to consider the extent to which the anti-Drury machinations could be proved and, if so, whether any violated federal law. On Wednesday, May 17, 1972, Lawrence Brown testified before the grand jury that he had made up the story about being approached the previous month by the mill executives to murder Wyman Westberry.

> DISTRICT ATTORNEY: All right, now, tell us about this fifteen-hundred-dollar offer to you, how that came about? Who were you supposed to kill—Westberry?
> BROWN: Wyman Westberry.
> D.A.: All right, tell us about that.
> BROWN: Well, it was a story that I was supposed to tell...
> D.A.: Who did you tell me had approached you about killing Westberry?...
> BROWN: I told you Tommy Thomas, Robert Harrison, and George Brumley. Those were the three guys I told you approached me...
> D.A.: Was there, in fact, any such meeting?
> BROWN: No.

Before the month was out, George Beaver swore that he had offered Brown $10,000 to make up the story about being hired to kill Westberry; Brown reversed himself again, this time saying he had been kidnaped by Thomas and others, who forced him to recant his original story; Beaver retracted his story in June, saying he had not, after all, tried to hire Brown to make up the story. In September, Gilman Paper Company fired Wyman Westberry. "Why are you firing me," Westberry demanded of a company official, "when I'm not guilty and not showing no information?" Shortly after his dismissal, Westberry filed a civil suit against Brumley, Harrison, and Thomas, seeking to recover damages based on their alleged plot to have him murdered.

The company's ostensible reason for firing Westberry was that it had learned he had been responsible, two and a half years earlier, for pouring acid on a black construction worker who had used a previously whites-only bathroom in the mill's maintenance department. Witnesses had come forward two years or so after the fact to denounce Westberry for earlier incidents. Testimony in his civil suit, which was tried while he sought arbitration to get his job back, cast Westberry as a violent racist.

Some time in late 1969, according to testimony, Westberry approached Raymond Dyals, a machinist and a member of the local union's grievance committee. Westberry complained that blacks were using the toilets in Gilman's maintenance department. He requested Dyals to bring his complaints before company officials; Dyals said Westberry wanted the company to prevent blacks from using the lavatory. A Gilman executive told Dyals "There was nothing that they could possibly do about it. It [integration] was here and we'd have to contend with it."

Dyals said he related to Westberry the substance of his conversation with the Gilman official. Westberry replied, Dyals recalled, "There was something that could be done about it. . . If the right stuff was thrown on there, it wouldn't take but one time and it would alleviate the problem."

The day before the incident the following March, a shipping supervisor saw Westberry enter the storeroom at the plant and request "something to put acid in." Westberry was given a glass beaker. That night, according to testimony from an instrument mechanic named J. T. Blount, Westberry drew "white liquor" from a metal tank in the plant's caustic room. (White liquor is what the workers call a caustic soda used in the processing of paper; it acts to soften pulpwood, or, as Blount described it, "eats the wood so you can cook it.") Westberry put the acid in what Blount described as a plastic jug.

The next day—the day of the incident—Westberry was leaving the restroom with James McGhin, a welder, just as a black man (whose name was listed in the transcripts as Rawls) was entering. "Who does he think he is," Westberry said to McGhin, "using our restroom?" Westberry picked up a beaker, which McGhin said contained white liquor, from a nearby shelf. Westberry told McGhin "he could get him [Rawls] out of there." They re-entered the lavatory, and Westberry climbed on a rack so that he could look down into the toilet. McGhin said he turned at that moment and left. "I heard the nigger screaming," he recalled.

Immediately, Westberry caught up with McGhin. "He got his so-and-so out of there," McGhin testified Westberry said. After the FBI entered the case in the fall of 1970, McGhin said Westberry visited him. McGhin said, "Wyman, you know this is the truth, just as good as anything." Westberry replied, "I'll do anything or give you anything you want if you will keep your mouth shut." Subsequently, when the incident was aired at a union meeting, Westberry rose and swore he didn't do it — "and I was sitting there knowing it," McGhin said, "and he [Westberry] dropped his head and wouldn't even look at me."

Some months after the incident, McGhin confided in a Baptist minister, William Carlton Owens, that he knew the identity of the person who had thrown the acid on the black employee. Owens testified that he urged McGhin to tell the truth to the investigators. McGhin didn't, but the night after the incident, he said, he revealed to a fellow welder, Marvin C. Jordan, that Westberry had poured acid on a black construction worker. McGhin swore Jordan to secrecy. Later, however, Jordan saw Westberry and asked him whether the story was true. Westberry said, "I didn't pour acid on him; I poured white liquor on him."

Blount, the mechanic who said he had seen Westberry draw white liquor from a caustic tank, heard about the acid-pouring incident "a day or two" after it happened. Asked why he didn't say anything at the time, he replied, "I might have been like a lot of the rest of them. I just don't want — the niggers was using our restrooms at that time and they was using our water fountains and our restrooms and I just didn't say anything about it."

Westberry consistently denied any responsibility for the attack on Rawls, who suffered first- and second-degree burns on his head and around his scrotum. Although he lost his civil suit, which was dismissed in 1973, Westberry won his labor arbitration. Testimony that had surfaced so long after the fact, and after Westberry had been the company's nemesis for two and a half years, was unacceptable to the arbitrator. Fallows, who decided to write a new article about Westberry, told me in 1981 that he had interviewed all those who had testified against Westberry in the Rawls incident, and, "while truth is at a premium in St. Marys, they all recanted."

Everyone, it seems, recants in St. Marys sooner or later. The fact is that Westberry went back to work at the mill and, despite the loss of his civil suit, remained determined to strike out at Brumley, Harrison, and Thomas. After he lost his civil suit, Westberry started on a new tack with old supporters. He reached Wellford and Schuck in Washington, urging them to pursue those in authority who could investigate the charges that the company had intended to kill him. At a Washington cocktail party, Schuck encountered a law school classmate, J. Stanley Pottinger, who was then the assistant attorney general in charge of the Justice Department's Civil Rights Division. It was to Pottinger that Schuck made his entreaty that the St. Marys case be reopened.

Pottinger turned the case over to Stephen Horn, a young lawyer who "was the new kid on the block" in the Civil Rights Division. Horn recalls that he "had nothing else to do at the time," so he pored over the available records pertaining to the St. Marys case. "It would go back and forth between us and the Criminal Division," Horn said. "It was like a jigsaw puzzle; I would take out the files, go over them, try to figure out where to put a piece, and then put it away again." Pottinger, Horn says, also was interested. "He's got a high level of curiosity," Horn recalled of his former boss, "and this was a curious case."

The case moved inexorably toward the convening of a grand jury in Savannah in June 1975. Indictments were brought against Brumley, Harrison, and Thomas in October, and after a nine-day trial in January 1976, the three were convicted of suborning perjury—persuading Lawrence Brown to lie to a federal grand jury when he testified that he had made up the story about the three trying to get him to murder Westberry. In other words, the Justice Department believed that the mill executives had, in fact, tried to have Westberry assassinated. An appeals court later wondered what had motivated the Justice Department. No federal crime was at issue; the case rested primarily on the uncorroborated testimony of Lawrence Brown, who had told several versions of the story already; the facts had been played out in detail in Westberry's civil suit less than two years earlier. Perhaps the reason was that a young attorney had little else to do, or, as Horn told me, that "the Justice Department certainly reacts more to cases involving publicity." Or perhaps it was Horn's and Pottinger's curiosity about a situation with more snarls and twists than a bowl of spaghetti.

Whatever the reason for bringing the case, there was never any doubt among the prosecutors as to why the defendants wanted Westberry killed. Horn, who prosecuted the case, told me, "The media certainly influenced the St. Marys case; in fact, the media made the case in the first place. Wyman Westberry had access to media—and media's interest in him led to the initial plan to kill him. But for his tenacity and talent in motivating the media, it wouldn't have happened."

On that point, and on almost none other, the United States Court of Appeals for the Fifth Circuit and the United States Department of Justice, Civil Rights Division, were in accord. In one of the more scathing opinions handed down by an appellate court, the judges, in October 1977, directed acquittal of the defendants on all charges. As strongly as the arbitration decision defended Westberry and suggested that the charges against him had been manufactured, the court of appeals' decision as strongly impugned Westberry and the case against Brumley, Harrison, and Thomas. Westberry, the court said, once before "pursued to exhaustion" his charges against the three men; he "was vigorously and relentingly pursuing a vendetta against Gilman, launching any available missile in the direction of his employer." At one point, the court referred to Westberry, somewhat gratuitously, as "the accused acid-thrower." Lawrence Brown was "a devastatingly impeached witness." When Brown first told his story to the Georgia Bureau of Investigation on April 19, 1972, a GBI agent listened on an extension as Brown telephoned Thomas and told him "he was ready to go ahead with the deal." Thomas responded, "Cool it. We will talk about it tomorrow at work." Five days later, Brown, fitted with a listening device, had a twelve-minute taped conversation with Thomas, "during which," the court noted, "Thomas described Westberry, Brown stated he was ready to go through with the deal, but Thomas told him to wait up a while."

The recorded conversation between Brown and Thomas was fishy, but the court noted that it was devoid of any details, and that not even Brown suggested Brumley and Harrison had said anything at all. At the April 9, 1972, meeting at which Thomas supposedly tried to hire Brown to kill Westberry, Brumley and Harrison said nothing, merely nodded their heads. Less than a month later, Brown changed his story and, less than a month after that, changed it again.

The saga of St. Marys is an example of national media's hit-and-run style. Often, of necessity, the media are simplistic, present stories in stark, vivid colors with little, if any, shading, frequently overlook the pith of a story — and yet can devastate those on whom they focus their lethal rays. If the mill can be believed, media prompted Westberry, Drury, Beaver, Brown, and probably others, to concoct a scheme that would destroy powerful executives of Gilman Paper Company in St. Marys. If Westberry and the others can be believed, media prompted high-level executives to plot murder, suborn perjury, and seduce a variety of people falsely to attribute racial prejudice to Drury and Westberry.

It is not difficult to find those, whose lives were touched by St. Marys, who maintain that the United States Court of Appeals was bought by Gilman, or that the United States Department of Justice got in bed with liars and racists to bring a polluter to its knees.

Except for Fallows, who returned to St. Marys a decade after he met Westberry to write about him and changes in the town (a new United States Navy installation has diluted Gilman's economic stranglehold), national media never gave the place another tumble. It is the old story of the city-slicker, who, after a one-night stand, during which he coos how much he loves the farmer's nubile daughter, leaves her pregnant and alone and is never seen or heard from again.

The lesson to be learned is that one should be wary of the bold, seemingly knowledgeable judgments from which media rarely shrink and about which media rarely are correct.

I asked Lloyd Brown, an old friend and an editor of *The Jacksonville Journal*, to review the St. Marys story nearly nine years after he and I first looked at it together. (He was then *Newsweek*'s "stringer," or part-time correspondent, in the area.) Not only did I want to learn what had happened in the ensuing years; I wanted an independent judgment of how well—or poorly—the media had fared in 1972.

Brown found Brumley retired "in fine style" in the plush resort of Sea Island, Georgia. He located Carl Drury in Brunswick, Georgia, where he continues to prosper. Tommy Thomas and Wyman Westberry remain at Gilman, and Harrison, removed from all mill business, is running "a thriving law firm."

He talked to them all (except for Lawrence Brown, who avoided him), and he concluded that "all of the national media failed to get the real story. It may have been a more subtle, less salable story about a political struggle in the Georgia backwoods where neither side had any heroes and where economics, politics, and social status all played a part. It would have taken more time and effort. The truth does, sometimes."

13 ═══════════════

We Have to Get
Pieces on the Air

*I*N SEPTEMBER 1970, in the midst of the trial of Second
Lieutenant William L. Calley for having murdered defenseless men, women, and children in My Lai village in Vietnam,
public perception of the military's honor and character
appeared to have hit the bottom. Then, in Fort McPherson,
Georgia, bad slipped to worse. A bemedaled, ramrod-
straight, rock-hard genuine hero of two unpopular American
wars, Lieutenant Colonel Anthony Herbert, dimmed any
hope among military leaders that the behavior of Calley and
his murderous platoon could be viewed as anomalous to
general military conduct in Vietnam. Herbert—who had
been cited by General Matthew B. Ridgway as America's
outstanding enlisted soldier during the Korean War, who had
risen through the ranks to become a battalion commander in
Vietnam, where, in less than two months, he had been
awarded a Silver Star and three Bronze Stars—filed formal
charges that there had been other atrocities committed in
Vietnam, that he had reported them, that his commanding
officers had failed to take appropriate action to investigate

them, and that he had been relieved of his command because of his insistence that his allegations be pursued.

What followed throughout the 1970s and into the eighties provided an extraordinarily well-documented study of the operations and motivations of modern news media, and yet another glimpse into the horrors of inhuman behavior in war.

All the elements of modern journalism converged on Lieutenant Colonel Herbert: the thirst for conflict and controversy, the quest for visibility by reporters and editors, the disposition to "investigate" suspected misconduct in others, the propensity to emphasize revelation over substance, the predictable tides of inconstancy that lap around the celebrated, and the singular capacity for impressing on millions of minds a uniform perception of anyone or anything.

Herbert was at once the creature and victim of the confluence of history with the expansion and strengthening of American media. They united to make him and to break him. He was catapulted by them into the heady ether of public acclaim, later to be snatched by the same forces, discredited, thrust into obscurity.

Herbert was a tailor-made media hero for the time. From Tet in 1968, media generally had been critical of the conduct of the Vietnam War. By late 1969, large segments of the populace had demonstrated their own skepticism with sufficient energy to prod the Nixon administration into launching sharp attacks on the press, claiming that one-sided reporting of the war had been misleading Americans. The revelations about My Lai convinced millions more that the Vietnam War should be terminated as quickly as possible. Yet the administration and the military averred that the My Lai massacre, which had occurred in March 1968, during some of the most intense fighting of the war, was an aberration, involving inexperienced troops and green commanders. When Herbert leveled his charges, however, they seemed to demonstrate a pattern of criminal activity by American troops in Vietnam led by seasoned, high-ranking Army officers.

Further, the man making these charges was no cowardly deserter or draft-evader. This man had killed enemy troops with his bare hands, had been wounded in battle four times, and had insisted on leading his men into combat rather than watching from the relative safety of an observation helicopter. Herbert's charges justified the picture of Vietnam the media had been painting for nearly two years.

For the next year and a half, Herbert was lionized by the media. From reports on network news programs to accounts in national news magazines and the nation's most respected newspapers to appearances on national television talk shows, Herbert was presented as being almost without blemish. The Army, meanwhile, announced an investigation of Herbert's allegations. No countervailing information was issued, though, and Herbert's two primary targets — Brigadier General John W. Barnes and Colonel J. Ross Franklin — were not made available for interviews. Unofficially, however, the Army had begun to impugn Herbert's motives and his stability. I had been covering the Herbert story for *Newsweek* when I received a telephone call from Colonel L. B. Mattingly, the public information officer at Fort McPherson, where Herbert had been assigned soon after being stripped of his command in Vietnam. Mattingly informed me that Herbert was, in the Army's view, a "pathological liar," something he wanted me to publish without attribution. I published it — but I quoted Mattingly. Knowledge that the Army would resort to such tactics wouldn't help its case with the public.

In the spring of 1971, CBS News dealt the military another blow with its documentary *The Selling of the Pentagon,* which described the immensity of the Pentagon's tax-paid public relations effort to persuade Congress and the people to support the military. The production ignited a congressional inquiry into charges that CBS had edited the documentary in such a way as to distort the military's point of view. Congress demanded the "outtakes" — film clips not used on the broadcast—and threatened to cite CBS president Frank Stanton for contempt when he refused to supply them. Later, the congressional committee relented and dropped the action.

The Secretary of the Army had expunged from Herbert's record the adverse fitness report written by those against whom he had filed charges. He could continue his military career. Yet in November 1971, Herbert, who had continued vigorously to press his case against the Army, both in the military and in the media, stated that the Army's harassment of him and his family had grown too great for his wife and daughter to tolerate. He decided to retire from the service at the end of February 1972. Numerous editors across the nation were outraged. The Knight newspaper chain accused the Army of "making a scapegoat" of Herbert; *The New York Times* urged Herbert to keep up his "battle that involves...the integrity and effectiveness of the U.S.Army." *The New Republic* published an article maintaining that the Army's treatment of Herbert "is a disgrace to the Army and a tragedy for the nation."

Now the military started striking back more aggressively, though still surreptitiously. In September 1971, a special assistant to the Army chief of staff, William Westmoreland, had prepared, on official stationery, an eight-page "fact sheet" on Herbert and on his allegations, a draft of a letter to the editor (which those in sympathy with the military could send to their local newspapers), a chronology of events related to the case, and a series of suggested questions that journalists could put to Herbert. The material was sent to selected journalists, among them Paul Dean of *The Arizona Republic,* Morton Kondracke of *The Chicago Sun-Times,* Peter Braestrup of *The Washington Post,* and syndicated military affairs columnist S. L. A. Marshall. The result was a series of stories, published across the country, questioning the veracity of Herbert's allegations. According to the fact sheet, there was no record of Herbert's having reported war crimes until a year and a half after he had been relieved of his command. The

Army papers also said that his most serious charge—a refusal by Colonel Franklin to act on Herbert's report of the wanton killing of a half-dozen or so unarmed Vietnamese at Cu Loi village—could not be substantiated, and, in any event, Franklin was on leave when Herbert purportedly told him of the killings, indicating that Herbert was mistaken. Although the Army claimed that its investigation of the rest of Herbert's charges disclosed that the incidents had been disposed of appropriately or could not be corroborated, it steadfastly refused to make public its investigative files.

Herbert continued hammering at the Army in interviews and speeches around the nation. His goal, he said, was to strengthen the military by ridding it of a self-serving corps of officers whose primary service was to their careers, not to their country.

Among those who wanted to provide still another forum for Herbert was Barry Lando, an experienced reporter for *Time* and CBS News, who had joined the staff of *60 Minutes* as a producer in September 1971. Lando had met Herbert a few months earlier and had done a story about him for *The CBS Weekend News*. Lando thought Herbert would make an excellent subject for one of his early efforts for *60 Minutes*. It was a decision that would affect Lando's and Herbert's lives for more than a decade, result in enormous legal costs, emotional strain, and thousands of pages of sworn testimony that provide the basis for an intimate view of how the most popular news program in the world—and, to a large extent, how all of journalism—conceives, develops, and reports significant stories.

Not long after Lando began his new career with *60 Minutes,* he undertook a story, he said, "involving secrecy in government. I tried to throw it together in time for hearings that were due to begin on the subject...but I was unable to get the story together in time...so we decided to drop the whole thing." It was an unfortunate failure for Lando. On March 10, 1972, he wrote a memo to Mike Wallace regarding his earlier idea to do a story on Herbert:

First of all, I know that after the "Secrecy Fiasco" I should be trying to turn out a solid story as quickly as possible...but I continue to be fascinated by the Herbert case.

Wallace understood Lando's position, but did not believe that his new producer, one of several each *60 Minutes* correspondent works with, would be wise to pursue the Herbert story:

> We looked at what we had [Wallace would testify in a 1976 deposition in the Herbert suit]...and found that the story was going no place. Lando was new on the broadcast at that time and felt badly that one of his earliest projects had foundered. Hence, he was anxious to get going on some stories that would actually make air...The expenditure of time, effort, money on a project he describes as "Secrecy Fiasco" is not one that is treated lightly in our shop.

Lando, however, thought he had reason to pursue the Herbert story. His March 10, 1972, memorandum continued:

> I have talked with officers who say that:
> (1) Franklin was back in Vietnam, not in Hawaii, when that [Cu Loi atrocity] took place.
> (2) They heard Herbert reporting from the base by radio to his superior.
> (3) That the incident was common knowledge throughout the unit.
> (4) It was also common knowledge that Herbert was trying to get something done about it.

Lando also advised Wallace that Colonel Franklin, who had denied knowing about any atrocities committed under his command, was himself relieved of command a little more than a year after he had sacked Herbert, and that the reason involved something called "a body bombing" — throwing a prisoner out of a helicopter to his death. In addition, Lando had obtained a story supporting the tenor of Herbert's allegations:

Another former lieutenant who served under Herbert recounts how he had just finished watching a Vietnamese prisoner get a few teeth knocked out with a rifle butt...When Colonel Franklin flew in on his chopper, the prisoner's mouth was still cut and bleeding. But all Franklin wanted to know was why he was being questioned in the field and not back at headquarters. Another officer also tells about reporting a similar incident to Franklin and being told, "War is hell."

But Wallace still opposed the idea:

I felt...that there was no sense in doing a Herbert broadcast if it was simply going to be an elongated carbon copy of material which had been previously adduced in newspapers or television or in magazines. I said to Barry Lando, "If we can produce a broadcast that adds to the sum of human information about Colonel Herbert, if we can develop the story further, if we can shed new light on the apparent confrontation between Herbert and the Army, if we can investigate to some degree the role of the press in this whole business, then, conceivably, we will film and broadcast such a piece. If we cannot, then, Barry, forget it. We have to get pieces on the air, and we cannot spend a great deal of time spinning our wheels."

Don Hewitt said he "wasn't too interested in the story...I thought it was an oft-told tale." Hewitt told Wallace that, as far as he was concerned, Lando could continue looking into the idea "as long as it doesn't interfere with the story he was doing...a story in St. Marys, Georgia, a story about a company town." That story, one of Lando's earliest successes on *60 Minutes*, was aired in May 1972.

Lando still could not "make air" with a pro-Herbert, anti-Army story. On June 21, 1972, he submitted to Wallace and Hewitt a new summary of a proposed segment on Herbert. This time, the approach was quite different.

"He began to come up with some information," Wallace

recalled, "which cast some doubt, in my mind, upon the situation vis-à-vis Herbert and Franklin..."

Wallace told Hewitt that Lando had interviewed people who had contradicted Herbert's "oft-told tale." "I said," Hewitt remembered, "...that would make the story more newsworthy, because it would report news that had not been previously reported, that I was interested more in the Herbert story now than I had been then."

Lando had broken from the pack. He had proposed a story demonstrating that Herbert, whom most in the media were exalting, had been lying. Now there was a good chance for making air again.

Lando visited Major General Winant Sidle, the Army's chief information officer, and Colonel Leonard F. B. Reed, Jr., chief of the Army's news branch. "I may have stated to Colonel Reed," Lando said, "that I was getting more and more mixed up on the Herbert case." He told Reed that he suspected Herbert was not telling the truth. From that point, the Army agreed to make Barnes and Franklin, held incommunicado from most in the media, available for interviews with *60 Minutes*.

Lando did not ask anyone in the Pentagon to explain the circumstances of Franklin's removal from command, nor did he or Wallace persist in demanding that Franklin explain the circumstances of the alleged body bombing. (Franklin later was exonerated of that charge, although the reporters could not have predicted that at the time.)

Instead, Lando decided to concentrate on one bit of information that might resolve whether or not Herbert was telling the truth. Herbert had written and spoken extensively about the St. Valentine's Day Massacre, the murder of defenseless Viet Cong suspects at Cu Loi village on February 14, 1969. According to Herbert, he saw Vietnamese national police, under the supervision of their American adviser, murder several of those being questioned. He reported the incident to Colonel Franklin and, later, to General

Barnes. He wanted them to prosecute the American lieutenant who had stood by and done nothing to stop the killing,
even after assuming responsibility for the prisoners. Not only
did Franklin and Barnes refuse to investigate, Herbert
contended, but they instructed him to forget about the
incident. Later, however, Franklin maintained that he was in
Hawaii on February 14, 1969 — and he had documentation to
prove it — so Herbert could not have reported the Cu Loi
incident when he claimed he had. Lando examined the
evidence — a check signed by Franklin on St. Valentine's Day
for what appeared to be the full amount of the hotel bill —
and was convinced that Herbert was dissembling.

Lando and Wallace now turned the story into a concentrated effort to demonstrate that Herbert's allegations were
invalid. By February 4, 1973, when the program was
broadcast — entitled, with intended irony, "The Selling of
Colonel Herbert" — it seemed that Lando had all the evidence he needed.

> I thought he was a killer [General Barnes said on *60 Minutes*].
> I thought he enjoyed killing and I thought he would cause me
> a lot of trouble in the pacification. I don't think he understood
> the role.

Lando, who questioned Barnes for the program, asked
whether the general had any "evidence, hard evidence, to
show that he was a killer."

> BARNES: No, I have no hard evidence other than the fact I
> know that he enjoyed getting out with squads with an M-16
> and leading squads. No other battalion commander did that.
> LANDO: Couldn't this just be a sign of bravery?
> BARNES: Oh, it certainly could. But the same kind of thing I
> didn't want happening. . . when we got to the pacification role.

Barnes "elaborated his suspicions about Herbert":

> I can't pin this thing anywhere [Barnes said on the program],
> but I just got the feeling, with all these high body counts he
> had, that some of them were suspect. . . And I just didn't have

confidence in him. I'd lost confidence in him as a commander with the ability to control his people.

Wallace himself elaborated later in the program about Herbert's attitude toward the enemy.

WALLACE: Although several men who served with Herbert say it's not so, there are others who claim that Herbert was an officer who could be brutal with captured enemy prisoners himself.

Sergeant Bruce Potter, once a radioman under Herbert, appeared on camera with a lengthy anecdote about how Herbert had threatened to throw a prisoner out of a helicopter if he didn't talk. Off camera, Wallace told Herbert of the story. When Herbert denied it on film, Wallace tried to persuade him to call Potter a liar. Wallace next identified Bob Stemmies, a military intelligence sergeant, as saying that Herbert had once stood by and done nothing while interrogators beat a Viet Cong nurse. Herbert denied that charge. Mike Plantz, a helicopter pilot, claimed, Wallace said, that he had seen Herbert "beat up" prisoners on two occasions. "It's false, it's false," Herbert said.

Wallace made much on the *60 Minutes* segment about Bill Hill, one of Herbert's company commanders, saying that Herbert had become a liar.

WALLACE: Bill Hill, one of your top company commanders...
HERBERT: Yes...
WALLACE: ...has told us that Herbert "is the best battalion commander I've ever had, but for some reason he's become a liar. It's all so much garbage."
HERBERT: If he's still in the Army, he will do the same as other officers will do, I'm sure, in order to keep their career going. These men are not going to destroy themselves.
WALLACE: In other words, he has simply chickened out and is going along with the Army line against Herbert?
HERBERT: I don't know.
WALLACE: Well, that's what you're suggesting.

HERBERT: I don't even know he said it. You're telling me he said it. But I'm sure he did say it if you say he did.

Actually, Bill Hill had made several other statements, although *60 Minutes* did not choose to report them. Barry Lando's notes show that on December 5, 1972, Hill told Lando, "As best I know, Herbert reported it [the Cu Loi massacre]; at least on battalion net. I heard one." On January 2, 1973, Hill gave Lando the line used on the program — and much stronger stuff. "Herbert probably most brutal man you ever run across when it comes to caring about human beings," Lando's notes have Hill saying. "He not the same man I knew in Nam." On March 16, 1973, after the *60 Minutes* segment was broadcast, but before his piece appeared in *The Atlantic Monthly*, Lando called Hill again. Had Hill seen Franklin on February 14? "I didn't say I saw him there. I said I *thought* he was there. Hell, I thought he was there but there was no way to be certain. Always running around; see him every few days. When I sat down to think about it, I couldn't be certain."

Within a week after conducting the Pentagon interviews, Wallace and Lando received the only investigative material on Herbert's charges that the Pentagon would agree to disclose. It consisted of statements made under oath by Captain Jack Richter Donovan, Jr. According to attorneys in the case, Lando was given the statements because they were supposed to show how Herbert inflated enemy body counts following combat by his battalion. In fact, they cast the Herbert investigation in a new light. On May 16, 1971, Donovan was interviewed by Army investigator Frank G. Bourland at Fort Sheridan, Illinois. Donovan told Bourland that some time in February or March 1969, after a combat action coordinated by Herbert, "Herbert came into the Tactical Operations Center at Landing Zone English and reported that approximately six detainees had been lined up and shot and that one of the detainees had his throat cut."

Donovan, continuing his statement, pointed out that

Herbert had reported that forty-nine enemy were killed and about fifteen weapons were captured. Herbert, he said, reported that "most of the weapons had been picked up by the Vietnamese elements supporting the operation. I recall that the U.S. advisers denied that they had, in fact, recovered any captured weapons and stated that the body count had been grossly exaggerated. I was present in the Tactical Operations Center when Herbert entered and made his after-action report."

To this point, the problems Donovan's statement created for the *60 Minutes* approach to the Herbert case could be overcome. On the one hand, Herbert apparently had reported immediately — in the presence of Donovan and two other soldiers the captain identified as Sergeant First Class Otto Morgan and Lieutenant Colonel Henry Boyer — that six detainees had been executed and one's throat had been cut. (According to the Army's summary findings, no one could "substantiate" Herbert's story of a throat-cutting; they failed to say he had reported such an incident to at least three people.) On the other hand, the statement renewed questions about the validity of Herbert's body counts, something Franklin had challenged from the start. What followed, however, shot holes in the *60 Minutes* position that Herbert had not reported the murders to Colonel Franklin:

DONOVAN: [to the investigator]: Following the report, we drove up to Brigade Headquarters...Lieutenant Colonel Herbert discussed the incident with the brigade S-3 [operations staff officer]. I do know for certain that Lieutenant Colonel Herbert reported the killing of the six detainees [or approximately six detainees] to Colonel Franklin — but I do not recall if Herbert reported the incident to Franklin immediately following the combat action. At that time, I was in Brigade Headquarters with Lieutenant Colonel Herbert, checking on intelligence information. I was standing about five feet from the location where Franklin and Herbert were talking when I heard Herbert tell Franklin about the detainees being lined up and shot by Vietnamese forces...Her-

bert was talking directly to Franklin, and, in my opinion, he
could not help but hear what Herbert had said. I do not recall
Franklin's response if, in fact, he made a response...The
information relative to the detainees was part of a continuing
conversation between the two...no longer than a month
following the action. The incident was a big issue for Herbert
because the [American] advisers were disputing his account of
the action...I cannot really say what Herbert's motive
was...concern for the detainees who had been shot or the fact
that his body count and report of weapons captured were
being disputed. For several weeks...almost on a daily basis,
Herbert would mention the incident, stating he had reported
[it] to Brigade. I know of no inquiry or investigation that
followed the incident.

Donovan was asked whether he was discussing a reported
combat action at Cu Loi on February 14, 1969, and he said he
was.

Five weeks after Donovan's interview by Bourland, on
June 23, 1971, Donovan was summoned to the Pentagon for
additional questioning. The investigator, Ralph R. Scott,
pointed out that while Donovan was still in Vietnam in
December 1970, he had told an Army investigator that he had
"no hearsay information concerning war crimes to report."
But, Scott said, Donovan's May 1971, statement was "rather
detailed...Would you explain the apparent contradiction?"

Donovan said the first agent (Leonard Comras) emphasized
that he wanted Donovan's "actual observations [and]
...information I had about war crimes committed other than
what Lieutenant Colonel Herbert had alleged." Donovan said
he provided the information about Cu Loi, but "this was by-
passed by the first agent." Then, he said, he wanted to clarify
some aspects of his more detailed statement. Donovan
explained that after he and Herbert arrived at Brigade
Headquarters, Herbert entered the S-3 office and Donovan
was in the radio complex of the Tactical Operations Center
(TOC),

standing five to ten feet from the wall separating the S-3 office and the TOC. I overheard a conversation taking place between Lieutenant Colonel Herbert and an individual I thought at that time to be Colonel Franklin. At no time did I hear the individual make any specific statement, but just based upon the sound of his voice, I deduced it was Colonel Franklin in the office, although I never specifically saw the individual and only heard a limited [amount] of the conversation. I was never told by Lieutenant Colonel Herbert that he talked to Colonel Franklin at that particular time. What I did hear was Lieutenant Colonel Herbert making remarks to the individual about persons being shot on the beach by the National Police at Cu Loi. Prior to this trip to Brigade, Lieutenant Colonel Herbert had been talking extensively about Cu Loi and that people were lined up and killed and that a war crime had been committed...

The way in which Lieutenant Colonel Herbert related the individuals being shot was in a form that seemed to me to have been reasonably clear that there was a war crime in a sense that people were lined up and shot, but this was largely due to the fact that I had heard Lieutenant Colonel Herbert mention it on several occasions. Thinking back, Lieutenant Colonel Herbert did not make it abundantly clear he was reporting a war crime, but, in fact, seemed to be a reiteration by Lieutenant Colonel Herbert of the facts concerning the accuracy of his body counts and weapons captured.

Donovan, though he continued to waffle while giving his Pentagon statement, and continued to stress the likelihood that Herbert's principal interest resided in defending his body count, nonetheless consistently replied that he had believed Herbert was reporting the murders at Cu Loi to Colonel Franklin:

SCOTT [investigator]: ...Did you actually hear anything said by the individual to whom Herbert was talking?
DONOVAN: I heard no specific words...other than single-word acknowledgments of Lieutenant Colonel Herbert's remarks. The tone of Lieutenant Colonel Herbert's voice and the manner, in general, in which he was speaking seemed typical of most of the conversations he had with Colonel

Franklin. Although I did not pick out any particular words
...and I was in the radio room, it was my impression that this
was the sound of Colonel Franklin's voice...

SCOTT: Could Lieutenant Colonel Herbert have been talking
to someone other than Colonel Franklin, or are you certain he
was talking to Franklin?

DONOVAN: No, I cannot be absolutely certain that it was
Colonel Franklin. The tone of the conversation seemed to
indicate to me that it was Colonel Franklin in the office. I
cannot rule out the possibility that Lieutenant Colonel
Herbert was reporting a war crime to Colonel Franklin. The
portion I heard was very brief, and I was not devoting my
complete attention to the conversation. Since I cannot say
what came before or after what I heard, I cannot say that
Lieutenant Colonel Herbert was not making a full report to
Colonel Franklin.

After reading Donovan's testimony, Lando arranged to see
Franklin again. They met in Franklin's office on January 10,
1973. "I told Franklin that the new information that I had
spoken to him about were statements by Donovan and the
equipment was set up..." Lando recalled. "I handed him the
statements, told him to take a look at them, and then we
began the interview. I simply asked him to start off by
explaining the Donovan statements: How would he explain
them? What was his explanation?"

LANDO: ...Is there a chance that you, or any other officer,
could just have tuned out a part from what Herbert was saying
because of past experience?

FRANKLIN: There was an awful lot of that. Herbert would
tell, frankly, just incredible stories and this was a daily
occurrence, and frequently his appearance in the TOC, it was
not to transact business, conduct operations; it would just
deteriorate into these very, very, at best, far-fetched war
stories. And I would say there's certainly a possibility that
people could just—he said such fantastic things, sometimes;
they were known to be incorrect—that people could very
easily disregard them: tune out, turn off.

LANDO: Could you, yourself, have done that?

FRANKLIN: Yes. I have done that frequently with Herbert. He would just go on and on and I would start thinking about something else because, if I didn't, I would become, frequently, too irritated. Herbert worked for me, and it just made me feel bad and it was awkward for me just to hear him tell these stories which were patently false—and again, they weren't official statements; they were just stories. But you don't miss, you don't tune out, when somebody talks about six people getting killed—no. That—had he mentioned that to me, I would certainly have, I believe, recalled it and also had taken some sort of action—pushed it further, asked more questions that required certain actions of Colonel Herbert.

Lando read to Franklin the portion of Donovan's statement in which he maintained that Herbert had presented the incident in a form which made it "reasonably clear" that a war crime had been committed.

FRANKLIN: No, certainly not, because, again, regardless of who did it or to whom it was done, when a lieutenant colonel makes a statement of this nature, it's very serious.

LANDO: Is it at all possible that something like this could have happened, that there could have been a conversation like this two or three weeks after the action, as Donovan said, with yourself?

FRANKLIN: I don't think it's possible that he could have stated that six detainees were lined up and killed, murdered. It certainly is possible that he could have made comments to the effect, criticizing the ARVN or criticizing American advisers—vague, general comments about the mistreating of their own people—that certainly is possible. But, no. A statement to the effect that six people were murdered in cold blood? No. That couldn't have slipped by without both being remembered by me and being remembered by others.

No part of the interview with Colonel Franklin on January 10, 1973, appeared on the *60 Minutes* segment about Herbert. There was no reference either to Donovan or to any statement casting doubt on Franklin's assertion that Herbert never had reported the Cu Loi murders to him. On the segment, Wallace asserted that Herbert had provided the names of "several people who can testify that Franklin was in Vietnam on February 14... We contacted almost every one of them. None could confirm Herbert's claim. Several men serving under Herbert say they had heard Herbert say, while in Vietnam, that he had reported the February 14 killings, but none were certain that he had actually reported them."

Donovan, however, had sworn that Herbert had reported specifically, among other things, the murder of six detainees; he said he and two others were present in the Tactical Operations Center "when Herbert entered and made his after-action report. Following the report, we drove up to Brigade Headquarters..." It was then that Donovan could not be certain whether Herbert had reported the murders to Franklin immediately or some time later. Nonetheless, according to Donovan, Herbert had told of the killings in his after-action report.

There was no uncertainty in the *60 Minutes* broadcast. On January 4, 1973, three weeks before Mike Wallace would interview Herbert and a month before the segment would be broadcast, Wallace, Lando, and a camera crew went to the Pentagon to interview Franklin, Captain James Grimshaw (one of Herbert's admiring company commanders), and others. By then, *60 Minutes* had chosen its heroes and villains.

With a touch of wry humor, Lando, on the day of the interviews, took a copy of Herbert's book, *Soldier,* to the Pentagon. He asked Franklin, perhaps the principal antagonist in the book, to autograph it for him. Lando remembers the inscription: "With thanks for all that you have done in this."

Wallace recalled discussing the possibility of the Army's suing Herbert. "I believe," Wallace remembered, "that it was I who said to Colonel Franklin that if his total story stood up, conceivably he had the possibility of an action... The only additional remark I remember making to Colonel Franklin was 'If you were in Vietnam at the time you say you were not, Colonel, it's your ass.'" (Later, eight months after the *60 Minutes* segment was broadcast, Franklin did file a $3 million suit against Herbert. It subsequently was dismissed. Franklin told me in 1975 that he had "dropped the suit for financial reasons. The lawyer quit. We were up against guys [Herbert] with unlimited resources." It was while he was being deposed in that case that Franklin made the statement "No officer or anybody ever mentioned a war crime or atrocity to me — or, if they did, I never failed to take action.")

When Wallace interviewed Franklin that day, he asked the colonel why he had been relieved of command some months after Herbert had been stripped of his battalion. Franklin refused to discuss the matter, and Wallace did not pursue it. Lando had interviewed Franklin about it a month earlier — also at the Pentagon — on December 4, 1972. Lando's notes quote Franklin: "Crew units supporting us dropped body on our Tactical Operations Center and there was investigation by First Cavalry. Four years on command equivalents and three bad months...I relieved day after." Lando said, "At one point I had suggested to [Wallace] it be included in the program," but it was not.

On the broadcast, Wallace criticized *The New York Times* for giving "big play" to the story that Herbert had passed a lie-detector test, "but when the Army said that Colonel Franklin, the man Herbert had accused, had also passed a lie-detector test...there was not a word about it in the *Times*." Yet Lando and Wallace never examined the test or the results. "We decided," Lando recalled, "that if the Army was willing to make the test available to us, that would mean they really had nothing to hide about it, and that what they said was true." Franklin was less sanguine about the test. In a sworn statement, taken in connection with his lawsuit against Herbert, Franklin remembered that when the test was concluded, he turned to the polygraph expert and asked, "'How about it, chief, am I telling the truth?' He said, 'You're

the only one who knows that, Colonel.' I felt very degraded."
Herbert's test was administered by a nonmilitary professional, Benjamin Franklin Malinowski; the results were made
public. When Herbert's lawyer asked Wallace whether he
and Lando had ever discussed a man named Malinowski,
Wallace replied, "It sounds like a cellist."

The climax of the program was an on-camera, face-to-face
confrontation arranged by *60 Minutes* between Herbert and
Captain Jim Grimshaw. Herbert had written in *Soldier* about
a heroic deed of Grimshaw's for which Herbert recommended
that his company commander be awarded the Silver Star.
Unknown to Herbert, Grimshaw and his wife were in the
studio, watching Wallace's interview with Herbert on a
television monitor. In the confrontation, Grimshaw maintained that he was under no pressure from the Pentagon
(where he had been interviewed previously by Wallace, and
where he had said that Herbert had "gone beyond...the
undeniable truth" and that Herbert had not been relieved of
command because of his allegations of war crimes). In the
face-to-face encounter, Grimshaw stood his ground; he maintained that two of the three incidents involving him in *Soldier*
weren't true.

Although Grimshaw's appearance on *60 Minutes* provided
the climactic confrontation between Herbert and a man who,
to Herbert's face, said Herbert had told less than the truth,
unused portions of the interview with Grimshaw, filmed at
the Pentagon on January 4, 1973, disclosed that Grimshaw's
views were not wholly represented on the segment as
broadcast:

WALLACE: Was Franklin in the country at that time
[February 14]?
GRIMSHAW: ...The only thing that Herbert told me was,
[he] briefly described the incidents of what he had seen, said it
wasn't — that's not the thing that is to be done. He cautioned
me of ever getting myself or my command involved in
anything like that, and that he had reported it. When he said

he reported it, I feel that he either reported it to...Colonel
Franklin or General Barnes...
WALLACE: ...Well, did Herbert make a big deal of that kind
of thing?
GRIMSHAW: I don't remember him making such a big deal
out of it...He talked to me as a commander to commander,
and once in a while he'd mention this war-crime business, and
it was all a caution of saying, "Don't get yourselves involved in
it." Now, you've got to remember there's a guy who a
lieutenant colonel talking to a captain...He's not going to
personally involve me in everything that he sees or does.

Wallace went on to castigate many of the media—
principally *The New York Times*—for not making more of an
effort to check out Herbert's story, which, he said, "was far
from clear-cut..." The media, a former Army investigator
said on the program, were "looking for another hero [and]
tended to accept [Herbert's] allegations uncritically." The
investigator, who had examined Herbert's charges against
General Barnes, said, essentially, that Herbert's charges did
not stand up. Franklin said that his own refusal to talk to the
press should not have resulted in antagonistic news stories.
He disputed the notion "that if you won't talk to the press,
then they can say anything they want...But there's still a
responsibility to tell the truth." Barnes was more charitable:

> During the long investigation on me, the Army's policy was
> not to put out any statements at all because of prejudice to
> others involved...Therefore, the press had no place else to go
> for information but back to Herbert, where the source was.
> And I just think that the press did what they could but they
> weren't given both sides of the stories. Right or wrong...I
> think that's what happened.

The most persuasive aspect of the program, in terms of
demonstrating that Herbert's story may have sprung some
leaks, was its focus on whether Franklin was in Hawaii at the
time Herbert said he reported to him—first by field radio

and then in person — the incident at Cu Loi. Franklin asserted that he was in the Ilikai Hotel in Honolulu and did not return to Vietnam until February 16, Vietnam time. Herbert said Franklin was lying.

WALLACE: Checking with the Ilikai Hotel in Hawaii, we found that Colonel and Mrs. Franklin had indeed been registered there from February 7 to late in the afternoon of February 14. That would already have been February 15 in Vietnam. Colonel Franklin also gave us a canceled check signed by himself and made out to the Ilikai Hotel for the exact amount of the hotel bill. The check was dated February 14. And we spoke with two Army officers who were in Hawaii at the same time. They say they flew back to Vietnam with Colonel Franklin, taking off from Honolulu late on February 14, arriving at Cam Ranh Bay in Vietnam on February 16, local time.

Herbert clearly was surprised when Wallace showed him the check, dated February 14 and signed by Franklin. He even suggested that he could have been mistaken about the dates — but that was not the crucial point.

WALLACE: . . . Herbert had tried to put the whole question of his reporting or not reporting atrocities in a different light.
HERBERT: Let's say I didn't, just for the sake of the discussion. It would make absolutely no difference if I waited five years to do it. The motive [of why I reported the atrocities] would make no difference whatsoever. The question is: Did the crimes occur or didn't they?
WALLACE: Oh?
HERBERT: Were Colonel Franklin and General Barnes well aware of them or weren't they? I say they were, and I say I reported them, and it's still there and it still stands.
WALLACE: No. The point is there's no dispute that war crimes occurred in Vietnam. The dispute, it seems, is this: you've called Franklin a liar. . . You've called Barnes a liar. . . You said the Army, really, deprived you of your military career because you insisted upon reporting war crimes and they wanted them covered up. And that's really what the issue is here.

Lando reiterated the point even more strongly in an article he wrote in the May 1973 issue of *The Atlantic:*

> The key point to the whole Herbert affair was not whether atrocities had occurred—the Army admitted that some of those described by Herbert did happen—but whether Herbert had actually reported them, and, because he insisted on trying to get them investigated, had had his career ruined by a military establishment intent on covering up war crimes. It was only by claiming to be a martyr that Herbert had gained such national prominence.

The key point of the allegations made by Herbert was *precisely* that atrocities had occurred—and that they had occurred regularly—primarily because of the unwillingness of commanders rigidly to enforce their troops' adherence to military codes of conduct.

The achievement of national prominence by an individual, though perhaps unwarranted, surely is not a "key point" in the life of a nation or its military establishment. Yet Wallace and Lando had maintained that, from a journalistic aspect, the story of "atrocities" had been told and was not worth telling again; the journalistic key was whether Herbert could be pulled from his pedestal—and that there was a *60 Minutes* story only if he could be.

That, of course, was not Lando's initial view. The Army had released its "findings" on Herbert's allegations in November 1971, and, as late as the following March, after Herbert's retirement from the Army, Lando had proposed a story supporting Herbert's position. One reason may have been the Army's laconic summary of the Herbert case and its continuing refusal, despite entreaties from Lando and other journalists, to release any of its investigative materials.

The Army, for instance, disposed of Herbert's principal allegation that a massacre of five Vietnamese detainees had occurred at Cu Loi on February 14, 1969, with a paragraph:

> Four individuals were located who claim witnessing the execution of detainess by the Vietnamese police on 14

February 1969...The lieutenant adviser who accompanied
the Vietnamese unit denies seeing or hearing about any
detainee killings...There were no witnesses to Lieutenant
Colonel Herbert's alleged report to Colonel Franklin, nor was
any evidence found to substantiate Lieutenant Colonel Herbert's charges...The American adviser did not have command authority over the South Vietnamese unit. Since all
alleged offenders were Vietnamese nationals, the investigation
was forwarded...to appropriate Republic of Vietnam officials.

All other charges were treated in the same fashion. To the
charge that a soldier mutilated the body of a Vietnamese, the
Army replied that "the incident was investigated...Two
persons were convicted by general court-martial." To the
charge that interrogators — Americans and Vietnamese under
American supervision — tortured prisoners, the answer was
that "these allegations are still under investigation. No
comment can be made pending completion...Herbert stated
that he orally reported the incident to Colonel Franklin.
There were no witnesses to this alleged report, and no
evidence was found to substantiate the claim." To the charge
that American interrogators forced water into the nose and
mouth of a detainee, the report said that "two persons, both
now returned to civilian life, who participated in the investigation, admitted the use of water during the interrogation."
Herbert said he reported the incident to Franklin; Franklin
denied it.

It was more than a year later — on February 4, 1973 — that
60 Minutes broadcast its lengthy segment on Herbert. The
Army still had not released another word on the alleged
atrocities, an issue that obviously had not been resolved. The
Army offered no answers as to whether American advisers had
responsibility for murders committed by the Vietnamese
whom they advised; the Army failed to elaborate on the
torture performed by its interrogators. The Army did not
explain how, if several of these incidents had occurred, the
brigade commander, Barnes, and his deputy, Franklin, had
failed to hear about them from anyone. Yet Barnes and

Franklin claimed that they were unaware of such crimes. The questions were neither asked nor answered on *60 Minutes*.

The media, it appeared, no longer were attracted by atrocities; that story had been done. Now, it appeared, it was more important to discover whether Herbert had lied—not about atrocities having been committed, but about whether he, personally, had reported those atrocities, to whom he had reported them, and when.

The *60 Minutes* broadcast and the ensuing article by Lando in *The Atlantic* dissolved Herbert's celebrity. Invitations to speak on college campuses and elsewhere for substantial fees dwindled, then disappeared. Discussions to sell the dramatic rights to *Soldier* for a large sum were ended.

In late 1973, Herbert sued CBS, *60 Minutes*, *The Atlantic Monthly*, Wallace, and Lando for $44.7 million. The development of his case suggests the enormous human investment of energy, time, money, emotion, and sheer single-mindedness required for a counterattack against major media. By late 1975, after Herbert's lawyers had taken thousands of pages of sworn, pretrial depositions (Lando's testimony alone filled 2903 pages), they insisted that they needed specific answers regarding the editorial process. Because Herbert had conceded that he was a "public figure" and therefore must prove that he was libeled with "actual malice," he could not pursue his cause unless the journalists were required to explain how and why certain materials were chosen for or excluded from the *60 Minutes* segment. In January 1977, a United States district court ordered that such questions be answered. The following November, a United States court of appeals reversed that decision, saying, in a 2-to-1 ruling, that a reporter cannot be forced to disclose "how he formulated his judgments on what to print or not to print." In April 1979, the United States Supreme Court voted, 6 to 3, that to deny Herbert access to information about the editorial process would be "placing beyond the plaintiff's reach a range of direct evidence relevant to proving knowing or reckless falsehood." Lawyers for CBS and the other respondents then began taking their depositions from Herbert and others. By mid-1981, the arduous and costly task of taking sworn, pretrial depositions had been completed. What with further pretrial motions, responses to the motions, reponses to the responses, availability of court dates, conflicting schedules of the principals and their lawyers, the anticipated length of the trial itself, and the appeals process, no one connected with the case would or could predict when a final adjudication might be expected.

"To say that a citizen in the United States can sue CBS is ludicrous — it's impossible," Herbert maintained, explaining that he wasn't just *any* citizen. "First of all," he added, "I have a military retirement that goes on the average of $15,000 to $20,000 a year. I have that money. I have money that I made in speaking engagements, a very high-priced speaker around the college circuit. I've had high-priced jobs as a doctor of psychology. Every cent that I've had — I don't own a single thing. I don't own anything — nothing. I don't own a house. I don't own a car. Every cent I have has gone into this case — plus I am indebted to one helluva lot of people that have loaned me money on the fact that I will pay them back someday, somehow, such as a helluva lot of friends who have carried me at different times.

"Item two is that I hit it with a law firm that was willing to go ahead with this. Friends have carried me down to buying food. No individual could do it. The big corporations try to starve you out. That's the fault of the courts. They [big corporations] hope witnesses die, and the courts let them drag this thing out. The courts play the role of big business. It goes back to Malcolm X's statement, 'Justice is for just us white folks.' The law has been made by the wealthy; it has been made by big business and their lawyers to benefit them in every way and keep the small man from doing it."

Gerard McCauley, Herbert's literary agent and his long-time friend, said that "what *60 Minutes* did was reduce the issue to whether or not Herbert was a liar. What was overlooked then, and has been ever since, was the extent to which American troops committed or condoned atrocities and to which their commanders covered up the evidence. So the program succeeded in getting the Army off the hook, the administration, Franklin, Barnes — the whole lot."

Through action taken by his lawyers in connection with his libel suit, Herbert was successful in prying loose from the Army its full investigation of his charges. In 1975, I was able to look at those documents. I urged that *Newsweek* do a story about these findings which the Army had summarized so glibly in November 1971. *Newsweek* turned down my suggestion: atrocities in Vietnam were no longer news.

I spoke then to Franklin and, through an intermediary, to Barnes — the first time I had ever reached them. Herbert, General Barnes stated, "has impressive credentials and therefore the capability of being listened to and used by those people or groups anxious to discredit the Army and, particularly, the war in Vietnam. His interest in vindicating himself coincides with those who want to discredit the United States Army and the war in Vietnam."

Franklin was "100 percent" certain that Herbert never had reported any war crimes to him. "He's a liar," Franklin told me. "The guy who had the biggest propensity to commit a war crime was Herbert. One of the reasons he was relieved was his propensity to use unrestricted violence... You've got yourself a real loser." Franklin told me he had taken a Vietnamese family of five into his home, then at Fort Benning, Georgia. Clearly, he was not antagonistic to the Vietnamese people. Besides, he said, "there's a fine line between toughness and brutality. How can you have a secret in a brigade? You would have seen this. If you've got things like that going on, the commander is responsible, whether he knows about it or not. No army in any battle acted with more restraint than the American Army, across the board," in Vietnam. My Lai, he added, was "a crazy thing."

According to the Army's investigation of Herbert's charges — the material it never has released publicly — the 173rd Airborne Brigade, commanded by Barnes and Franklin from late 1968 for nearly a year, had more than its share of "crazy" occurrences.

Robert Bolton Stemme (probably the man identified on *60 Minutes* as "Bob Stemmies," who supposedly saw Herbert standing by and doing nothing while a Viet Cong nurse was beaten) reported an incident in which a "detainee" was kicked to death. Although he stated that a Viet Cong nurse was present, there was no mention of her having been beaten by anyone, much less by Herbert. Another soldier reported the destruction of a village and the murder of its inhabitants by two soldiers. They were "disciplined" by being "relieved of duty on occasion," their platoon leader testified, "but we were so short of men, we had to take them back." Another member of 173rd Airborne Brigade reported that a Vietnamese villager was shot by a private first class, who then cut the ears from the man—while he still was alive. The private's punishment for murder and mutilation was confinement for ten months and a $1000 fine.

Army investigator Frank Bourland took a detailed statement from an American soldier in Herbert's brigade on the techniques used by interrogators at Bong Son between November 1968 and October 1969, the approximate period that Barnes and Franklin were in charge of the 173rd Airborne. "During that period," the solder swore, "there were a few occasions where a captured Viet Cong–North Vietnamese detainee was determined to have vital information and would not divulge the information through use of normal interrogation techniques on our part—that is, psychological approaches without use of violence, trickery, et cetera. In those few instances, we...would use the water technique, electrical wire technique, dummy grenade technique, and the slapping-with-the-hand procedure."

This expert had seen "instances where prisoners have died as a result of their wounds while being interrogated, but not as a result of the interrogation. I know of no instances where American soldiers have significantly harmed suspects during interrogation." He then recalled "one occasion, at Landing

Zone English...a male prisoner ran and leaped into a half-barrel of burning diesel fuel...I heard later that he had died."

A South Vietnamese soldier attached to the 173rd Airborne Brigade testified to another curious "suicide" by a prisoner. After striking the prisoner in the face with the scabbard of his field knife, the American interrogator "grabbed [him] by the back of the head and neck and forced his head into a pail of water, but not for long, then rolled [him] over on his back...and then urinated on the man's face. A few minutes later, [he] took a small wooden stick and struck [the prisoner] on the back of the hands several times with no results...He himself felt that perhaps it was time to consider that [the prisoner] had told the truth." It was too late. The prisoner did not regain consciousness and died a few hours later. The interrogator told his Vietnamese assistant he "was not certain why the man died, but stated he might have committed suicide by holding his breath too long."

The Army's investigation turned up evidence that some officers of the 173rd Airborne may even have altered autopsy reports on Vietnamese prisoners to minimize suspicion of foul play by American interrogators.

In August 1975, when I acquired the documents pertaining to the Army's investigation, I asked Major Brigham Shuler of the Army's Criminal Investigation Division why they had not been released before. He answered, "The Army had a political interest, if you will, in not releasing information at that time on these things happening in the 173rd."

Among the documents not originally released was one dated March 4, 1971, from Ralph Scott, the Army criminal investigator who questioned Captain Donovan in June 1971. It was short and to the point:

BASIS FOR INVESTIGATION: On 4 November 1970, Lieutenant Colonel Anthony B. Herbert...reported that about 14 February 1969, at Cu Loi, Republic of Vietnam, accompanied by an American adviser, South Vietnamese soldiers murdered five Vietnamese detainees.

INVESTIGATIVE SUMMARY: Investigation revealed that on 14 February 1969, during a combat operation of the Second Battalion, 503rd Infantry, 173rd Airborne Brigade, at Cu Loi, Quang Nhai Province, Republic of Vietnam, unidentified South Vietnamese troops, accompanied by...American adviser [name deleted], murdered approximately eight (8) Vietnamese detainees. Investigation further revealed that subsequent to the murders, the Vietnamese troops looted and burned the village. Additionally, two Vietnamese detainees, prior to being released to American intelligence, were beaten by the Vietnamese troops.

Although it was determined by the Army's investigation that "the American adviser did not have command authority over the South Vietnamese unit" and therefore was helpless to stop the killing, a sworn statement from one of Herbert's platoon leaders at Cu Loi indicated that an American with a distaste for murder could indeed make a difference:

After cleaning up the village, we found that we had killed nine Viet Cong, that I counted, and we had captured five or six Viet Cong...Outside the village were about twenty National Policemen and one American adviser, who I had seen in the village during the action. The detainees were apparently released to the National Police. As I approached that group outside the village, I saw a National Policeman shoot one of the detainees who had been kneeling down and apparently was being questioned...[but] would not answer. The same National Policeman started questioning another detainee in the group who was also kneeling. That National Policeman and another one shot that detainee. I grabbed the National Policeman who was doing the questioning and had Hoa [his Vietnamese scout] tell him that I would shoot him if any others were killed...

INVESTIGATOR: Do you know the name of the American National Police adviser?

PLATOON LEADER: No. But a few days later, when we were conducting a sweep of the same village, I saw him there with the same force. He told me that he could not do anything with that National Policeman who had been doing the questioning, and he implied that he was afraid of him.

When *60 Minutes* was preparing its segment on Herbert, it did not have access to any of the investigative material, though it had issued a request for the Army to release it. (The Army released it only when forced to in connection with Herbert's suit.) Still, Lando had interviewed a number of people who supported Herbert's story, yet none of them appeared on the *60 Minutes* segment nor was quoted on the program. Lando had been told by a helicopter pilot, Larry Kahili, that Herbert had shown consideration for Vietnamese civilians, that he had suggested enemy wounded be treated as if they were friendly troops — and that he, Kahili, would be willing to repeat his statements on camera. Others — Captain Laurence Potter, Major Francis Tally, a Captain Dorney — had given Lando favorable information about Herbert's treatment of Vietnamese. During the taking of depositions in Herbert's libel suit, Herbert's lawyer, Jonathan Lubell, asked why Lando, Wallace, and their editors included the statement from Mike Plantz about Herbert mistreating a prisoner but not any of the statements describing his just behavior. Lando's lawyer, Richard C. Green, objected.

LUBELL: I am asking him if he discussed with Mike Wallace...as to the basis for including some statements and excluding others.
GREEN: I repeat my objection on the grounds you are calling for a discussion about editorial judgment.
LUBELL: Mr. Green, there comes a point where editorial judgment cannot be a blanket for reckless or deliberate distortion of fact.

Lando, however, had hard evidence. He had Franklin's canceled check of February 14, 1969, demonstrating that the colonel had been in Hawaii when Herbert says he confronted him with a report of the killings at Cu Loi. Lubell elicited from Lando a statement that Franklin had told him he had arrived in Hawaii on February 9 for five days of leave. But the hotel bill that Lando had in his possession showed full charges for February 7 and 8.

> LUBELL: You say you spoke to Colonel Franklin about this matter of the seventh and eighth billing...?
>
> LANDO: I think I may have just asked him if he knew why the charges were the same during that period...I think he said he didn't know.
>
> LUBELL: Did you ever ask him whether he ever checked being charged for a full room rate for those two days?
>
> LANDO: No.

Lubell pointed out that the hotel bill showed a reduced rate for February 14.

> LUBELL: Were you ever advised by any investigator of yours that reduced rate may have been the result of only one person occupying the room on that date?
>
> LANDO: That is correct; but at the same time I was advised by Western Hotels in Washington that the reduced rate may have been an early checkout rate.
>
> LUBELL: Did you come to the conclusion that the view of Western Hotels in Washington was more accurate than the view of your investigator in Hawaii?
>
> LANDO: ...As far as I was concerned, it was a toss-up. The key thing was that there was a full charge for the night of February 13.

Lubell, in his questioning, pointed to inconsistencies in Lando's logic. If Franklin had left later in the day on February 13, he still could have been charged for a full day at the hotel and have been back at his post on February 14. Besides, Franklin said he hadn't left until February 14 — and if he was lying about that, his story would be as suspect as Herbert's. On *60 Minutes*, Wallace said two Army officers had returned to Vietnam with Franklin, taking off from Honolulu late on February 14. He did not disclose, however, that one of the officers reported that before returning to Vietnam, Colonel Franklin had put Mrs. Franklin on a plane in Honolulu; the other, though, remembered Mrs. Franklin seeing *them* off.

Lubell was trying to show that the full room charges proved that Franklin and his wife shared the room at the Ilikai from February 7. The reduced rate on February 14, Lubell argued, indicated that Franklin had left and Mrs. Franklin had stayed behind. The hotel bill showed a "balance due" of $25 (it had not been paid in full, as *60 Minutes* reported); the check, therefore, could have been predated.

When Wallace was being deposed by Lubell, he was asked, "In the investigation that you say was going on to try to get a full picture, one of the issues, was it not, was Herbert's attitude toward the commission of atrocities in Vietnam?"

Wallace answered, "No."

"You didn't think that was relevant?" Herbert's lawyer asked.

Wallace replied:

> ...I stipulated [on the program] that everybody knows that war crimes took place. What we were talking about in the broadcast was: was Colonel Herbert's career broken by the military because of his insistence upon reporting war crimes to his superiors, and was there a cover-up by his superiors? That was the issue...
>
> LUBELL: ...Weren't you trying to explore what Herbert's attitude toward atrocities was? Didn't you think that was one of the things being investigated?
>
> WALLACE: ...I don't know anybody...who's in favor of atrocities. Are you asking me if I believe Colonel Herbert was in favor of atrocities?
>
> LUBELL: No. I'm asking you if one of the subjects you were looking into was what was Herbert's attitude toward war crimes or atrocities in Vietnam.
>
> WALLACE: I would imagine he was against them. Forgive me for imagining.

But Wallace conceded that he told Lando, in effect, that if he "could get a couple of statements from people who would show that Herbert was committing acts of brutality, that would enhance the program."

The attitude of Wallace, Lando, and *60 Minutes* toward Herbert by that time was exemplified best by Wallace's choice of words in describing Herbert during the Pentagon interviews of January 4, 1973. Unknown to Wallace, Army technicians were tape-recording the interviews he was conducting. When the crew stopped to change film or to make other adjustments, the Army's tape continued to record the conversations. On April 1, 1976, when Wallace was being deposed by Jonathan Lubell, the subject of the Army's tape recording was raised. Lubell questioned Wallace while Herbert and Wallace's attorney, Carleton G. Eldridge, Jr., looked on:

LUBELL: Do you recall on January 4, while you were at the Pentagon, and in that room where the...Army had the tape going, do you recall a statement by you that "the Army built this son of a bitch up"?
WALLACE: Yes.
LUBELL: And you were referring to Colonel Herbert?
WALLACE: Yes.
LUBELL: Was that your view of Colonel Herbert on January 4?
WALLACE: That he was "built up" or a "son of a bitch"?
LUBELL: Let's break it down: that he was a "son of a bitch."
WALLACE: I might call, "Carl [referring to his attorney], you old son of a bitch." I might call...I certainly would not call Colonel Herbert a son of a bitch to his face. But, Mr. Lubell, if I might be permitted an amplification. I was stunned at the amount of profanity on that tape...And I think that in the context of, forgive me, a *macho* conversation, that I indulged myself in a series of expletives. I did not then, nor do I now, regard Colonel Herbert as a son of a bitch in the sense which you seem to suggest.
LUBELL: The other part of the statement, that the Army had built Colonel Herbert up — was that your position at the time?
WALLACE: It's perfectly apparent that the Army had great respect for him, had peddled him around the world, had used him for recruiting, had done myriad things with a man they

very much admired. Now, the Army didn't want to talk about him anymore.

Herbert did not learn of Donovan's statements until 1975, when his attorneys obtained the report of the Army's investigation. *60 Minutes* had seen Donovan's replies two and a half years earlier but had never disclosed them.

Lubell asked Wallace about his reaction to the Donovan statements. Wallace replied that he more or less washed his hands of them. "They seemed to be contradictory," Wallace said in his April 1976 deposition, "and therefore led us, effectively, no place. . . I don't recall what [Lando] told me at that time. . . Lando talked to. . . numerous people. It was a complicated investigation. I was involved with many, many other projects during the course of that time. I depended on Barry Lando because I knew him to be a careful, faithful, devoted investigative reporter. Therefore, from time to time, he would make certain statements to me or summarize certain of his investigations for me. . . I was satisfied that he was trying very, very hard to understand fully, from both sides, the position of Herbert and the position of those who denied Herbert's charges, or who disagreed with certain things that Herbert said."

Lubell asked Lando whether he had ever included in any draft he prepared for the *60 Minutes* Herbert story Franklin's comments that Herbert may have made "vague, general comments" criticizing South Vietnamese soldiers or their American advisers.

LANDO: I don't think [Franklin's] answer ends there.
LUBELL: The question ends there. Did you include, in any draft of the program, a reference to that statement of Colonel Franklin?
LANDO: That was not his complete statement.
LUBELL: In the program, Mr. Lando, did you include complete statements of everybody that appeared in the program as aired?
LANDO: I think a complete answer to the questions, yes.

LUBELL: Are you saying that no answer to any question that you presented on the program was less than the full answer on the filmed interview?
LANDO: I'm not talking about a word-for-word answer. That was not Franklin's answer to the question that was asked here.
LUBELL: That's not responsive.
LANDO: What do you mean by "full answer"? I'm not talking about word for word...It may not have had the full answer, word for word...I don't really know how to go beyond those terms—the basic answer; what the person basically answered to a question.

Nor did *60 Minutes* include any of the following exchange between Wallace and Grimshaw during their January 4, 1973, interview:

WALLACE: Do you know other examples of when he shaded the truth?
GRIMSHAW: No. And, as I've stated in my sworn statements, my letter to him, I felt this guy's integrity was unquestionable. He never lied to me when I was there serving under him; I know he didn't lie to me...

Yet Lando said that his "conclusion was that Grimshaw could no longer be sure whether or not Herbert had ever lied to him in Vietnam..."

Lubell asked Lando whether he had expressed interest in 1971 in collaborating with Herbert on a book. Lando admitted his interest but said it had ended even before he developed doubts about Herbert's story. Lubell then asked Lando whether, after the surprise confrontation between Herbert and Grimshaw, he had engaged in an angry exchange with Herbert in which Lando burst out, "I'll get you"? Yes, Lando said. Herbert had been accusing him of waging a "vendetta" because Herbert had not agreed to collaborate on the book with Lando.

"Herbert continued to press this line following the interview," Lando remembered. "I told Herbert that I believe that if he went too far that I would 'get' him. Herbert said,

'What do you mean by that?' And I said, 'Libel.' That was how the remark happened to be made..."

Since February 1978, when Herbert appealed to the Supreme Court to allow a public figure in a libel suit to probe the editorial process, the thousands of pages of sworn testimony in connection with his case have been available to the public. But despite the attention from the media to the result of the Supreme Court's decision in *Herbert* v. *Lando,* and the extensive editorial criticism of that decision, no journalist has studied the report of the Army investigation and written about it — either to examine Herbert's contention or to examine the anatomy of a major libel suit that had initiated a major Supreme Court decision affecting news media.

Why would *60 Minutes* present a segment heavily weighted against Herbert when it possessed a great deal of mitigating material? I do not believe Lando was waging a vendetta against Herbert, or, if he was, that he would or could have used *60 Minutes* as a weapon. I do not believe Herbert's contention there was an understanding between the White House and *60 Minutes* that if CBS "got" Herbert, the White House would use its influence to quash a proposed contempt-of-Congress action against Frank Stanton for refusing to provide outtakes of *The Selling of the Pentagon.*

What I believe happened is that there was a reportorial response of the kind not limited to *60 Minutes* or Mike Wallace or Barry Lando or television news. It is the nature of modern journalism to develop and pursue those stories, whether important in the scheme of life or not, which the closed society of journalists believes are newsworthy. "Newsworthy" may mean "important"; it may also mean "exciting," "controversial," "revelatory," or merely "different." Newsworthy is what makes air on television, makes page one in a newspaper, makes "the book" at a news magazine. Another pro-Herbert story in 1972 or 1973 may have been important; it would not have been exciting, controversial, revelatory, or different. "We have to get pieces on the air," Wallace told Lando in March 1972, "and we cannot spend a great deal of time spinning our wheels." In June 1972, after Lando presented Wallace with a memorandum questioning Herbert's veracity, Wallace replied, "Keep after it. Develop what you can." Hewitt said that he and his boss, Bill Leonard, were "much more interested" in the story now that Herbert's credibility was in doubt.

Modern journalism was at work in the case of Anthony Herbert. A few bright people — some would say dedicated people — believed what they wanted to believe for whatever reasons they chose to believe it about an Army officer celebrated as a hero and martyr. They may have been right or they may have been wrong. Their presentation, however, incorporated no sense of doubt; at its conclusion, the better part of forty million Americans would think Anthony Herbert was a liar. Yet *60 Minutes'* correspondents and editors, given the information they had, were in no position to know, much less tell the rest of us, the truth about Lieutenant Colonel Herbert.

On May 22, 1973, at the Hilton Hotel in New York, the National Academy of Television Arts and Sciences presented Emmy awards to Mike Wallace for "outstanding individual achievement" and to *60 Minutes* (represented by Don Hewitt and Barry Lando) for "outstanding achievement for regularly scheduled magazine-type programs" for the segment entitled "The Selling of Colonel Herbert."

Truth, apparently, is not always a requirement to journalism's rewards.

14

Pimples, Warts, and Everything

WHEN TOM BROKAW was in the midst of negotiating the most lucrative contract ever bestowed on a journalist, Steve Friedman, executive producer of NBC's *Today*, commented aptly that Brokaw "is the Dave Winfield of television news; he's the biggest free agent around." Dave Winfield, when he was free to sell his services to the highest bidder, was paid in the neighborhood of $2 million a year to play baseball for the New York Yankees. Brokaw, when he renegotiated his contract, was paid in the neighborhood of $1 million a year to play newsman for NBC. Journalists, like baseball players, are in business primarily to provide diversion; both should be considered superior if their batting average is around .300. Like baseball and other forms of mass entertainment, journalism has grown rich. Journalism has grown powerful, as well. Power begets pretension and pomposity, which, in turn, vitiate the institution wielding the power. That's what has happened among modern news media—and that's why their role and inherent limitations ought to be understood.

At its best, journalism is a good-natured gossip. It reports items of interest—sometimes amusing, sometimes tragic. It spread rumors and, occasionally, a bit of lip-smacking sensationalism. It chats about our neighbors, our town, and the latest foibles at city hall or in Washington. Like gossips, journalists usually pass along information from somebody who learned it from someone else. No matter how reliable or well intentioned the journalist, the story is likely to be somewhat askew by the time we hear it.

That's why a .300 batting average connotes success for a journalist. For journalism to mislead or confuse us, the practitioner doesn't have to be wrong; only his or her information or the source of the information need be wrong.

For example, during events following the nuclear plant accident at Three Mile Island, the Associated Press ran a story, datelined Harrisburg, Pennsylvania, warning that the hydrogen bubble inside the reactor could explode within two days, releasing highly radioactive material into the atmosphere. The AP reporter accurately reflected the fears and predictions of experts at the Nuclear Regulatory Commission in Washington; he checked his story with Washington-based spokesmen, who confirmed it. The story moved on the wire, was picked up by others, and became the basis for the later recollection of most of us that thousands of families were hours from disaster. Reporters, having no reason to question the Washington sources, tended to disregard the on-site NRC officials, who argued that the bubble, though an obstacle to a simple shut-down of the reactor, could not possibly explode. The experts in Washington were wrong; later, they would explain that the on-site NRC representatives had "better technical judgment [and]...practical knowledge...We've made an error in...calculation."

In that case, journalistic error resulted not from the journalist or from his source, but from incorrect information given to the source. One of the NRC commissioners would admit later, "The reporting—where it was off base—was off base because *we* were off base."

For readers and viewers, though, it didn't matter who was

off base: the font of the information, the conduit of that information to the media, or the media. The result was that incorrect information was blasted into our memories. Journalism will *always* be wrong unless the basic information is correct, its interpreter fully comprehends it and fairly represents it, and the reporter fully and fairly represents what he has learned. If any of those elements is lacking, the consequence is misinformation.

Reporters and their audiences would profit from contemplating more regularly the limitations of journalism.

The odds against journalism's ability to transmit valid information in fluid, complex, and controversial circumstances grow even longer as the number of editors on whom we must rely to determine what news the nation will learn grows smaller. The fewest editors who decide what most of us will know are, of course, those working in network television news.

"We are an emotional medium," Roger Mudd says of television. "The impact of the tube is not on the mind. It's on other senses—the eyes and the spleen and all that. That's where we're good, and that's what makes it so powerful—and so dangerous. If I let that really worry me, if I let that get to me, I would be paralyzed. I could not say a word, I could not speak, I could not think. You almost have to block that out of your mind—that everything you say has this quadruple magnification, that every arch of the brow and every tic of the lip is fraught [with meaning].

"What you try to do is to be as true to yourself as you can, and if you believe something to be true, you say it. It's a daily battle, and you're well on your way to winning it if you're aware of it."

No one can expect more of a reporter—except to understand that believing something to be true doesn't make it so.

The subjects examined in *Media Unbound*, in terms of how they were treated journalistically, were chosen advisedly. In almost every case, I sought a subject considered controversial by a broad segment of those who spend time reading and viewing news and discussing news events — the Vietnam War and nuclear energy, for example. The goal was neither to defend nor attack any event or viewpoint, but, rather, to demonstrate how easily a uniform (and sometimes uninformed) journalistic presentation can implant misinformation in our memories. Further, I wished to dispel the notion that journalistic presentations are "slanted" because of any ideology; the reasons, I tried to show, are much more mundane.

Whatever shortcomings I impute to journalists, I shared as a reporter on daily newspapers for eight and a half years in Alabama, Georgia, and North Carolina; as press secretary to Senator Birch Bayh, an Indiana Democrat, for five years; as a *Newsweek* correspondent for eight and a half years in Atlanta, Los Angeles, and Washington, D.C. And when I impute shortcomings to journalism, I do so in the spirit of Oliver Cromwell asking that his portrait reflect "all these roughnesses, pimples, warts, and everything as you see me; otherwise I will never pay a farthing for it." Journalism is far too powerful and important to require — or to profit from — flattery.

Acknowledgments

Bibliography

Index

ACKNOWLEDGMENTS ═══

The Author's
Mental State

ACKNOWLEDGE" means not only to express gratitude, but also to own up to something. Because much of this book deals generally with circumstances surrounding the mental state of journalists, it is only fair that I relate my own possible prejudices as well as my appreciation.

Gerard McCauley qualifies on both levels. He is my literary agent and, with his family, among my wife's and my dearest friends. He has been a source of encouragement and succor in ways that have been extraordinary and that, if described, would only embarrass him. McCauley also represents Anthony Herbert, a long-time friend of his. I met Herbert while I was a *Newsweek* correspondent, long before I knew McCauley. Our encounters then were, on the whole, governed by my professional interest in him. Since McCauley became my agent (and, later, my friend) in 1975, Herbert and I have been together socially on several occasions at McCauley's home and once at mine. I had no hand in Herbert's book, *Soldier*, nor do I have any interest — professional, financial, or otherwise — in any of his projects, whatever they may be. I am interested in his litigation against

60 Minutes, et al., only for journalistic reasons, all of which are evident in this book.

Robert Chandler, a CBS News vice president who had authority over *60 Minutes*, numbered among his other duties supervision of promotion of the news operation. In that context, he and I talked seriously on two occasions about the prospect of my providing services to CBS News. Once, while I still was with *Newsweek*, he and Richard Salant, then president of CBS News, interviewed me for a position as the organization's director of public affairs; I didn't get the job. Subsequently, after I had established a public affairs consulting firm in Washington, I tried, unsuccessfully, to persuade Chandler to retain me. Both occasions concluded with mutual civility and respect.

In my incarnation as a public affairs consultant, I never had any clients nor received any income, directly or indirectly, from any individual, business, or organization connected with any aspect of any topic I have examined in this book (except for my professional relationship with McCauley). I emphasize that particular point as it relates to power companies, nuclear energy, and the drug business.

Having exhausted my acknowledgments in one sense, I wish to add my gratitude to my wife, Nancy, who allowed me to "talk" this book over a number of months — a method by which I defined my purposes, sharpened my views, and caused those close to me hours of tedium. Ellen Joseph's editing was uniformly incisive; it minimized sloppy writing and sloppy thinking. Mary Legatski provided me with a small library of source materials; my son, Joseph, helped prepare the bibliography. And yes, authors, there *is* a copy editor called Pixie Apt, whose professionalism, thoroughness, and caring more than made up for my embarrassment at being lectured by her (necessarily, I'm afraid) for grammatical and syntactical slips.

If there is a person without whom this book could not have been written, that person is Mary Schneider, who, except for a fanatic devotion to anything connected with Ohio (she'll never forgive Pete Rose for leaving the Cincinnati Reds "just for the money," nor those who caused Woody Hayes's dismissal as Ohio State University's football coach because "a dumb player from the other team ran into his fist"), nears perfection as an assistant. Her research, her ideas, her comments, her loyalty—all were indispensable in the preparation of *Media Unbound* and in the conduct of my business affairs.

Finally, I wish to express my unending gratitude to journalism, which, for nearly all my adult years, has fed me, clothed me, and allowed me to romp through life with a maximum of pleasure and a minimum of angst. I don't know how the grownups manage.

Bibliography

Abrams, Floyd. Letters to the Editor, *New York Times*, 20 Apr. 1981.

Adams, Al. Interview with the author (via telephone). Decatur, Illinois, Aug. 1981.

Adams, William, and Fay Schreibman, eds. *Television Network News*. Washington, D.C.: George Washington University, 1978.

Adler, Renata. "The Justices and the Journalists" (review of *The Brethren*), *New York Times Book Review*, 16 Oct. 1979, pp. 1 et seq.

Altheide, David L. *Creating Reality*. Beverly Hills: Sage Publications, 1976.

Arlen, Michael J. "The Air: The Interview," *New Yorker*, 10 Nov. 1975, pp. 141 et seq.

———. *The Camera Age*. Toronto: McGraw-Hill Ryerson, 1981.

Army, Department of. Fact sheets compiled in the case of Lieutenant Colonel Anthony B. Herbert, dated 5 Nov. 1971, 17 Nov. 1971, 7 Dec. 1971. Reprinted in *Army*, Feb. 1972, pp. 6–11.

Army, Department of, Criminal Investigation Division. Sworn statements and other investigative materials compiled in 70-CID121 (investigation into charges by Lieutenant Colonel Anthony B. Herbert).

"Arson and Profit." *20/20*, 7 Feb. 1980.

Bagdikian, Ben. *Information Machines: Their Impact on Men and the Media.* New York: Harper & Row, 1971.

Banker, Stephen. "Beware of TV's Scoops," *Panorama,* Jan. 1981, pp. 37 et seq.

Banks, Louis. "The Rise of the Newsocracy," *Atlantic Monthly,* Jan. 1981, pp. 54–59.

Barbash, Fred. "*Alton Telegraph* Libel Judgment Sends Fearful Message to Press," *Washington Post,* 25 Aug. 1981, p. A3.

———. "A Story and a Tragic End: Paper Accused of 'Hounding' Jurist," *Washington Post,* 17 Mar. 1980, p. A1.

Barber, James David. *The Pulse of Politics: Electing Presidents in the Media Age.* New York: Norton, 1980.

Barber, James David, ed. *Race for the Presidency.* Englewood Cliffs, New Jersey: Prentice-Hall, 1978.

Barnes, Brigadier General John W. Statement to the author acquired through the office of the director, public affairs, United States Army. Washington, D.C.–Taiwan: Aug. 1975.

Barth, Alan. *The Loyalty of Free Men.* New York: Viking Press, 1951.

Base, Ron. "Will Success Spoil '60 Minutes'?" *Today,* 9 Sept. 1979.

Bennett, Charles C. Statements to Select Committee on Aging, U.S. House of Representatives, regarding DMSO. Washington, D.C., 24 Mar. 1980; Atlanta, 27 Mar. 1980.

Bergreen, Laurence. "The Strange Saga of a Painkiller," *TV Guide,* 26 Jul. 1980, pp. 2–6.

"Better Than Expected." Editorial, *New York Times,* 12 Feb. 1980.

Blumenthal, Sidney. *The Permanent Campaign.* Boston: Beacon Press, 1980.

Blustein, Paul, with Daniel Machalaba and Ann Hughey, "Washington Post Blames Its Untrue Story on 'Complete Systems Failure' by Editors," *Wall Street Journal,* 20 Apr. 1981, p. 4.

Braestrup, Peter. *Big Story.* New York: Doubleday Anchor, 1978.

Bray, Howard. *The Pillars of the Post.* New York: Norton, 1980.

Brennan, Justice William J. "Why the Press Misreads the Court," excerpts from an address at Rutgers University, *Washington Post,* 21 Dec. 1979.

Broder, David S. "Is Carter Vulnerable?" *Washington Post,* 12 Mar. 1980, p. 1.

———. *The Party's Over: The Failure of Politics in America.* New York: Harper & Row, 1971.

———. "The Press Is Guilty of Consumer Fraud," *Washington Post,* 3 June 1979, p. D1.

———. "Processed Out," *Washington Post,* 12 Mar. 1980.

Brown, Lloyd. Report to the author of interviews with George Brumley, Carl Drury, Robert Harrison, and others, plus additional research regarding St. Marys, Georgia, and the Gilman Paper Company. Jacksonville, Florida, Spring 1981.

"Brzezinski's Zipper Was Up," *Time,* 31 Dec. 1979, p. 58.

Buchwald, Art. "Capitol Punishment: They'd Rather Send Dan," *Washington Post,* 15 Apr. 1980.

Buckley, William F., Jr., "Alarming, Given the Source," *Washington Post,* 18 Nov. 1981, p. A19. Universal Press Syndicate.

Buksbaum, David. Interview with the author. New York, 28 Apr. 1980.

"Bum Steer," *60 Minutes,* 11 Sept. 1977.

Caddell, Patrick. Interview with Peter Ross Range, *Playboy,* Feb. 1980, pp. 63 et seq.

Carmody, Deirdre. "Editors Concerned by Court's 'State of Mind' Decision," *New York Times,* 19 Apr. 1979, p. B11.

———. "Newspapers Debating Effect of Court Rulings," *New York Times,* 7 Apr. 1980.

Carmody, John. "The TV Column: NBC's 'Sting' Stakeout on W Street," *Washington Post,* 5 Feb. 1980.

Carpenter, Teresa. "From Heroism to Madness," *Village Voice,* 12 May 1980, pp. 1 et seq.

———. "Murder on a Day Pass," *Village Voice,* 25 Feb. 1980, pp. 1 et seq.

Cater, Douglass, and Richard Adler, eds. *Television As a Social Force: New Approaches to TV Criticism.* New York: Praeger Publishers, 1975.

CBS News with Walter Cronkite, 18 Feb. 1980.

CBS Reports, "The Selling of the Pentagon," 23 Feb. 1971.

———. "Teddy," 4 Nov. 1979.

Chandler, Robert. Interview with the author. New York, 1 May 1980.

———. Letter to Wendell J. Kelley, New York, 21 Jan. 1980.

Ciolli, Rita. "Entrapment: A Narrow Defense," *Newsday,* 7 Feb. 1980, p. 14.

Cohen, Richard M., and Jules Witcover. *A Heartbeat Away.* New York: Viking Press, 1974.

Collins, Thomas. "Media Defend Disclosures," *Newsday*, 5 Feb. 1980.

Compaine, Benjamin M., ed. *Who Owns the Media?* New York: Harmony Books, 1979.

"Company Town," *60 Minutes*, 7 May 1972.

Cooke, Janet. "Jimmy's World: 8-Year-Old Heroin Addict Lives for a Fix," *Washington Post*, 28 Sept. 1980, p. A1.

Crouse, Timothy. *The Boys on the Bus*. New York: Random House, 1973.

Crout, J. Richard. Statement to Select Committee on Aging, U.S. House of Representatives. Washington, D.C., 24 Mar. 1980.

Current Biography Yearbook. Charles Moritz, ed. New York: H. W. Wilson, 1977.

Daniels, Lee. "Colonel Herbert Shows Tenacity in Legal Contest," *New York Times*, 19 Apr. 1979.

Dash, Samuel. *Chief Counsel: Inside the Ervin Committee and the Untold Story of Watergate*. New York: Random House, 1976.

Diamond, Edwin. *The Tin Kazoo: Television, Politics, and the News*. Cambridge: MIT Press, 1975.

Dickey, Christopher. "The Press...Zooms in on...El Salvador," *Washington Post*, 3 Apr. 1981, p. C1.

Dornsife, William P. "The TMI Accident, As It Really Happened," paper of the American Nuclear Society. Las Vegas, Nevada: June 1980.

Dorsey, John, ed. *On Mencken*. New York: Knopf, 1980.

Duval, Lieutenant Ed. Interview with the author (via telephone). Akron, Ohio, Sept. 1980.

Efron, Edith. *The News Twisters*. Los Angeles: Nash Publishing, 1971.

"The End of the 'Jimmy' Story." Editorial, *Washington Post*, 16 Apr. 1981.

Epstein, Edward Jay. *News from Nowhere: Television and the News*. New York: Random House, 1973.

"Ex *Post* Facto," *Time*, 26 Oct. 1981, p. 97.

Fairlie, Henry. "Fairlie at Large: Why the Fuss About a Little Bribery?" *Washington Post*, 17 Feb. 1980, p. C1.

Fallaci, Oriana. Interview in *Playboy*, Oct. 1981, pp. 100–103.

Fischkin, Barbara. "FBI's Master of the Sting," *Newsday*, 11 Feb. 1980, p. 4.

Fisher, Roy M. "Unnamed News Sources: An Uncharted World," *Washington Star*, 1 May 1981, p. A11.

FitzGerald, Frances. *Fire in the Lake*. Boston: Little, Brown, 1972.

Franklin, Colonel J. Ross. Interview with the author (via telephone), Columbus, Georgia, Aug. 1975.

Friendly, Jonathan. "Illinois Paper Seeks Libel-Case Support," *New York Times*, 12 May 1981.

Furgurson, Ernest B. "Anniversary of Chicago," *Baltimore Sun*, 28 Aug. 1969, p. A18.

Gailey, Phil. "The Trail of the Rumor on Blair House's 'Bug,'" *New York Times*, 18 Nov. 1981, p. A24.

Gans, Herbert J. *Deciding What's News*. New York: Pantheon Books, 1979.

Garment, Suzanne. "Political Thicket: Washington Stalks the Wild Rumor," *Wall Street Journal*, 6 Nov. 1981, p. 34.

Gates, Gary Paul. *Air Time: The Inside Story of CBS News*. New York: Harper & Row, 1978.

Germond, Jack W., and Jules Witcover. "Lack of Local TV Makes Losers of Jersey's Voters," *Washington Star*, 21 Apr. 1981.

Glessing, Robert J., and William P. White. *Mass Media: The Invisible Environment*. Chicago: Science Research Associates, 1973.

Golden, Soma. "The Editorial Notebook: Meanwhile, Inside the Debate," *New York Times*, 24 Sept. 1980, p. A30.

Good, Paul. "Why You Can't Always Trust '60 Minutes' Reporting," *Panorama*, Sept. 1980, pp. 38 et seq.

Goodale, Paul. "The Burnett Award," *New York Times*, 9 Apr. 1981.

Goodman, Ellen. "Media, Media Everywhere," *Boston Globe Newspaper Company*, 22? Aug. 1980.

Graham, Sandra. "Illinois Power Pans '60 Minutes,'" *Wall Street Journal*, 27 June 1980.

Green, Bill. "Janet's World: The Story of a Child Who Never Existed — How and Why It Came to Be Published," *Washington Post*, 19 Apr. 1981.

Greenfield, Jeff. Commentary on the return of the hostages from Iran, *CBS Sunday Morning*, 25 Jan. 1981.

Greenfield, Meg. "Carter and the PR Trap," *Newsweek*, 26 Jan. 1981, p. 84.

――――. "Chronic Political Amnesia," *Newsweek,* 22 Sept. 1980, p. 96.

Halberstam, David. *The Powers That Be.* New York, Knopf, 1979.

Halberstam, Dr. Michael. "Through the Looking Glass: A Second Opinion," *Washington Journalism Review,* Jan.–Feb. 1980, pp. 73–74.

Harwood, Richard. "The Electronic Eye: Real Carter Adversary," *Washington Post,* 12 Aug. 1980, p. A1.

Herbert, Anthony B. Interview with the author. Katonah, New York, 28 June 1980.

――――, with James T. Wooten. *Soldier.* New York: Holt, Rinehart & Winston, 1973.

Hewitt, Don. Deposition regarding *Herbert* v. *Lando,* 15 Jan. 1976.

――――. Interview with the author. New York, 1 May 1980.

Horn, Stephen. Interview with the author. Washington, D.C., 9 Apr. 1981.

"How Safe Is Safe?" *60 Minutes,* 8 Feb. 1976.

Illinois Commerce Commission. Order 79–0071, regarding Illinois Power Company proposed general increases in electric and gas rates, 28 Nov. 1979.

Illinois Power Company. "Analysis of CBS Letter Dated January 21, 1980," Decatur, Illinois, 29 Jan. 1980.

"Inside Afghanistan," *60 Minutes,* 6 Apr. 1980.

"The Iran File," *60 Minutes,* 2 Mar. 1980.

"Iran Timing Aided Carter, Caddell Says." Associated Press dispatch from Milwaukee, published in *Washington Star,* 3 Apr. 1980.

"Israel's Toughest Enemy," *60 Minutes,* 16 Feb. 1975.

"Israel's Toughest Enemy, Update," *60 Minutes,* 21 Mar. 1976.

Jacob, Dr. Stanley W. Statement to Select Committee on Aging, U.S. House of Representatives. Washington, D.C., 24 Mar. 1980.

Just, Ward. "Newspaper Days: Great Moments in American Journalism (or, The Sorrows of Gin)," *Atlantic Monthly,* Jan. 1980, pp. 37–39.

――――. "Newspaper Days: Politics—We Are the Hostages," *Atlantic Monthly,* Apr. 1980, pp. 99–101.

Kampelman, Max M. "The Power of the Press: A Problem for Our Democracy," *Policy Review,* Fall 1978.

Kaplan, Justin. *Lincoln Steffens.* New York: Simon & Schuster, 1974.

Kissinger, Henry. *White House Years.* Boston: Little, Brown, 1979.

"The Kissinger-Shah Connection," *60 Minutes,* 4 May 1980.

Kowet, Don. "Do Those '60 Minutes' Crusades Pay Off?" *TV Guide,* 10 Mar. 1979, pp. 18 et seq.

Kraft, Joseph. "Lippmann: Yesterday, Today and Tomorrow," Los Angeles Times Syndicate, 11 Sept. 1980.

_____. "What to Do About Leaks," Field Enterprises, 14 Feb. 1980.

Kristol, Irving. "The Underdeveloped Profession," *The Public Interest,* Winter 1967, pp. 49–50.

Kuralt, Charles. Commentary on reporting, *CBS Sunday Morning,* 7 Sept. 1980.

Lando, Barry. Depositions regarding *Herbert* v. *Lando,* May 1974–June 1975.

_____. "The Herbert Affair," *Atlantic Monthly,* May 1973, pp. 73–81.

_____. Interview with the author. New York, July 1980.

Lesher, Stephan. "Company Town: The Agony of St. Marys," *Newsweek,* 22 May 1972, pp. 82–83.

_____. File to *Newsweek* regarding St. Marys, Georgia, and Gilman Paper Company. St. Marys, Georgia, 12 May 1972.

Lewis, Anthony. "Dangers of the Sting," *New York Times,* 8 Feb. 1980.

Lofton, John. *The Press As Guardian of the First Amendment.* Columbia, South Carolina: University of South Carolina Press, 1981.

"Looking Out for Mrs. Berwid," *60 Minutes,* 30 Mar. 1980.

Lubell, Jonathan. Interviews with the author. New York, Aug. 1975 and Aug. 1981.

Lukas, J. Anthony. *Nightmare: The Underside of the Nixon Years.* New York: Viking Press, 1976.

MacDougall, A. Kent. "Flaws in Press Coverage plus Business Sensitivity Stir Bitter Debate" (and succeeding articles in a series), *Los Angeles Times,* 3–8 Feb. 1980.

Machalaba, Daniel. "After ABC Invades Akron for Big Story," *Wall Street Journal,* 16 Apr. 1980, p. 1.

"Maine: The Fourth Man." Editorial, *Washington Post,* 12 Feb. 1980.

Mander, Jerry. *Four Arguments for the Elimination of Television.* New York: William Morrow, 1978.

Mankiewicz, Frank, and Joel Swerdlow. *Remote Control: Television and the Manipulation of American Life.* New York: Times Books, 1978.

Marshall, Burke. "Two Scandals, Not One," *New York Times,* 8 Feb. 1980.

Mayer, Allan J., with others. "A Searching of Conscience," *Newsweek,* 4 May 1981, pp. 50–55.

Maynard, Robert C. Letters to the Editor, *Wall Street Journal,* 7 May 1981.

Mazo, Earl. *Richard Nixon.* New York: Harper & Row, 1959.

McCauley, Gerard. Interview with the author. Katonah, New York, 30 June 1980.

McFadden, Robert D. "Daily News Editor to Fight Questionable Reporting," *New York Times,* 11 May 1981.

McGinniss, Joe. *The Selling of the President.* New York: Trident, 1969.

McLuhan, Marshall. *Understanding Media: The Extension of Man.* New York: McGraw-Hill, 1965.

"Media Politicking." Editorial, *Washington Post,* 2 Jan. 1981.

Meyer, Karl E. "The Trials of Truth on Television," *New York Times,* 15 May 1981, p. A30.

Michaels, Marguerite. "News as a TV Movie in 60 Smashing Minutes," *Parade,* 11 Feb. 1979, pp. 4 et seq.

———. "Walter Wants the News to Say a Lot More," *Parade,* 23 Mar. 1980, pp. 4 et seq.

Miller, Mark Crispin, and Karen Runyon. "And That's the Way It Seems," *New Republic,* 14 Feb. 1981, pp. 19 et seq.

Mintz, Morton. "FDA Aides Probed in Testing of DMSO," *Washington Post,* 1 Aug. 1980, p. A2.

Mollenhoff, Clark R. "Unnamed News Sources: Where Myths Are Apt to Be Born," *Washington Star,* 1 May 1981, p. A11.

de Montaigne, Michel. *The Complete Essays of Montaigne.* Trans. Donald M. Frame. Stanford, California: Stanford University Press, 1976.

Montgomery, Paul. "Deception Denied by Reporter for Voice," *New York Times,* 11 May 1981, p. D12.

Mossetig, Michael, and Henry Griggs, Jr. "TV at the Front," *Foreign Policy,* Spring 1980, pp. 67–79.

Mudd, Roger. Interview with the author. Washington, D.C., 20 Mar. 1980.

Mueller, John E. *War, Presidents and Public Opinion*. New York: John Wiley, 1973.

"News Blackout in Iran," *CBS News Special Report*, 14 Jan. 1980.

The News Media and the Law, vol. 4, no. 1, Washington, D.C.: The Reporters Committee for Freedom of the Press, Mar.–Apr. 1980.

"Newsmen Dealt Blow on Defense in Suits for Libel," *New York Times*, unsigned, 19 Apr. 1979, p. A1.

Nixon, Richard M. *Six Crises*. New York: Doubleday, 1962.

"Nuclear Construction Costs," *60 Minutes*, 25 Nov. 1979.

"Nuclear Construction Costs, Update," *60 Minutes*, 14 Dec. 1980.

Oberdorfer, Don. "All Sides Resort to Diplomacy by Journalism in Iran Crisis," *Washington Post*, 20 Dec. 1979, p. A17.

———. *Tet!* New York: Doubleday, 1971.

———. "Why the Hostage Crisis Held Us All Hostage," *Washington Post*, 1 Feb. 1981, p. C1.

O'Connor, John J. "TV News Faces Own Crisis in Iranian Situation," *New York Times*, 20 Dec. 1979, p. C26.

Patterson, Thomas E., and Robert D. McClure. *The Unseeing Eye: The Myth of Television Power in National Elections*. New York: Putnam's, 1976.

Perkins, David, ed. *English Romantic Writers*. New York: Harcourt, Brace & World, 1967.

"Personalities," *Washington Post*, 6 Apr. 1981.

Powers, Ron. *The Newscasters: The News Business as Show Business*. New York: St. Martin's Press, 1977.

"The Princess and the PBS." Editorial, *Washington Post*, 14 May 1980.

Quinn, Sally. *We're Gonna Make You a Star*. New York: Simon & Schuster, 1975.

Ranney, Austin, ed. *The Past and Future of Presidential Debates*. Washington, D.C.: American Enterprise Institute, 1979.

Rather, Dan. Interview with the author. New York, 30 Apr. 1980.

———, and Gary Paul Gates. *The Palace Guard*. New York: Harper & Row, 1974.

———, with Mickey Herskowitz. *The Camera Never Blinks*. New York: William Morrow, 1977.

Reasoner, Harry. Interview with the author. New York, 29 Apr. 1980.

Reid, T. R. "The Pack Aboard the Plane," *Washington Post*, 21 Jan. 1980, p. A1.

Report of the President's Commission on the Accident at Three Mile Island (The Kemeny Commission Report), Oct. 1979, pp. 137–141, 149–165.

"The Results of the Iowa Results." Editorial, *New York Times*, 27 Jan. 1980.

"The Riddle of DMSO," *60 Minutes*, 23 Mar. 1980.

Rosenfeld, Megan. "Super Plumber of the Abscam Leaks," *Washington Post*, 13 Mar. 1980.

"Rough Ride on the Primary Trail," *Time*, 7 Apr. 1980, p. 91.

Rubin, Barry. "Iran," *Washington Journalism Review*, Apr. 1980, pp. 35–39.

Safire, William. "Essay: History on Its Head," *New York Times*, 9 Apr. 1981, p. A23.

———. *Safire's Political Dictionary*. New York: Random House, 1978.

Said, Edward W. "Iran and the Press: Whose Holy War?" *Columbia Journalism Review*, Mar.–Apr. 1980, pp. 23–33.

"Saigon Diary," *Wall Street Journal*, 3 Nov. 1981 (Part One), 4 Nov. 1981 (Part Two).

Sansweet, Stephen J. "'Absence of Malice': A New Film Challenges Press Ethics," *Wall Street Journal*, 6 Nov. 1981, p. 35.

"A Saudi Squall on Public TV." Editorial, *New York Times*, 9 May 1980, p. A30.

Schardt, Arlie, with Lucy Howard and others. "TV's Rush to Judgment," *Newsweek*, 28 July 1980, pp. 72–75.

———, with Tony Clifton, Nancy Stadtman, and Mary Lord. "TV: Held Hostage?" *Newsweek*, 24 Dec. 1979, p. 27.

Schorr, Daniel. *Clearing the Air*. Boston: Houghton Mifflin, 1977.

———. Interviews with the author. Washington, D.C., 7 Mar. 1980 and 3 Apr. 1980.

Schuck, Peter, and Harrison Wellford. "Democracy and the Good Life in a Company Town," *Harper's*, May 1972, pp. 56–66.

Schwartz, Harry. "A Heart Drug's Long Road to the Marketplace," *Wall Street Journal*, 22 Jan. 1982, p. 30.

Schwartz, Tony, "Brokaw Says He's 'Talking to All Three Networks,'" *New York Times*, 23 May 1981, p. 48.

————. "The Ethics Question in TV Investigative Reporting," *New York Times*, 23 Apr. 1981.

————. "Reruns on '6o Minutes' Spurs Debate," *New York Times*, 15 May 1980, p. C26.

————. "Wallace Taped in Ethnic Remark," *New York Times*, 12 Jan. 1982.

"The Selling of Colonel Herbert," *60 Minutes*, 4 Feb. 1973.

"The Selling of the Pentagon," *CBS Reports*, 23 Feb. 1971.

Shales, Tom, "Gunga Dan," *Washington Post*, 7 Apr. 1980.

————. "Journalism by the Jugular," *Washington Post*, 26 Apr. 1981, p. H1.

————. "On the Air: Rather," *Washington Post*, 12 Mar. 1980.

————. "Petty for Teddy: The Anti-Kennedy Bias in TV News Reporting," *Washington Post*, 30 Jan. 1980, p. B1.

————. "TV's Day of Trauma," *Washington Post*, 31 Mar. 1981, p. D1.

————. "TV's Troubles," *Washington Post*, [no date] 1981.

Shaw, Daniel L., and Maxwell E. McCombs. *The Emergence of American Political Issues: The Agenda-Setting Function of the Press*. St. Paul, Minnesota: West Publishing, 1977.

Shaw, David. "'6o Minutes': A TV Habit, Flaws and All," *Los Angeles Times*, 10–11 June 1980.

————. "The Trouble with TV Muckraking," *TV Guide*, 10 Oct. 1981, pp. 6–10.

Shribman, David. "Ubiquitous Allen Takes His Case to the Public," *New York Times*, 2 Dec. 1981, p. B4.

Shuler, Major Brigham. Interview with the author (via telephone), Washington, D.C., Aug. 1975.

Sirica, John J. *To Set the Record Straight*. New York: Norton, 1979.

60 Minutes, "Bum Steer," CBS Network, 11 Sept. 1977.

————. "Company Town," CBS Network, 7 May 1972.

————. "How Safe Is Safe?" CBS Network, 8 Feb. 1976.

————. "Inside Afghanistan," CBS Network, 6 Apr. 1980.

————. "Iran: December 1980," CBS Network, 14 Dec. 1980.

————. "The Iran File," CBS Network, 2 Mar. 1980.

————. "Israel's Toughest Enemy," CBS Network, 16 Feb. 1975.

————. "Israel's Toughest Enemy, Update," CBS Network, 21 Mar. 1976.

————. "The Kissinger-Shah Connection," CBS Network, 4 May 1980.

_____. "Looking Out for Mrs. Berwid," CBS Network, 30 Mar. 1980.

_____. "Nuclear Construction Costs," CBS Network, 25 Nov. 1979.

_____. "The Riddle of DMSO," CBS Network, 23 Mar. 1980.

_____. "The Selling of Colonel Herbert," CBS Network, 4 Feb. 1973.

_____. "So You Want to Write a Book?" CBS Network, 7 Jan. 1979.

_____. "What About Dan Schorr?" CBS Network, 25 Sept. 1976.

"*60 Minutes*/Our Reply," Illinois Power Company. Decatur, Illinois: 3 Dec. 1979.

Smilgis, Martha, with Mary Cronin. "Incredible? Or Abominable?" *Time*, 13 Oct. 1980, pp. 80–81.

Smith, Desmond. "The Small World of NBC News," *New York*, 29 June 1981, pp. 24 et seq.

_____. "The Wide World of Roone Arledge," *New York Times Magazine*, pp. 37 et seq.

Smith, Stephen, with Mary Cronin. "The New Face of TV News," *Time*, 25 Feb. 1980, pp. 64 et seq.

_____, with Elizabeth Rudulph, "A Convention Hall of Mirrors," *Time*, 28 July 1980, pp. 54–55.

Snyder, Louis L., and Richard B. Morris, eds. *A Treasury of Great Reporting*. New York: Simon & Schuster, 1949.

Socolow, Sanford. Interview with the author. New York, 1 July 1980.

"So You Want to Write a Book?" *60 Minutes*, 7 Jan. 1979.

Steel, Ronald. *Walter Lippmann and the American Century*. Boston: Atlantic–Little, Brown, 1980.

Steffens, Lincoln. *Autobiography of Lincoln Steffens*. New York: Harcourt Brace Jovanovich, 1958.

Stein, Harry. "How '60 Minutes' Makes News," *New York Times Magazine*, 6 May 1979, pp. 28 et seq.

Taylor, Paul. "Carter Drops Plans for Suit Against *Post*," *Washington Post*, 25 Oct. 1981, p. A7.

_____. "*Post* Apologizes to Carter for Gossip Column Item," *Washington Post*, 23 Oct. 1981, p. 1.

"Teddy," *CBS Reports*, 4 Nov. 1979.

Tivnan, Edward. "The Cronkite Syndrome," *The Dial*, Nov. 1980, pp. 44 et seq.

"Tracing the 'Arab Scam,'" *Newsday,* 7 Feb. 1980, pp. 7 et seq.

Tyrrell, R. Emmett Jr. "'Leaks Have Become a Vice,'" *Washington Post,* 18 Feb. 1980.

United States v. *Brumley,* No. 76–1895, United States Court of Appeals, Fifth Circuit, 14 Oct. 1977.

"Use of DMSO for Unapproved Indications," *FDA Drug Bulletin,* Nov. 1980, pp. 20–21.

Van Vliet, W. James. "Barbuto Pleads Guilty," *The Cleveland Plain Dealer,* 21 June 1980.

Volkman, Ernest. "The Press Creates Its Candidate," *Media People,* Dec. 1979, pp. 47–52.

Wallace, Mike. Deposition regarding *Herbert* v. *Lando,* 1 Apr. 1976.

————. "An Essay," *Parade,* 15 June 1980, p. 12.

————. Interview with the author. New York: 2 May 1980.

Warner, Edwin. "The Troubling Ethics of Abscam," *Time,* 18 Feb. 1980, p. 21.

Waters, Harry F., with Eric Gelman and Mary Lord. "Dan Rather, Anchor Man," *Newsweek,* 25 Feb. 1980, pp. 71 et seq.

————, with Eric Gelman, George Hackett, and Lucy Howard. "TV's War After Cronkite," *Newsweek,* 9 Mar. 1981, pp. 52 et seq.

————, with George Hackett. "Turning the Tables on '60 Minutes,'" *Newsweek* 16 Mar. 1981, p. 62.

Weisman, John. "The Strange Case of Geraldo Rivera," *TV Guide,* 6 Dec. 1980, pp. 21–28.

————, and Sally Bedell. "Something Is Missing in TV's Political Coverage," *TV Guide,* 5 July 1980.

Wellford, Harrison. Interview with the author (via telephone), Washington, D.C., Aug. 1981.

"What About Dan Schorr?" *60 Minutes,* 25 Sept. 1976.

"What About Dan Schorr?" Transcript of interview with Daniel Schorr by Mike Wallace, 24 Sept. 1976.

White, Theodore H. *Breach of Faith: The Fall of Richard M. Nixon.* New York: Atheneum, 1975.

————. *In Search of History: A Personal Expedition.* New York: Harper & Row, 1978.

————. *The Making of a President: 1960.* New York: Atheneum, 1961.

————. The Making of a President: 1964. New York: Atheneum, 1965.

————. The Making of a President: 1968. New York: Atheneum, 1969.

"Who Picks the President?" Nick Kotz, ed. The Washingtonian, June 1980, pp. 106 et seq.

Wicker, Tom. "A Chilling Court," New York Times, 20 Apr. 1979.

Will, George F. "How to Deal with Iran," Newsweek, 24 Dec. 1979, p. 84.

Wise, David. The Politics of Lying. New York: Random House, 1973.

Witcover, Jules. Marathon: The Pursuit of the Presidency, 1972–1976. New York: Viking Press, 1977.

Woodward, Bob, and Scott Armstrong. The Brethren. New York: Simon & Schuster, 1979.

————, and Carl Bernstein. All the President's Men. New York: Simon & Schuster, 1974.

Young, Andrew. "Grounds for Optimism," New York Times, 12 Mar. 1980, p. A27.

Zito, Tom. "Old Soldier's Media Battle," Washington Post, 1 Oct. 1979, p. B1.

INDEX